STROUD'S BUSES

STROUD'S BUSES

A Century of Motorised Public Transport in the Stroud Valleys

N P Daniels

Llyfrau Hiraethog

Llyfrau Hiraethog

Argraffiad cyntaf 2003

First published 2003

ISBN 0-9545166-0-5

Design and typeset by
Matador Publishing, Market Harborough, UK

Cyhoeddwyd yng Nghymru gan

Llyfrau Hiraethog
BP 35
Rhuthun
Sir Ddinbych
LL15 2ZB

Published by

Llyfrau Hiraethog
PO Box 35
Ruthin
Denbighshire
LL15 2ZB

To Stroud's bus men and women, past and present,
whose vital contribution to the social and economic life of Stroud
often goes unrecognised

CONTENTS

ACKNOWLEDGEMENTS

I am grateful to so many for contributing towards this volume. It is fitting to start by thanking a number of retired bus company employees (and where appropriate their spouses), for many of their memories. All were blessed with an attitude towards public service now so rarely seen in today's fast moving world. Chief among them were Senior Inspectors Jack Ireland and the late Mrs Ireland, Vic Watkins and Mrs Watkins, and John Holmes, Chief Clerk Ken Shelley and Mrs Shelley, Driver Brian Ede, District Traffic Superintendent Geoffrey Gould and Conductress Audrey Gay. Their invaluable recollections, records, photographs and anecdotes formed more than a backbone upon which this book has been based.

Local transport historians Kim Hewgill, Michael Ede, Andrew Fruscher, Robert Arkell and Brian Ward-Ellison have been both helpful and supportive in their contributions, sharing of records and photographic collections, as has David Lloyd for allowing me to use some of his published material on the GWR bus service in Stroud.

I should also like to acknowledge the permission given by Robert Crawley to use some of the material in his two books on the history of Western National and its antecedents which, together with material at the Omnibus Society's library and the Monk Collection, have proved of inestimable value in gaining a picture of Stroud's developments up to 1950.

Stroud Branch Library contains archived copies of the *Stroud News, Stroud Journal* and *Stroud News & Journal* and I should like to thank staff there, especially Helen Foulkes, and at the Gloucestershire Collection at Gloucester Library and the Gloucestershire Record Office, for their assistance. Retired editor of the *Stroud News & Journal,* Dennis Mason OBE was kind enough to share his thoughts on bus services on a number of occasions over his long career with the paper and its predecessor.

With Gloucestershire County Council playing a major part in public transport from the early 1970s, I am also grateful to retired or former transport co-ordinating officers Roger Macklin, Geoffrey Kerr and Michael Taplin.

Former Cheltenham & Gloucester Omnibus managing director Norrie Thomas was most candid in his recollections on and views about the years between 1983 and 1993. Clive Norman of Stagecoach regional office at Cheltenham and Deric Pemberton supplied much of the corroborating details for these years and the following ten.

Others helping with this project include Howard Beard, Malcolm Bell, Carl Berry, Peter Cook, Alan Davies, Stanley Davis, Stephen Dowle, Nigel Furness, Keith Hall, Adrian Hewlett, Mrs Pat Parker, Andrew Lawton, Mike Mason, Richard Masterman, Andy Mitchell, Neil Murray, John Potter, William Staniforth, Nigel Uttings, David Withers and Michael Wadman. Mark Cleave produced the map. If I have forgotten anyone, as I surely have, I can only apologise.

This work would have been impossible without the particular help and support of three people. The first is the permission granted by Richard Johnson to use information collected by his late father, David. David Johnson was a well known and highly regarded local preservationist with a particular interest in the town and someone who over the years had built up a impressive photographic record of developments.

Secondly, I am very grateful to Richard Waters. Richard allowed access to his considerable collection of timetables, vehicle data and memorabilia. His knowledge and understanding of Bristol Omnibus and its predecessors has allowed me the luxury of being able to question, discuss and refine ideas and arguments. Richard has offered corrections, suggestions and additions and his help in reviewing the work must also be acknowledged.

Thirdly, it is to former Stroud Valleys manager Christopher Blick BEM JP that I owe the greatest debt. His enthusiasm for the project, his suggestions and his willingness to unearth, and where necessary smooth the way for contacts has proved invaluable as has his collection of photographs and other material. He was also good enough to give the draft its final review before printing.

Finally, a project such as this demands much time and effort and I gratefully acknowledge the patience of my wife and family in this regard.

INTRODUCTION

Events on the buses serving the Stroud Valleys reflect just about all the changes seen nationally in the provincial bus industry. Yet there was always something different about Stroud' buses, something that may even be described as unique.

Much of this uniqueness can be attributed to the topography of the area. The Stroud Valleys and the steep and dominant Cotswold scarp lend themselves magnificently to picturesque and memorable bus operations. The valleys may be industrialised but the string of charming villages nearby offer quite a different perspective. Even in today's minibus era, the twists and turns of narrow country lanes and steep pitches test the proficiency of many a local bus driver. Settlements atop the Cotswolds rise to 700 feet above sea level or more, within three miles of the town centre. Ascending the narrow lanes more suited to the horse and cart in the days before power steering posed a significant challenge. This was the more so during the first snows of an early winter at such altitudes.

Bus operations were unique in other ways. Up to the break up of the former Bristol Omnibus Company, Stroud's road staff were described as "the gentlemen (and ladies) of the northern division". This not only reflected their skill in negotiating the area's byways but their undoubted courtesy towards passengers. In fact, up to this time, the local industry might best be described as a family, very closely knit and very self-reliant. Ventures such as the annual Carol Bus were a strong testimony to this.

And then there were the red buses operating in the twenties, thirties and forties. Although they disappeared at the time of a significant reorganisation – itself a major chapter in Stroud's bus history and one of national importance – older people still hold fond memories of the vehicles and crews. Similar memories of the pre-1950s Western National green buses still abound.

This volume, therefore, traces a history of Stroud's bus services, its vehicles and sometimes its personalities. It is not exhaustive but examines the early optimism associated with the arrival of the GWR motorbus at the turn of the twentieth century and the important part played by early pioneers such as Arnold, Reyne, Merritt and Rowlatt, when many rural districts found themselves integrated for the first time with a changing world. It examines the major contribution made at the coming to town in the twenties of the "National" – that company's first outpost in the west – and subsequent competition. It continues with stability, co-existence, the vital part played by the bus service during the Second World War and subsequent passenger growth, nationalisation and merger.

Thereafter, the volume observes a sad, slow decline during the age of the motor car. Fare increases and conductor redundancies follow, as did service cuts and further economies. After the brief optimism of a newly privatised industry of the mid- eighties, the history concludes as the service develops into one serving those less able or unwilling to drive. The current service is as important for those using the bus as it was in its heyday. The bus in Stroud remains vital to the town's economy, carrying between one and a half and two million passengers per annum.

In compiling a history such as this, there has been much reliance on people's memories and local press accounts. Memories fade and the media can misreport. Nevertheless, the responsibility for any inaccuracy rests solely with the author. By letting me know of any such errors I will be able to rectify matters during any future reprints. Such corrections will also be maintained on a web site at www.stroudvalleys.co.uk together with any additional material received. In fact, in addition to errors, I would be more than pleased to hear from anyone who might wish to add to or amend anything herein. Your general comments would also be most welcome.

N P Daniels BSc MCIT MILT
Ruthin, North Wales
daniels@stroudvalleys.co.uk

CHAPTER 1

1900–1919
THE MOTOR OMNIBUS ARRIVES

Mechanised road passenger transport may have started in Stroud in 1905 but the threat it posed to the railway 100 years ago in 1903 was responsible for the Great Western Railway's local railmotor service. Since October that year, in addition to its main line services from Swindon to Gloucester via Stroud, which began in 1845, the GWR had successfully operated its local steam railmotors from Chalford westward along the valley carved by the River Frome to Stonehouse. The frequent service was one of the first of its kind and used a self-powered single or two car steam railmotor without locomotive. It stopped at stations and a series of newly constructed local halts along the way.

In 1901, GWR was concerned that the horse bus service between Chalford and Stroud carried eight times the passengers using the train. Trains were too infrequent and stations too far apart. The swift installation of local trains and halts was not simply a reaction to horse bus traffic, however. At the turn of the 20th century, there was a real possibility that the Stroud Valleys would see road-based electric tramways. This started with an application in 1902 by Thomas Nevins, the American responsible for Cheltenham's electric trams, to build competing light railways in parallel with the GWR's between Chalford, Stroud and Stonehouse, between Nailsworth and Stroud alongside the Midland Railway and between Stroud, Painswick and Cheltenham. Both the GWR and MR succeeded in ensuring that these plans failed because they could prove they were competitive with existing rail services but, undeterred, an application to Parliament followed for the construction of road-based electric tramways or trolleybuses along the same routes. This venture involved local industrialists and was led by Stroud clothing manufacturer and social reformer George Holloway. This posed a significant threat to the GWR and one more likely to succeed. The GWR had experience of the impact of such road based tramways in the Cambourne and Redruth areas of Cornwall. The result was the swift introduction of the Stroud railmotor service, which operated more regularly than existing trains and stopped more frequently, giving the railway an edge over the competition that never materialised.

Painswick was due to be included in the stillborn electric tram network and to say that the town was disappointed when plans were not progressed was an understatement. It had already failed to attract the railway in spite of the incorporation of the Painswick Railway Company under the Painswick Railway Act of 1889, whose plans for a branch from Merrywalks in Stroud to just south of Painswick church had come to nothing.

Things were to change in 1904. This was a year of considerable optimism in Stroud for there was much talk within the town of the possible arrival of the motor omnibus, to be operated some four miles north to Painswick, by the Great Western Railway. Hitherto, for its local transport, in addition to the railmotors, Stroud had to rely upon a small but important network of horse buses operated by local people.

The Painswick Valley at the turn of the 20th century was industrialised with a number of mills and consequently the town itself was a prosperous one. In addition, many wealthier folk could afford to move in the opposite direction to the general industrial migration of the time and had settled in the "Queen of the Cotswolds", as it was then known, away as far as they could from the newly industrialised valley bottoms. In fact, over the centuries, Painswick had developed ahead of Stroud, although Stroud had by then overtaken it. Even so, Painswick was a town of importance but at about 500 feet above sea level, one that was realistically unreachable by conventional railways.

It was in December 1904, then, that the GWR finally published its plans for a motor omnibus service linking Stroud GWR station and Painswick and the story proper of motorbuses was to begin. This would be one of the company's first such ventures. In spite of the excitement upon the local streets, the necessary licenses from Stroud Urban District Council were not a formality. Stroud elected an urban district council, which in 1891 had adopted the Town Police Clauses Act 1889 and, as such, had the power to license omnibuses, hackney carriages and their drivers, whether horse drawn or motorised.

Stroud's first motor omnibus route was between the GWR Rail Station and Painswick. This view of one of GWR's first buses is at the GWR's Painswick "headquarters", the Falcon Inn. *Howard Beard collection*

The Council's Streets & Lighting Committee sat on 3 January 1905 to consider omnibus licenses. Before the committee were two applications: the first to be received was from a Stonehouse man by the name of Mr R H Stotesbury who was applying for four motor omnibus licenses. The second was from the GWR, for three. Although the committee resolved to grant both applicants their wishes, the matter continued at length at full Council the following day.

The debate centred on the fact that Stotesbury, as a private individual, was prepared to invest upwards of £7,000 in a fleet of motor vehicles that would meet the needs of the area. A council member felt that the GWR had brought forward its plans upon hearing of a potential rival. Another believed that a failure to license the GWR would create a monopoly for Stotesbury, while a third argued the reverse: even if the Stonehouse operator was granted four licenses to the GWR's three, no man would be prepared to compete against such a powerful company as the GWR and that this would itself create a monopoly.

It is clear that councillors' sympathies were mainly directed towards the local man, Stotesbury. It was also clear that GWR's opposition to the light tramway proposed just a few years earlier could influence members. However, it was felt that there was sufficient opportunity for

Stotesbury to operate between Stonehouse, Nailsworth and Stroud while the GWR concentrated on Painswick. There was praise for the GWR in preparing to start operations immediately, whereas there had been disappointments in the past. The chairman felt that as the applications from both parties were the first of their kind in Stroud, it was only fair to grant them both.

The council debates indicate that the GWR motor bus was no forgone conclusion. More for negative rather than positive reasons, GWR obtained its three motor omnibus licenses on a vote of seven to five and the service began quickly, as had been promised, on Monday 9 January 1905. What eventually happened to Stotesbury and his four licenses appears to have gone unrecorded.

Using two vehicles and witnessed by a considerable crowd of townsfolk, GWR operated a trial run from the GWR station at 1400 hrs on the preceding Saturday, carrying councillors, public dignitaries and GWR management. Crowds gathered en route and a considerable number waited at Painswick, some hoping in vain for a lift. The journey took slightly less than half an hour, in spite of the sharp ascent and apparently greasy roads, and therefore achieved an average of some 8 mph. That on the return was for 20 minutes. The fact that the trial was so well supported demonstrates both its novelty and importance to both towns. In fact, during normal running, crowds gathered for some

GWR vehicle no. 18 arrives at Stroud GWR Station by rail from Cornwall.
Howard Beard collection

time at each of the timetabled departures at both ends.

Local mill owners and businessmen warmly and openly welcomed the service. There was a sense that Painswick was at last connected by a modern means of communication, and without the black posts and overhead wires of an electric tramway as previously proposed. Henceforward, Painswick would be brought within three hours travel of London – or so it was claimed.

The vehicles themselves were two 12 mph Milnes Daimler 20 hp petrol engined single decks, one of open construction although later rebuilt as an enclosed vehicle. Seating 22, the vehicles were upholstered in leather. Seats were tiered upwards towards the rear and partly overhung the near and off sides and when full, as they often were, gave the impression of being top heavy. These were joined by a Milnes Daimler open top double deck a few weeks later.

Mr Bailey was in charge of the enterprise, followed a year later by Mr A W Hoult. The first bus was said to be driven by Sammy Adams, something of a local character and someone who drove buses for a further 25 years. Other early GWR drivers were George Guildford and Tom Stafford, both of whom retired as bus men in the sixties. The timetable saw eight return trips to begin with, although by 1908 this had been increased to 11, with five on Sundays. Scheduled single journeys took 25 minutes each way. The GWR rather grandly described the Falcon Hotel, where two of the buses were oustationed, as their "headquarters" in Painswick. The main garage and repair shop was at the rear of Stroud GWR station.

Among the considerable back slapping and sincere congratulations of the time, there was the small matter of the existing horse bus provider between Stroud and Painswick. This was Maurice Ireland who since about 1893 had been providing a passenger service between the two towns. All those involved in the early opening of the GWR service – perhaps with the exception of the GWR itself – wished that Ireland be treated liberally by the GWR. Many expected him to be taken over or go out of business. In fact, Ireland continued with his horse bus for some years after the new service, offering four return trips on Mondays to Thursdays with an extra round trip on Fridays and Saturdays. This was gradually reduced in number during the First World War. Undaunted by the new motor omnibus, Ireland purchased two double decks of his own after the First World War, in March 1919, when he resumed a similar pattern of service to that operating before the war, albeit with considerable competition from GWR. Ireland was no stranger to competition, having experienced a fair amount in the horse bus days against Mark Soul who took over from earlier operator, Thomas Spring, probably in 1914.

By 1920, Ireland had two AEC "B" type buses and had diversified into motor bus operation from Painswick to Cheltenham on certain days. However, it was on 1 April 1920 that Ireland sold to the National Omnibus & Transport Company Ltd who had commenced motor bus services in Stroud in 1919. National was acquisitive at the time and there is no doubt that Ireland would have received a fair price. The fact that Ireland was able to sustain his business for 15 years in the face of such formidable competition as the GWR is a tribute both to his hard work and to the support of local people.

Around the time of the new GWR service, one of Ireland's horses died. Some felt moved to say that this was through shock at seeing motor omnibuses. However, this death raised a debate in Stroud about the conditions under which all passenger-hauling horses were kept and used. Stroud's gradients were steep and some believed that horses were seen drawing too often. Some hoped that such horses would be spared by more motor buses, though this was still some way off.

A problem associated with the GWR buses was the amount of dust they generated as they passed through Stroud. This was because of the nature of the roads at that time. There were calls for the council's water cart to make more frequent trips around the town.

There is no doubt that the GWR service to Painswick proved popular. 1 March 1905 saw the extension of a route to Cainscross. At this time, a double deck was introduced to operate as a supplementary road service between Stroud and Chalford to ease overloading on the railmotors. Passengers in comparing bus and railmotor came out in favour of the latter. Therefore, it was perhaps as well that the bus was short lived as by 10 June, additional railmotors had arrived and the Chalford bus service was withdrawn. The Cainscross leg was terminated at the same time, as it proved less successful than the GWR had hoped. Cainscross remained within easy walking distance of the town centre and even when buses began to operate along this road with considerable frequency, it took a while for passengers to change their travel habits.

May 1905 saw what was probably Stroud's first motor bus accident. A GWR bus upon approaching the Falcon at Painswick lost its brakes and the vehicle began to slip backwards down the steep hill. The driver was unable to stop the vehicle except by turning it into a ditch, overturning it and four people suffered bruising. It is also worth recording that three years later, one of Ireland's employees, Brian Ireland (no

The short lived GWR double deck bus service which supplemented railmotors between Stroud and Chalford from March to June 1905, is seen awaiting departure in April 1905 at Stroud GWR Station. *Jack Ireland collection*

relation), was involved in what was probably the first serious bus accident in the area. In October 1908, while manoeuvring his horse and bus at Painswick, he found himself pinned against the wall by the bus itself. He died of his injuries the following day and at age 32, tragically left a wife and eight children. Mrs Ireland then took in laundry, specialising in bus company uniforms, something she did well into the Western National years at Stroud. Of their eight children, two became bus drivers, one a bus fitter and two sisters were cleaners with Red & White.

By September 1905, the GWR was seeking permission to hang "tablets" from gas lamps to denote stopping places or to erect new poles where no lamps existed. October 1906 saw GWR motor buses operating from Painswick to Cheltenham as a separate route entirely to that operating to and from Stroud, with an hour's running time, although through running between Stroud and Cheltenham was to begin within two months. This became the first longer distance bus service operating in the Stroud area, pre-dating similar developments by some 13 years.

Painswick's continued development owed much to the GWR motor bus. Similar towns and villages made wealthy by the area's early wool cloth trade struggled to compete with valley bottom mills and industries, which were established by the turn of the century.

En route for Chalford, the GWR double deck picks up at Bowbridge. Open top double decks were still in use in the early thirties in Stroud and still being manufactured in Britain in 1927. *Howard Beard collection*

Settlements such as Minchinhampton and Bisley actually declined in importance whereas Painswick, connected as it was to the GWR network by motor bus, continued to thrive even though use of the bus was less for rail connections than journeys into Stroud itself.

The Painswick – Cheltenham leg was suspended during the First World War, although the GWR maintained its services between Painswick and Stroud. As petrol was short at this time, GWR converted its buses to gas with tanks on the single deck roofs or on the upper deck of double deck vehicles. Following the war, a Maudsley arrived in Stroud from duties in Liskeard, Cornwall, having itself been replaced by an AEC.

Meanwhile, possibly from 1907 and certainly from 1910, Nailsworth had begun to benefit from motor bus operations. These were initially run as horse buses by Frank Arnold who, by 1913, was operating four return motor bus journeys on Mondays to Fridays, six on Saturdays and two on Sundays, some of which connected with GWR trains at Stroud. Arnold first used a Thornycroft single deck but latterly had purchased two double decks, first a Ryknield and then a Caledon. He competed with Davis' horse bus for a while, which had started in 1889 and which, by 1910 operated twice on Mondays to Thursdays and three times on

AF 84, CO 84 and BH 09 line up at Stroud GWR Station in c.1908 with staff. All are Milnes Daimlers. Note at this time that BH 09 on the right is not fully enclosed. *Howard Beard collection*

Fridays and Saturdays. Davis was still recorded as running as late as 1917. Arnold was also operating motor buses on certain days to Avening by November 1910, some through from Stroud and others from Nailsworth. Mr Saul applied for a license to operate a motor omnibus

Frank Arnold operated early motor omnibuses between Stroud, Nailsworth and Avening, where Thornycroft AD 1680 is seen. *Howard Beard collection*

Arnold's earlier of two double decks, a Ryknield with registration AD 1786, at Nailsworth. *Howard Beard collection*

in March 1910 on a similar route to Arnold's but this was transferred to Arnold in July that year. Meanwhile, what was referred to as the Bath Tramways Company appears to have been running an additional motor bus service between Nailsworth and Stroud in 1910, without applying for the necessary vehicle and driver licenses and in 1911, Mr O Jeffrey was granted licenses and he, too, worked the Nailsworth road. There were complaints in June 1911 that Arnold and Jeffrey were racing but this was settled amicably with an agreement between the two.

The popular motor bus between Stroud and Nailsworth was far more convenient than the parallel train. For one thing, the bus stopped at intermediate points such as Inchrook, North Woodchester and Lightpill. For another, the MR passenger rail service offered good access to Stonehouse but those travelling to Stroud found it frustrating. It was necessary either to walk from the nearest station on the line at Dudbridge to Stroud or await a connecting train known as the "Dudbridge Donkey" or "Donkey Ride" to Stroud's MR station at Wallbridge. Even then, this was some distance from the central area. The newly arrived National was to take over Arnold on 17 March 1920 even before it bought out Ireland.

By 1908, Mr W J Combe of Eastington was operating a motor bus service between Eastington, Stonehouse and Stroud with two trips from Eastington and three from Stonehouse on weekdays, save Thursday afternoons, for many years Stroud's traditional half-day. Jack Pegler was by 1919 operating a motor bus service between Stroud and Framilode twice a week.

No further motor buses appear to be recorded during the period from 1905 to National's arrival in 1919. This was in spite of periodic calls for the GWR to provide more services. The potential capital and revenue costs were off-putting and insufficient people had the necessary driving and mechanical skills to maintain what amounted to fairly unreliable early vehicles on the area's under-maintained roads. Instead, the horse buses continued either daily or on certain days only.

The aftermath of the First World War was to change things completely during the twenties and it was immediately after the war that the National rode into town.

CHAPTER 2

1920–1929
A PATTERN EMERGES

Conditions were right in the 1920s for the considerable expansion of the motor omnibus. With the exception of the pioneering GWR operation, up to the First World War, such motor bus services as there were had largely replaced horse drawn operations. This was about to change. Wartime thrift had resulted in much of the population building up healthy savings and with little else on which to spend this during the post war austerity years, travel itself benefitted significantly. New routes and excursions blossomed. To deliver these services, there returned from the trenches a new workforce skilled in driving, vehicle maintenance or both. Advances in vehicle technology and even a suitable pool of ex-military vehicles for conversion had improved reliability and lowered costs. At this time, there were few and localised licensing restrictions and motor bus development was relatively easy and straightforward. New entrants with their war time capital invested in what they saw as enterprises with a good return while existing companies were set to expand.

One such expanding company was the National Steam Car Company Ltd. With its origins in vehicle manufacture, from 1909 the company began to operate buses as well, solely within London. An agreement between the London bus operators of 1913 limited National's expansion and it began to look outside the capital. It first took over the Chelmsford services of the Great Eastern Railway. National then opened branches at Colchester and Bedford.

Why did National choose Stroud? At this time, companies with territorial ambitions had begun to expand throughout Britain but had largely overlooked much of the West Country, with its lower population densities. Pioneering concerns such as National had reached the point where, in order to maintain the growth in profits associated with earlier years, expansion in the west was inevitable.

Parts of the West Country were beginning to see the development of territorial companies but motor bus operation was still patchy. Local carriers using horse buses still served much of the region. The GWR had been at the forefront of the train companies in providing motor buses as feeders, including one at Stroud, but such services were somewhat random. Tramway development among the plethora of small and medium sized towns was largely impossible. It was therefore natural that National should look towards the West Country as the last part of England to offer development potential.

The industrialised Stroud Valleys was one such area, which perfectly matched National's model for further growth. First, it was urbanised in the sense that the valley floors were populous, industrious and productive. The cloth and wool trades were enjoying rapid development. The Golden Valley eastwards from Stroud, for example, was so named because of the number of flourishing businesses therein.

Secondly, the town itself was fast developing as the commercial centre serving this blossoming industry. Thirdly, as indicated from its persuasive literature from the twenties, National recognised the tourism potential both in terms of access to the bracing hills above the town and the ready market for excursion work. Fourthly, although the railways had developed along some valley floors, halts and stations were limited to key settlements only. The success of the local railmotors would not have gone unnoticed to National. Finally, bus services were fragmented and in the hands of local carriers and, with the exception of the GWR motor bus to Painswick and a few others, the horse was the dominant motive power.

However, one particular circumstance for National proved to be pivotal. Two Stroud industrialists, Messrs A B Cooke and G W Powell, had between them formed a company by the name of Gloucestershire Carriers to begin motor bus passenger services in Stroud. Cooke and Powell had arranged the necessary funding through the same company used by National and it was this finance house that brought both concerns together. What followed was mutually beneficial to both parties. National found a venture almost ready to go and acquired the company. Gloucestershire Carriers never operated but Cooke and Powell were content to concentrate on their substantial core mill interests, somewhat the richer after National's offer.

It was therefore on 19 December 1919 that the National Steam Car Company Ltd began its operations in Stroud under the local management of Mr Algy Wood. This was its first and pioneering outpost in the West Country although branches at Yeovil, Taunton, Bridgwater and Trowbridge soon followed. On 13 February 1920, the company was reconstituted as the National Omnibus & Transport Company Ltd.

National initially operated two vehicles on two routes. One paralleled the railmotor between Chalford and Stonehouse via Stroud in what was to become the forerunner of Stroud's most important local route. On weekdays, it operated nine times a day to both Chalford and Stonehouse, with six journeys on Sundays. Fares from Stroud to Stonehouse were 3d and from Chalford to Stonehouse, 7d. The vehicles were both ex-London General and, as was the custom, ran on solid tyres, pneumatics being introduced in Stroud as elsewhere from the mid-1920s with solid tyres phased out by 1932. Buses averaged no more than 12 mph.

The second route operated between Nailsworth and Painswick via Stroud and Pitchcombe. This provided seven journeys to Nailsworth and six to Painswick on weekdays plus five to Nailsworth and four to Painswick on Sundays. The National fare between Stroud and Painswick was 1d less that GWR's. The service competed with the motor bus operations of Arnold between Stroud and Nailsworth and both the GWR and Ireland between Stroud and Painswick. Whereas GWR terminated at its station in Stroud, the National opted for nearby King Street which, at this time, was the heart of the commercial area.

Just as at the GWR motor bus announcement of 1904, Stroud celebrated at the prospect of more buses, this time to be operated by a firm of the calibre of National. Both routes proved immediately popular and their arrival changed the social landscape of the Stroud Valleys forever.

If the public's welcome of the new services was keen, that of the licensing authority was more measured. In December 1919, the Stroud Urban District Council's Streets & Lighting Committee granted a provisional license to National for one month only. This was upon the understanding that the timetable would be strictly adhered to. At the first full Urban District Council of January 1920, while accepting that the National bus service was undoubtedly of benefit to the area, concern was expressed that the service was anything but punctual, with some departures operating half an hour late. A further one-month license was granted and the Council asked that the Company reconsider its schedules.

This National did for on 17 January 1920, revisions were made. National reduced its service to six weekday buses to Chalford, seven to

Stonehouse and five to Painswick while adding an eighth to Nailsworth. Running times were extended by 10 minutes between Stonehouse and Chalford. Further amendments were made on 7 February, principally introducing an extra journey between Nailsworth and Painswick.

It is likely that the frequent number of "stops" (there being no designated bus stopping places at this time) and the state of the local roads and in particularly the solid tyres upon them were contributory to the early unreliability. Metalling of roads took place in the 1930s and bus services had to wait a decade or more before this major investment was to bring its tremendous benefits and, even then, the rudimentary surfaces would easily be churned by bus wheels. Many of Stroud's roads in the twenties had a tendency to see motor vehicles get stuck and this was actually where the horse bus was able to score, as hooves could more easily dig into the relatively soft road, where necessary.

By the time of the next Council, the number of buses at Stroud had grown to six, requiring 10 drivers. The National sent a delegation from London to seek a more permanent license and explained that the original timetable had been something of a temporary one to determine by experience the conditions under which services operated and the running time required. The company pointed out that timetable revisions had helped, although they did admit to experiencing difficulties, including finding suitable premises. There was a promise of a double deck to help with loadings. The Council accepted that there had been improvements and permanent licenses were duly granted.

Things moved fast. On 17 March 1920, National acquired its first Stroud area operator. This was Frank Arnold who had operated between Avening, Nailsworth and Stroud. Arnold's double deck Caledon was transferred to National, numbered as 2112, but soon taken off the road as unfit. The previous spring, there were occasions when the Nailsworth service did not operate at all owing to breakdowns, even though the early drivers each carried whole tool kits to try to keep buses going. The take-over strengthened National's Nailsworth service which now ran broadly hourly at 13 times a day on Mondays to Fridays, 15 on Saturdays and seven times on Sundays. The train between Nailsworth, Woodchester and Dudbridge offered just four journeys on weekdays.

The garaging facilities also improved at this time with the acquisition of a site known as Badbrook Garage on Slad Road. National had hitherto used somewhat unsatisfactory premises under railway arches four and five at Wallbridge although the Painswick Inn yard,

Gloucester Street, was used before that as Wallbridge was not ready. With the acquisition of Arnold's business came premises at Cossack Square, Nailsworth, used as an outstation till 1936. Additional premises for two buses at Britannia Square in Nailsworth were obtained between 1924 and 1931.

It is not surprising that National's activity in Stroud came to the attention of a neighbouring territorial operator, the Bristol Tramways & Carriage Company Ltd. Tramways at this time were operating in a deep blue and white livery and the terms "Bristol Blues" and "Blue Taxis" were widely used. From its heartland in the city of Bristol, Tramways had undergone rapid though patchy motor omnibus expansion in Bath and Weston-super-Mare before establishing branches in Cheltenham and Gloucester in 1912 and 1913 respectively. Uneasy at the newcomer within easy travelling of its northern plants, Tramways began hourly services from Nailsworth, which bifurcated at Stroud every two hours to either Gloucester via Stonehouse or Cheltenham via Painswick. These required two Gloucester- and two Cheltenham-based vehicles and were advertised to operate from early April 1920. In 1921, the Nailsworth – Cheltenham service 46 had become hourly and that to Gloucester (service 51) remained at two-hourly intervals. However, Tramways was unsuccessful in obtaining the necessary license from Stroud Urban District Council and, initially, passengers boarding the services at Stroud could only do so upon the production of a valid return ticket. This restriction was lifted after only a matter of weeks following full licensing along the routes.

National, too, wished to expand in a northerly direction, beyond Painswick to Cheltenham. Here, in June 1920, it saw opposition from the council in Cheltenham where there was some reluctance among council members to license the necessary vehicles and drivers. There were complaints about the affect such vehicles would have on the public highways and that the addition of a further operator along this particular road would only exacerbate what was already described as a cut throat situation between the GWR and Tramways. The Bristol company pointed out that the council in issuing Cheltenham licenses had in the past tended to look more favourably upon local proprietors than the larger concern. Its local manager now argued that in this case Tramways was the local firm and that National was, in fact, an interloper. After much debate, Cheltenham concluded that the additional bus service was an amenity in the public interest, that competition was healthy and that additional services might bring more people in to the town.

Meanwhile, in September 1920, National opened a small branch at Wotton-under-Edge, providing services between Wotton, Kingswood and Charfield rail station and between Dursley and Uley. Although the facility closed within twelve months, the continued expansion was of concern to Bristol Tramways, even though the Bristol company had yet to start services south of Nailsworth. The matter of National's expansion in an area considered by Bristol Tramways to be its own – by now including National services in Bridgwater, Weston-super-Mare, Glastonbury and Burnham-on-Sea as well as Stroud and Wotton – was referred to the London & Provincial Omnibus Owners' Association and in December 1920, fares and timetables over common sections of road were mutually agreed.

In 1920 and 1921, National operated at least 11 buses in Stroud with native registrations plus, for a short period, Arnold's Caledon. These were five AEC YC types with open top double deck bodies seating 44 and constructed by National itself, two AEC YC charabancs with 28 seat bodies and three AEC single deck buses with 36 seat Dodson bodies.

Expansion by National throughout 1921 was frustrated only by the lack of availability of buses. Nevertheless, agreement with Tramways saw the extension of National services from Nailsworth beyond Stroud and Painswick to Cheltenham. In August 1921, services were extended beyond Avening to Tetbury, then to Malmesbury and again in 1923 to Chippenham but the Wotton enterprise closed, with buses transferring to a newly opened branch at Trowbridge in Wiltshire. This move summed up the "gold-rush" years of the early 1920s: if services were incapable of returning sufficient profit, they would be sacrificed for those that possibly could. It was somewhat ironic that a number of Trowbridge services later also failed and were abandoned during their early years.

September saw services from Stroud to Cirencester (followed a month later by separate services between Cirencester, Fairford, Lechlade and Farringdon). 1921 also brought with it the appearance of route numbers, as follows:

1   Stroud – Nailsworth
2   Nailsworth – Stroud – Cheltenham
3   Stroud – Tetbury – Malmesbury
4   Chalford – Stroud – Stonehouse
5   Stroud – Cirencester
6   Cirencester – Lechlade – Farringdon

Services were renumbered in October 1922 beginning with 46 to 55 and, when these were depleted in 1925, from 64 onwards.

The agreement reached in December 1920 by both National and Bristol Tramways considered the position at that time but failed to secure future territorial limits. This left the Bristol company free to outflank National in moves that demonstrated the Klondike-like rush of the early motor bus era. To do this, and in contrast to National's vehicle shortage at the time, Bristol had built up a considerable stock-pile of vehicles made by its own motor construction works. In 1921, Tramways opened a branch at Wells and the associated routes limited the northerly expansion of National services already in place in Somerset. Simultaneously, Tramways began route extensions from Chipping Sodbury to Tetbury and Malmesbury and extended from Marshfield to Chippenham. Next, Bristol introduced a Cheltenham to Cirencester service followed a month later by an extension beyond Frampton Cotterell to Wotton-under-Edge, itself only recently vacated by National – how National must have regretted that move! The final blow to National also occurred at this time: services began to Chippenham, Cirencester and Farringdon from a newly opened branch at Swindon, a move that dramatically reached over existing National territory.

In the space of just one year, a planned and well-executed manoeu-vre had seen Bristol Tramways effectively isolate National's Gloucestershire operations. Lack of buses at National had been a contributory factor. While there was still considerable scope for growth in the further reaches of the west country south of Tramway's new frontier, National henceforward would need to satisfy itself with expansion within its surrounded Stroud operations, rather than any enlargement beyond it.

It must not be forgotten that while Tramways played out its territo-rial game of chess with National, there were other motor bus entrepre-neurs starting and developing in the Stroud area, following the favourable post-First World War conditions. Operating as The Blue Bird Bus, one such was Ernest Lewis of Frampton-on-Severn who ran to and from Stroud. National bought this firm's Frampton to Stroud service in November 1926 while Lewis continued to Gloucester for a few more years.

From about 1919, Perkins Motor Bus Service operated at 1400 on Mondays and Wednesdays from Leonard Stanley to Stroud, returning from Stroud at 1600. Before this, Spratt had operated horse buses. It is not known whether Perkins had any connection with the popular

Staff at the National Omnibus & Transport Company Stroud Branch in the early 1920s at Badbrook Garage. Back row, left to right: H W King, Mr Curtis and three unidentified staff. Front row: J Day, J Mills, ?, Mr Lester, ?, Sid Light (Uncle to local author Laurie Lee), Valder King. *Jack Ireland collection*

Thorp Brothers' motor buses of Leonard Stanley which operated from the mid-twenties to the Stanleys on a more frequent basis but Perkins appears to have left the scene by 1922. The Thorps were two brothers who operated a route each from Stroud to Coaley via the Stanleys and Frocester and from Stroud to Gloucester via the Stanleys.

Another was Major Henry Roland Napier Rowlatt who, as owner of the Bear Inn on Rodborough Common, began motor omnibus operations from Stroud to the Bear for staff transport and as a means of ensuring that his guests arriving at Stroud's rail stations could reach his establishment. Soon after, by 1923 in fact, he extended services beyond The Bear to and from Minchinhampton as public omnibuses, operating six return trips on weekdays and three on Sundays, and the fleet grew to two Morris vehicles and two Vulcans plus a Reo.

Rowlatt found a competitor on his service to and from Minchinhampton. Carrier John Merritt – or Merrett as it was also spelt – of that town expanded into public omnibuses in about 1920 and traded as Grey Motors or Grey Bus Services. The first "bus" was a military surplus Ford T lorry converted for public use with a rear entrance and primitive longitudinal wooden seating. Early services between Minchinhampton and Stroud ran on demand but developed into a timetable operating initially on Tuesdays, Fridays and Saturdays. By the end of the decade, using a small fleet of Chevrolets, Grey Bus Services extended daily from Stroud to Minchinhampton, Stroud to Avening via Nailsworth and Stroud to Tetbury and Malmesbury, by then all in overt competition with National.

The importance of all these early services to the development of Stroud and its Valleys cannot be over-emphasised. The main method of passenger transport for those living away from a rail line up to the First World War had been by horse bus. These were limited by many constraints: seating capacity, frequency of operation – usually two or three times per week – and, not least, speed. Though some of the early motor buses were less than totally reliable, they were a giant leap forward and came at a time when the shop keepers of Stroud itself were keen to encourage rural residents to view and buy their wares.

The motor bus also opened the Cotswold upland areas above Stroud. Stroud's upland Commons of Burleigh, Littleworth, Rodborough, Selsey and Minchinhampton were little more than two or three miles from the town's centre but with the limitations of the horse bus, they might as well have been at the other end of the country. The term used at the time for Stroud's Commons was "the highlands" which illustrates nicely the fact that such areas were perceived as remote and inaccessible.

From 1903, it had been possible for Stroud urban residents to catch the railmotor to Ham Mill Halt or Brimscombe Bridge and walk the steep inclines to Minchinhampton Common. To do this, walkers had to climb about 500 feet over a distance of about a mile – not particularly conducive to a day out on the Common or a round of golf on the established links! After the First World War, Stroud became popular with visitors from the Midlands and motor buses to Minchinhampton (and indeed elsewhere), as provided first by Grey Bus Services and Rowlatt's Bear Bus Service and later by National, ensured that Stroud's natural beauty became easily accessible to locals and tourists alike. In fact, National exploited this to the full by publishing in the late 1920s a descriptive guide to the twists, turns, pitches and viewpoints associated with its Stroud services.

With National set for expansion locally alongside smaller operators from 1923, the situation in Stroud developed into something of a competitive free-for-all. National buses from Stroud reached Bisley as service 53 and Birdlip as 52 in 1923. Another new service that year was the 54 between Stroud and Frampton-on-Severn, which competed with Lewis' Blue Bird Bus Service, and, somewhat, with the Thorp brothers. A third was the 55 to Minchinhampton via Amberley which competed head on with those operated both by the Grey Bus Service and by Major Napier Rowlatt. In fact, a National driver was summoned and fined £3 plus costs in 1927 having been caught racing the parallel Grey Bus service. A fourth was between Stroud and Cashes Green, numbered 64, a route provided solely by National. The following year saw an extension from Bisley to Oakridge on the 53 and the establishment of a new route between Stroud and Whiteshill (56).

By this time, a new and formidable Stroud competitor to National was emerging. These were the services operated by Nicholas "Dick" Reyne. In providing local bus services, Reyne became something of a local hero at this time. As an Australian airman who arrived at Aston Down airfield as part of the Australian Expeditionary Force shortly before the end of the First World War, he elected to stay in the Stroud area to marry his Minchinhampton bride. Blessed with a keen and sharp business ability, he realised the potential offered by the motor omnibus. It is quite possible that it was Reyne's father-in-law, who worked for National, who actually sewed the initial seeds. Reyne's genuine approach to providing a local customer focused service, his ability to listen to passengers' requirements and his willingness to open up motor bus routes in rural districts untouched by others because of their poorly maintained roads, which in actual fact were often no more than well worn tracks, ensured a significant following. In later years, Reyne was elected as a councillor on Stroud Urban District Council. He is well remembered in Stroud to this day. It is unclear at exactly what stage Reyne entered the local bus market. He is understood to have become associated with the Grey Bus Service of Minchinhampton at an early stage, probably before 1924.

When Rowlatt offered his business for sale in March 1926, National stepped in to ensure that the Grey Bus Service did not strengthen its position, such was the potential threat. The Rowlatt purchase was interesting in that the agreement ensured the retention of "The Bear Inn" on National's vehicle running boards and within its timetables (where it has remained ever since, though of more importance nowadays to the nearby hamlet of Houndscroft and the Bownham Park housing estate than to those travelling to The Bear itself). National was to provide late evening services on three nights each week upon the conclusion of cinema performances which was interesting as

Rowlatt's last journey was at 1910. Rowlatt also negotiated a number of staff passes for use on National services to and from The Bear. Although Rowlatt's Bear premises were used as an outstation for a while, this was soon after logically moved to Minchinhampton itself.

Having acquired a Minchinhampton route against Merritt & Reyne's Grey Bus Service, in 1926 National began its attempt to secure its position against what was probably its most fierce competitor anywhere in Britain, Reyne himself. For the most part, Grey Buses were operated as a separate business to the Reyne's other firm and it was this, trading as Red Bus, that was to become so popular with Stroud's passengers. Its vehicles were characterised by both their colour and the kangaroo logo within a broad oval, placed on the sides of the vehicles.

Red Bus had shortly beforehand started to expand, using drivers who also doubled as cleaners and fitters. In partnership with Mr M A Whittington and using premises once occupied by the Little Mill at Lansdown, Reyne started services to valley mills, operating at first not on a regular, clock-face timetable like National's but at times suited to workers. This proved both popular and profitable. Reyne was able to purchase a second vehicle and by June 1926 held a further two licenses and began operating to areas unserved by any motor bus. On more rural runs where passengers would be well known to the driver, it was possible for regular passengers to have their fares chalked up until pay day and this, too, proved popular. In three years Reyne's routes included services from Stroud to Horsley and Wickwar, from Nailsworth to Minchinhampton, from Stroud to Dursley via Eastington, from Stroud to Bussage and France Lynch (male passengers having to walk if the bus was fully laden, to enable to the bus to climb Toadsmoor Hill), and to Horns Road and Summer Street in the urban area of Stroud itself. By the close of the decade, free from any of the constraints and agreements as between territorial operators, Red Bus was able to penetrate the Stroud to Gloucester market both via Edge and Painswick and that to Cheltenham via Painswick as well as buses operating to Malmesbury. Whittington is understood to have sold his interests in 1927, leaving Reyne in sole charge.

In 1926, therefore, National began a service 67 between Nailsworth and Horsley. Activity in Nailsworth continued with services to Nympsfield which later that year were extended first to Dursley via Uley and was later still to start from Stroud. Then came the 68 to the Stanleys, 53A to Bussage via Bisley, a service to Sheepscombe and a new route 69 to Cirencester via Minchinhampton, which lasted from February to November 1926 only. To do this, National added to its

Blue Star operated express services through Stroud from 1928. Leyland Lioness FH 5724 was bodied by Strachan and lettered accordingly for use on the service. *Roy Marshall collection*

existing vehicles a 1922 Burford with Hickman bodywork, and three Guy BA types with Dodson 30 seat bodies.

National further consolidated its position in Stroud as it moved from its Slad Road premises to Brick House in London Road. Plans were swiftly drawn up for a brand new garage on the adjacent land and this was to include a 5,000 gallon petrol tank. Completed in 1927 by a Paganhill firm, it was extended in 1936, additional parking provided on site in 1963 and in fact housed Stroud's buses until 1993. It was in 1927 that the booking office and back offices at 8A George Street were opened, replacing the offices at Locking Hill (from 1920) and Rowcroft Retreat (at the commencement of service in 1919).

Also in 1927, Stroud Urban District Council granted further omnibus licenses for Greyhound Motors for a Malmesbury to Stroud operation via Nailsworth. Greyhound successfully applied for extended weekend services later in 1927 but had withdrawn by December 1928 when a Mr Sherston was approved and duly licensed to operate. Red Bus began operation to Ruscombe (following Western National's 1927 service to that village, which lasted only months) and later that year between Cheltenham and Birdlip. Also that year, a Mr Hopson began working Mondays, Tuesdays, Wednesdays, Fridays and Saturdays between Stroud, Sapperton and Cirencester. Unsurprisingly, National complained about pirating on its routes, especially to and from

Nailsworth. Congestion was becoming serious, too, and there were reported to be as many as 270 journeys running in the town on Saturdays in 1927.

The story of Stroud's first motor bus routes pivots around National and Red Bus. Nevertheless, Bristol Tramways and the Thorp Brothers were still operating in Stroud at this time as was the GWR. The GWR's pioneering motor bus service of 1905 carried on regardless of the number of services amassing on the roads from Stroud to Painswick. An agreement between National and the GWR dating from July 1921 led to the withdrawal of GWR services between Painswick and Cheltenham upon National's withdrawal of some local services between Stroud and Painswick. Tramways' motor buses were also operating on this road. The agreement also meant that GWR would not compete significantly throughout National's territory.

After many years of service, the original Milnes Daimler GWR buses were withdrawn in 1922 and replaced by AECs. In 1925, Stroud received Burfords. There was some non-competitive GWR expansion in 1926 when it began two short services to Rodborough in May and Kingscourt in July respectively and it extended its service beyond Painswick to Cranham on summer Sundays in August. By this time, all its buses were stored adjacent to the GWR station yard at Cheapside where a corrugated iron garage capable of taking double decks had been built and painted in GWR colours.

Meanwhile, between 3 and 12 May 1926, trades unions called upon all workers in Britain to cease work in support of the miners' wage dispute. Within two days of this General Strike, most of Stroud's industry was on short working and 1,300 people thrown out of work with crowds applying for the Dole. Both GWR and LMS local trains in the district stopped completely as 200 railwaymen – 98 per cent of the local rail workforce – struck. A skeleton express service did reach Stroud, however.

The three GWR buses in the town were pressed into rail replacement services operating at 0700 and 0800 from Chalford to Gloucester via Stroud and Stonehouse, principally for season ticket holders whose rail passes were honoured on the bus service. Thereafter and until the evening returns from Gloucester were required, the buses would operate "as required" between Stonehouse and Chalford via Stroud.

The General Strike was something of a watershed. National drivers did not join the stoppage and the company was able to provide 100 per cent of its services, augmenting those between Stonehouse, Stroud and

Chalford and between Stroud and Painswick, the latter presumably because GWR buses to Painswick were employed on other duties. This all indicated to rail operators that the public were happy to forsake the railways for road transport and it galvanised rail operators to take direct action in trying to acquire more road passenger interests, something that would lead to changes by the end of the decade.

No account of early bus services in Stroud would be complete without reference to the tours and excursions operated from the town. These were a valuable part of local operators' businesses. The period of National growth at Stroud coincided with the replacement of the charabanc by the motor coach, thereby improving passenger comfort considerably. The old 1920s "charas" ran on solid tyres, were open save for a retractable soft-top and had a series of bench seats, all of which tended to be accessible from the nearside only. With their gradual replacement by National motor coaches, tours from Stroud had become both extensive and popular by the mid-twenties, even though charas continued to be used throughout the decade. Coaches reached as far afield as Bristol and Clifton, Bath, Weston-super-Mare, the Malvern Hills, Abergavenny, the Black Mountains, Fairford and Bibury, Severn Beach, Bath, Northleach, Stow and Broadway, the Wye Valley, Oxford and Stratford-on-Avon. Afternoon and evening "drives", or mystery tours as they became known, were also popular.

National produced a series of brochures and promotional literature extolling the virtues of its excursions from Stroud as elsewhere and offering much detail as to the routes and points of interest. It was the routes as well as the destination that was of equal interest and here the motor coach scored over parallel excursions offered by LMS and GWR. In fact, from 1927, the GWR went one better with the introduction of a six-day "Land Cruise" from Stroud to Oxford via the Forest of Dean, Wye Valley, Malvern Hills and Stratford-on-Avon. The trip lasted six days, cost 12 guineas and employed Maudsley motor coaches. Meanwhile, National's regular, senior coach drivers became expert in tourism related matters as they acted as guides. Local proprietors also offered similar tours, Weston being especially popular. In addition to tours and excursions, local bus providers would often lay on special buses or duplicates for specific events, including to local shows.

In March 1928, Reyne inaugurated an express service daily between Stroud and London via Reading at a 15/- fare, using locally registered DF 4605, a Thoryncroft coach. It departed Stroud at 0830 and returned daily from London at 1500, the journey time being 4 hours 40 minutes, including a refreshment break at Wantage. In time, there was

one additional return trip added and the service was extended to operate from Gloucester in 1929, for which DF 6916 and DF 9186, two
Leyland Tigers with London Lorries bodies, were purchased. Express
services had been virtually non-existent before the First World War
but also in 1928, Blue Star Coaches set about operating express services
from Gloucester to London also via Stroud and Reading, using a 26
seater which boasted pneumatic tyres, semi-bucket spring backed seats
and a "heating apparatus". Blue Star was taken over by Red & White
soon after. By 1930, there were up to six operators employed on express
services between Gloucester and London. Blue Star operated once a
day and offered the same return fare from Stroud to London as did Red
Bus.

Meanwhile, in 1929, Merritt's Grey Bus Service operated between
Stroud, Tetbury and Malmesbury, possibly replacing Sherston. This
operated four weekday journeys to Malmesbury, plus a couple of shorts
to Tetbury. Merritt's son summoned National in January 1929 for
obstruction at Woodchester, but the case was dismissed. Silvey of
Epney started a service between Longney and Stroud in 1928. Although
this service passed to Bristol Tramways, another branch of the Silvey
family continued to operate from Arlingham to Gloucester to 1969.

Structural changes were afoot for National in 1929. This resulted
from the Road & Rail Transport Act 1928 when the "Big Four" regional
rail operators of the time (including GWR) were able to invest in bus
operations. This was something that the rail concerns had been seeking
since the General Strike proved to them that rail no longer held a local
transport monopoly. National's operations at this time were spread
throughout the country but it was in the west that matters proceeded
most swiftly with broad agreement being reached with GWR even
before the Bill's assent. This led to the merger on 28 February 1929 of
GWR's bus interests with National's in the west of England under the
newly created Western National Omnibus Company Ltd, a name that
has only recently vanished from the sides of buses in Devon and
Cornwall. The National Omnibus & Transport Company was now the
holding company and its subordinate Western National assumed the
vehicles and control of the three GWR Stroud routes, although these
appeared in GWR's own publicity after that date.

At the same time, the GWR invested substantially in Bristol
Tramways. This was not significant for Stroud at the time but was to
become so in the following years.

Four AEC Reliance buses, three with Strachan and one with Dodson
32 seat bodywork plus a Guy 20 seat coach with Hoyal bodywork had

King Street, Stroud, c. 1927. The bus on the right, registration DF 1827, is most likely one of Reyne's Red Buses. *Peckham's of Stroud*

arrived by 1929. 1929 also saw the adoption of service 55A between Stroud and Minchinhampton via Brimscombe. With the arrival of Western National, all services were renumbered and Stroud's found themselves in the 200 series. The routes operated by National in Stroud at the end of the twenties were as follows:

220	Nailsworth – Stroud – Painswick – Cheltenham (formerly 46/51)
220A	Stroud – Painswick
221	Chalford – Stroud – Stonehouse (47)
222	Stroud – Chalford – Cirencester (48)
223	Stroud – Nailsworth – Tetbury – Malmesbury – Chippenham (49/49A)
224	Stroud – Nailsworth (50)
226	Stroud – Oakridge/Bussage via Bisley (53)
226	Stroud – Bussage via Bisley, Eastcombe (53A)
227	Stroud – The Stanleys – Eastington – Framilode (54)
228	Stroud – The Bear – Amberley – Minchinhampton (55)

229	Stroud – Brimscombe – Minchinhampton (55A)
225	Stroud – Slad – Birdlip (52)
230	Stroud – Whiteshill (56)
231	Stroud – Randwick via Cashes Green (64)
232	Stroud – Nailsworth – Horsley – Dursley (67)
233	Stroud – King Stanley (68)
	Stroud – Painswick (ex-GWR)
	Stroud – Rodborough (ex-GWR)
	Stroud – Kingscourt (ex-GWR)

As the decade closed, much of Western National's attention was focused on its growth in Somerset, Devon and Cornwall and also the expansion of express coaches. Its recently acquired Royal Blue business joined the Associated Motorways pool of express routes, which included Black & White at Cheltenham. Nevertheless, by 1929, Western National, Red Bus, Bristol Tramways, GWR and Thorp's between them had just about set out the pattern of bus services that would continue in operation at least to the early 1980s and in many cases beyond. While this completely changed village life in the area, it did offer rural communities the opportunity to take part in wider affairs. Right to its end, the decade had been an active one as companies vied for Stroud's routes and passengers, and this would remain so until the understandings of the early thirties.

CHAPTER 3

1930–1939
RED, GREEN AND BLUE

By the close of the twenties, the formation of Stroud's local bus service network was almost complete. There was considerable competition between operators, especially between Red Bus and Western National. In fact, competition in Stroud was as intense as it had been anywhere in Britain and such rivalry for routes and passengers between the Stroud concerns, including the earlier explorations of Bristol Tramways from Cheltenham and Gloucester, had ensured a remarkably quick route development – in the space of just 10 years.

Competition between bus operators had become something of a problem throughout Britain. Services burgeoned during the twenties as demand for travel grew. There were also very real concerns that, in an effort to out-compete others, some operators were literally running their vehicles into the ground, with little time available for even routine maintenance. There is no evidence to suggest that vehicle upkeep was a particular concern in Stroud. In fact, Stroud's Urban District Council had adopted the permissive legislation that gave at least some control of its buses. These were the Town Police Clauses Acts 1847 and 1889, the latter having been adopted in Stroud in 1891. The council employed an inspector to exercise quality control and investigate problems, and vehicles were licensed annually.

These Acts applied to individual local authority areas, having been drafted in the horse age. Now, the motor omnibus was easily capable of longer distances and it meant that buses used on inter-urban or longer distance rural services required more than one council license. Some authorities used the legislation to protect their own operations while others limited the numbers of vehicles in use. Yet in Stroud, most services were local in nature and required just one license per vehicle. It is perhaps as well that the adjacent Rural District Councils had not adopted the Acts. Cheltenham and Gloucester both licensed vehicles and Stroud's operators never experienced any problems in obtaining multiple vehicle licenses, other than in synchronising applications.

Once vehicle licenses were granted, there was no means of regulating the routes along which they operated, the times of their departures or fares charged upon them. In the areas where competition was at its most fierce – and Stroud was one of them – it was possible to witness some rather ugly scenes. Further, it was claimed that competition caused undue congestion on town centre streets and at termini, and even if Stroud benefitted from responsible operators with well maintained vehicles, there was certainly criticism of congestion, though what the complainants would have made of the traffic build up from the 1950s is anyone's guess.

The consequence of all this was that many in Britain felt that the system of unfettered competition had become unmanageable. The government intervened.

This was in the shape of the Road Traffic Act 1930. Henceforward, operators, vehicles and drivers would all be licensed, not by a purely local council with local concerns, but by newly appointed regional Traffic Commissioners. Drivers and conductors now required to have character references and medicals and were subject to criminal prosecution for working without licenses. The vehicles themselves were open to more rigorous inspections by ministry men. This contributed significantly to safety standards throughout the operating industry.

Most importantly, routes, timetables and fares were to be regulated and it is this, above all else, that was to ensure stability over the years to come. It is not surprising that the territorial operators such as Western National and Bristol Tramways welcomed such moves, keen to exchange free-for-all for order. The fight for passengers left the streets and entered the Traffic Commissioners' traffic court. Often, in deciding which of two (or more) competitive operators should hold one of the new route-specific "stage carriage licenses", the Traffic Commissioners would judge which provider had operated first or, if this proved impossible or a strong enough case was put before them, they would license more than one, but with a degree of equity.

Councillors still busied themselves with matters relating to buses and bus services and it would appear that it took some time for both them and the public to appreciate that Stroud Urban District Council's responsibilities had passed to the Traffic Commissioners.

There had previously been an agreement regarding service levels and fares as far back as December 1920 between Bristol Tramways and the

National drivers and conductors at Minchinhampton, 1931, from left: J Pond, G Davis, L Cooke, A Glastonbury, J Cooke, W Archer, A Liddicott. Western National outstationed buses at Minchinhampton to 1934. Note the ticket machines carried by conductors. *Jack Ireland*

National Omnibus & Transport Company but, as regards Stroud, this had a limited impact on a couple of specific routes only. It was therefore the Road Traffic Act that was responsible for a degree of stability not before seen in Stroud. No longer was the competition between Red Bus and National quite so headstrong and there was a degree of co-opera-tion. At the passing of the Road Traffic Act, Red Bus was very much an established operator in Stroud and was able to demonstrate that it had been the first operator on a number of routes. Even in competition with Western National, Red Bus was providing a public service. The Traffic Commissioners duly granted stage carriage service licenses both to Red Bus and Western National, as they did to Bristol Tramways' and Thorp's services in the area. Nevertheless, of the two bus services introduced by Western National in June 1930, only that from Stroud to Framilode (256) was licensed, the other, between Stroud, Eastington and Dursley (255) having been refused in May 1931, as the service was not sufficiently established and, in fact, paralleled a Red Bus route. Strangely, one of the two express services started in June 1930 failed to get a license, this being the 257A to Weston-super-Mare via Nailsworth. A similar service via Stonehouse (257) was licensed.

Even with this regulation, it is important to note that competition in the area was not extinguished, only lessened. With the exception of those routes governed by the 1920 agreement, return fare inter-avail-ability between operators was still unheard of. Nevertheless, between them the companies and Traffic Commissioners saw to it that the area's bus services moved towards a more co-ordinated timetable.

For example, direct services from Stroud to Gloucester via Edge were operated by both Red Bus and Bristol Tramways and, by 1933, had become more logical, with each company running alternate journeys, although each used a different Gloucester terminus! Services to Minchinhampton operated at 15 minute intervals via Amberley with Red Bus and Western National responsible for alternate journeys, those from Amberley via Box being Western National's and those via Tom Long's Post being Red Bus'. Services between Stroud and Nailsworth became more-or-less co-ordinated. Red Bus and Western National operated alternate half-hourly buses between Stroud and Chalford, with hourly Red Bus journeys connecting at Chalford for a service to Bakers Mill via the narrow Chalford High Street. The Bakers Mill feeder was designed for Frampton Mansell and Oakridge passen-gers but was withdrawn shortly afterwards.

Services operating in 1931 in Stroud were as follows:

Bristol Tramways Services
Nailsworth – Cheltenham via Stroud, Painswick (46)
Nailsworth – Gloucester via Stroud, Stonehouse (51)
Painswick – Gloucester via Brockworth (54)
Painswick – Gloucester (58)
Stroud – Gloucester via Edge (60)
Cranham – Cheltenham via Birdlip (63)

Red Bus Services
Stroud – Avening via Nailsworth
Stroud – Dursley via Nailsworth, Horsley
Stroud – Wickwar via Nailsworth, Wotton
Stroud – Gloucester via Edge
Stroud – Gloucester via Painswick
Stroud – Painswick
Stroud – Cheltenham via Birdlip
Stroud – France Lynch
Stroud – Stonehouse
Stroud – Chalford

Chalford – Bakers Mill
Stroud – Cirencester via Chalford, Daglingworth
Stroud – Minchinhampton via Amberley, Tom Long's Post
Stroud – Malmesbury via Minchinhampton
Stroud – Dursley via Eastington
Stroud – Dursley via Selsley
Stroud – Ruscombe
Stroud – Horns Road
Stroud – Summer Crescent
Nailsworth – Minchinhampton

Thorp's Services
Stroud – Gloucester via Leonard Stanley, Stonehouse
Stroud – Coaley

Western National Services
Nailsworth – Cheltenham via Stroud, Painswick (220)
Stonehouse – Chalford via Stroud (221)
Stroud – Cirencester via Chalford (222)
Stroud – Chippenham via Nailsworth, Tetbury, Malmesbury (223)
Stroud – Nailsworth (224)
Stroud – Birdlip (225)
Stroud – Oakridge or Bussage (226)
Stroud – Framilode via Eastington (227)
Stroud – Minchinhampton via Amberley, Box (228)
Stroud – Minchinhampton via Brimscombe (229)
Stroud – Whiteshill (230)
Stroud – Randwick (231)
Stroud – Dursley via Nailsworth, Uley (232)
Stroud – King Stanley (233)
Stroud – Painswick (252)
Stroud – Rodborough/Kingscourt (253)
Stroud – Framilode (256)
Stroud – Weston-super-Mare via Bristol (257)

Meanwhile, further structural changes to those made in 1929 were taking place within the operating companies. In what was a surprise move, May 1931 saw the National Omnibus & Transport Company, Western National's parent, being taken over by Thomas Tilling Ltd, an operator with its roots in London. It is of interest that Thomas Tilling's father moved from Gloucestershire to Middlesex from where

View towards Uplands Church, c.1932. In the foreground is Red Bus' Austral Garage at Lansdown, just before its closure. *Peckham's of Stroud*

Thomas Tilling himself began operating horse buses, moving into motor omnibuses and subsequently becoming interested in provincial operations at the same time as National, following the limits agreed by London operators in 1913. By 1930, Thomas Tilling Ltd, either by itself or jointly with others, had become one of the three major forces in British bus service operations.

It was a year later, in 1932, that GWR transferred its stake in Bristol Tramways to Thomas Tilling group subsidiary Western National. This effectively placed Western National in control of Bristol Tramways which was somewhat ironic given the efforts of both parties' to outdo each other in the Stroud, Wotton and Cirencester areas only a decade earlier. The effect was that both organisations were now part of the Tilling Group.

By 1932, Merritt's Grey Bus Services were operating six weekday journeys to Malmesbury and five on Sundays plus a couple of shorts to

Tetbury and up to half-hourly between Stroud, The Bear, Amberley and Minchinhampton, with hourly extensions to Avening which operated back to Stroud via Nailsworth. Operating in the reverse direction was a service at least up to half-hourly intervals between Stroud and Nailsworth with hourly extensions again to Avening, which operated in a circular service back to Stroud via Minchinhampton. Grey Bus also operated a curious route from Stroud to Nailsworth via Woodchester, Amberley and Box, which is the only known service to have used Culver Hill until revisions to the Nailsworth minibus in the eighties.

Yet another significant structural change occurred in 1933. Reyne, who had incorporated Red Bus from August 1932 and who had only recently merged his Grey Bus interests with the more substantial Red Bus business, sold in October 1933 to Red & White Services of Chepstow. Not only did this include Reyne's substantial Stroud network, Red & White gained the express service to London and a bus route between Gloucester, Maisemore, Staunton and Malvern, previously operated by Reyne. Red & White remained a large and growing independent in an era of territorial groupings such as Tilling. Red & White's origins were with the merger of otherwise disparate interests in the South Wales Valleys, Monmouthshire and the Forest of Dean. Its rapid expansion in the 1920s had included Blue Star Coaches, operators of an express from Gloucester to London via Stroud and Reading, taken over in 1929. Red & White was later to acquire a number of concerns in south central Wales, Oxfordshire and Berkshire and in 1939, Cheltenham District Traction, the operator of local bus routes in Cheltenham and successor to the town's tram system pioneered by Thomas Nevins.

Reyne immediately lent his business skills to the Red & White board, retiring as a director 13 years later. Against the odds, he had built up a business of some 30 to 35 buses and become something of a local hero. In 1933, Reyne operated some 35 per cent of local departures compared to Bristol Tramways' seven per cent and Western National's 57 per cent. The respect built up for Red Bus was not to diminish upon transfer to the Chepstow operator. Red & White enjoyed a considerable reputation for the quality of its operations, the condition of its vehicles – including its well finished paintwork – and the loyalty of its smartly turned out staff, all of which are still remembered fondly in Stroud. In fact, the Red & White driver regime was impeccable. Discipline was high, there was a day's suspension for both conductor and driver for operating early and serious offences would see driver or conductor having to journey to the Bulwark head quarters at

Chepstow. Much training was also undertaken at Chepstow.

It actually took Red & White a full year to absorb totally the Red Bus operation. Vehicles known to have passed from Red Bus to Red & White included 12 Albions, a type familiar to the operator, and a Leyland Lion. Six further Albions, a Leyland Lion, a Leyland Tiger and a Thornycroft found themselves elsewhere in Red & White territory, other than at Stroud. The remainder of Red Bus vehicles is assumed to have been withdrawn upon takeover.

One of Red & White's first moves was to transfer Red Bus' operations from Austral Garage at Lansdown to premises in Dudbridge. The move from Lansdown was warmly welcomed by people in this otherwise quiet, residential part of the town. For them, Red Bus' expansion had been hard to bear. After the move, not only was the neighbourhood quieter, traffic congestion was lessened. Austral Garage, appropriately named by Reyne, had originally been the Little Mill, dealing in grain. It was converted first to a cabinetmakers and since the First World War, was demolished in favour of motor repair workshops, taken over and extended by Reyne.

At the time of these changes in 1933, Stroud's buses were operating at about 77 per cent of the 1952 level of service (1952 being the year passengers numbers were at their height).

The Tilling Group became more than a little concerned at the expansion of independent Red & White in its midst and almost immediately got around a table to negotiate. There followed a milestone agreement between Red & White and Tilling Group subsidiaries Bristol Tramways and Western National. This rationalised and further co-ordinated services in the town, brought about route exchanges, eliminated most competitive practice, withdrew unprofitable mileage and enabled significant efficiencies to be made. Furthermore, the Traffic Commissioners were happy with the agreement.

The Commissioners may have been happy but was the general public? Certainly, they were not! The reorganisation came into operation on New Years Day 1934 and it was not all plain sailing. Criticisms included the speeding up of some services and it was principally because of this that passengers had apparently become alarmed. Buses were now obliged to run up and down Butterow Hill faster than before, on their way to Minchinhampton via Amberley and there was concern at the speeds buses passed through Pinfarthings, the other side of Amberley. This followed a cut in running time from a 28-minute single trip to just 19. Another was the service to Ruscombe, which had changed hands from Red Bus to Western National. There was concern

With its distinctive "piano front" body, Leyland Titan TD1 no. 3127, new in 1931, poses only a few years after the erection of Western National's London Road premises, a building that would serve the town into the nineties. The advertisement on the side is for Allenburys', an early baby formula. *Peckham's of Stroud*

that revisions to the timetable left drivers no option but to increase speed along the narrow and twisting lanes for which the route was particularly infamous.

On the other hand, there was criticism of the Nailsworth to Cheltenham via Stroud and Painswick service for completely the opposite reason. The bus was timetabled to wait both in Stroud and Painswick and was therefore considered too slow!

Apart from the trunk routes, there was a certain dissatisfaction with changes in departures. Revisions to services to Whiteshill, Slad and Birdlip, Dursley (Lister's Works) and France Lynch, though all minor in nature, appeared to cause some concern for workers, pupils or those workers returning home by bus for lunch (as was the custom in those days, for those who lived sufficiently close to their work). Again,

Ruscombe was a focus of complaints following the withdrawal of an early morning journey, changes to lunch hour buses and changes in fares. This followed the passing of the route from Red & White to Western National that month and a combined timetable with the Whiteshill service. There was concern that the Ruscombe and Whiteshill services should both be reinstated as separate routes.

There were further complaints. The embryonic Red Bus town services between Stroud and Summer Street via Horns Road had been withdrawn altogether and there was strong criticism in the town as these were felt to be remunerative. With the withdrawal of the Stroud to Dursley service via Nailsworth, there was no longer a service between Nailsworth and Nympsfield. Neither were there buses between Nailsworth and Minchinhampton and Nailsworth shop keepers and traders were vociferous and passionate in their complaints about both these decisions. Minchinhampton services via Amberley, which had seen four buses an hour operated by both Western National and Red & White, were now reduced to three an hour and even this reduction brought a raft of complaints. With the revisions to France Lynch and Bussage services now operating via Toadsmoor, Bisley (which had benefitted from a broadly hourly service) now saw buses about every two hours.

On a positive note, on the other hand, rationalisation between Stroud and Painswick caused little complaint as Red & White pulled out, leaving Western National on shorts and both Western National and Bristol on through services. A doubling of through buses between Chalford and Stonehouse via Stroud offered more through journey opportunities compared to the situation beforehand where alternate buses from both legs terminated at Stroud.

The Urban District Council became so alarmed at the overall public reaction that a delegation sought an urgent meeting with the chairman of the Traffic Commissioners, which was postponed once as the deputation was driven back by fog on the day of the first meeting! The complaints rumbled on through the winter. While there were adjustments made to some services and a compromise single trip time of 25 minutes between Stroud and Minchinhampton was introduced (and the previous waiting time at The Bear left out), it is a sobering thought that even in 1934, some very rural services were acknowledged to have begun losing money and as a result a number of the changes had become permanent, in spite of the outcry. Growth in passenger numbers, seen at the birth of the network in the twenties, could not be sustained. Such rapid expansion could not easily be repeated in subsequent years. The worldwide depression of the early thirties had also taken its toll. The rationalisation of 1934 was therefore timely.

By 1934, therefore, Stroud's passengers saw red, blue and green buses working in partnership in providing services for the area. This partnership and its pattern of service were to see only minor modifications to the end of the 30s. Some routes saw genuine joint working when operators took it in turns, working alternate journeys. These included Stonehouse to Chalford, Birdlip to Dursley via Stroud and Stroud to France Lynch. Nailsworth to Gloucester and to Cheltenham services were already joint operations by this time. Other routes operated on a curious week on/week off basis with either Red & White or Western National operating all journeys during any particular week. This arrangement included the Cirencester and Oakridge services.

One other peculiarity was that both Red & White and Western National retained their separate route numbering systems, even on joint routes. Red & White had introduced two digit numbers in Stroud upon taking over Reyne's Red Bus. Such numbers were retained but used in timetables only, never on buses themselves. Nevertheless, this dual numbering system would have caused some confusion.

To counter the negative stories about the co-ordination exercise's cutbacks, there was more optimistic news regarding fares. Western National at this time charged 5d single to Nailsworth, no return being available, 9d return to Minchinhampton, and 2/6 to Cheltenham. Much to the delight of Stroud's passengers, further negotiation secured a

3128 is another Western National 1931 Leyland TD1. In spite of the harsh working conditions at the time, the employee, assumed to be a fitter, seems happy enough to be photographed. *Chris Blick collection*

most popular understanding between the three operators over return ticket inter-availability. Nevertheless, this issue still caused some confusion where routes were particularly perverse. For example, there remained disputes over Minchinhampton services. Red & White and Western National return ticket holders could use either bus company along the jointly operated route from Stroud to Minchinhampton via Amberley. However, boarding a bus in Stroud for Minchinhampton with a Red & White ticket was not possible on Western National's route 229 via Brimscombe, as Western National was sole operator. Returns from Minchinhampton issued on 229 were stamped with the letter "B" as a means of identification and were not acceptable on Red & White journeys to Minchinhampton via Amberley.

1933 saw Thorp's services taken over. That from Stroud to Coaley and Far Green via the Stanleys passed first to Red Bus but upon agreement were combined with Western National's 223 between Stroud and King Stanley, the Coaley and Far Green section being withdrawn. The Thorp service between Stroud, the Stanleys and Gloucester passed to Bristol Tramways as number 117 but this was later withdrawn between Stroud and Leonard Stanley. From around this date, Tramways introduced service 110 between Stroud, Ebley, the Stanleys and Cam Mills, twice a day in each direction at work times.

Drivers' and conductors' working conditions during the late 1920s and early 1930s were harsh. Long hours and double shifts were the norm, often with a complete day's work from dawn to the last picture buses. It was a company offence for a conductor to sit down in his vehicle while passengers were aboard. Caps had to be worn at all times except during exceptionally hot weather when they could be removed, but only when the bus had left the town centre. Drivers and conductors were sent home if they forgot their badges and were subject to a day's suspension for being only five minutes late, without good reason. Those living some distance from the town centre who did not have their own transport had to walk or cycle to pick up the beginning of their shift. Sundays off were rare, although timetables did start later in the day. Unless drivers were on regular routes, duties were not posted up very far in advance, in Western National's case crews being told the previous day of the next day's duties. More notice tended to be available for Red & White's drivers.

Although it was not always the case, there were periods of staff shortage during the early and mid thirties. The labour market at the time was tight, a job on the buses was seen to be regular and reliable and therefore a safe bet. Before the war, Western National paid £2/10/-

for starter drivers, rising to 3 Guineas (otherwise known as £1/1/- or 21 shillings), while conductors received £-/32/6 (32 shillings, 6d). Notwithstanding the cumbersome old currency, such variable rates made life difficult for wages clerks. Conditions may have been primitive by today's standards, shifts longer and fitters engaged at garages were required to buy and bring their own tools and overalls but, with general increases in passenger demand throughout the thirties, it was still a growing industry offering stable employment.

There were a number of accidents involving buses during the 1930s. These involved pedestrians, cyclists and motor cars. This was hardly surprising given the increase in both traffic speeds (including buses) and traffic volumes on local roads, many of which were of necessity steep and had in the main been built to a standard for the horse and cart. A motor cyclist died in 1938 following a crash with a bus at Rooksmoor on the Nailsworth road. A particular tragedy was the death in Malmesbury of a four year old girl under the wheels of a Western National bus.

The most spectacular, however, was the case of Conductor Herbert Bliss in 1931. At this time, although there had been advances in vehicle design – for example, pneumatic tyres began to replace solid ones between 1925 and 1930 – the open top double decks delivered in the twenties were still in use. Drivers were under instruction, upon approaching Rowcroft railway bridge in the town to stop to give sufficient time for conductors to mount the open rear stairs to warn passengers to remain in their seats to avoid contact with the bridge. At the conductor's bell, the driver would proceed.

However, it had become common practice for the driver to take the bus under the bridge at a slow pace rather than first stopping. At the same time, the conductor would shout from near the top of the stairs for passengers to keep their seats. On the occasion of the accident, Herbert Bliss went too far up the stairs as the vehicle was moving forward, was hit by the bridge and knocked clean off the back of the bus to the road below. He was taken to hospital with a suspected fractured skull and required skin grafts from his thigh. He spent several months in hospital before returning to work on the buses, lived a normal life thereafter and died in retirement!

Vehicle reliability during the twenties and thirties was not always good. Each company was required to maintain a high engineering spares ratio. Well known and respected former Stroud senior inspector Jack Ireland recalls an incident on the last Minchinhampton-bound trip one day in 1930 when he was conducting on a Western National

Guy single deck. During the journey, the Guy's big end went. The driver had managed to coax the bus to Minchinhampton but the vehicle was due to be left there for the following day's first journey to Stroud. The driver therefore motorbiked back to Stroud to collect a replacement and upon return nursed the stricken bus to Stroud via Tom Long's Post. It was halfway down the steep and long Brimscombe Hill at the Yew Tree Inn that the driver decided, to save the engine, to freewheel, the prospect of meeting any traffic in the opposite direction being minimal. The speed gained was such that at the old hump back bridge near the Ship Inn, the vehicle's wheels lost contact with the road entirely and travelled over half a mile along London Road to Thrupp Brewery Lane after making the sharp left turn at Brimscombe Corner. It was at this bridge that one absent-minded driver grounded his Chalford-bound bus by turning right towards Minchinhampton by mistake.

Ireland also recalls, this time as a Western National driver in the late thirties, that a magneto in his early Leyland packed up one evening near Stonehenge on the return leg of a Cheltenham – Southsea – Cheltenham express duplicate. Coach drivers carried their own tool boxes for the numerous improvisations and minor running repairs they encountered away from base but this was more serious. Ireland had to walk two miles to Shrewton to find a telephone but upon inquiry found that Trowbridge, the nearest depot, was unable to help, so he tried Stroud. After some considerable time, Ireland could see in the distance the headlights of the Stroud replacement vehicle after its 50 mile journey only to see them disappear again as the driver took a wrong turn, towards Swindon. The garage foreman from Horsley did arrive with a new magneto having been awoken by the late night fitter. By this time, Ireland had to hunt for water which he obtained from two butts adjacent to a local cottage, the nearby brook being unreachable owing to slippery banks. This was now past midnight but the passengers, in relatively good humour, had spent the evening in the Catherine Wheel pub. Ireland recalls that two years later, while approaching Shrewton on the same duplicate, a passenger actually recalled the incident to him.

As the thirties progressed, both Red & White and Western National improved and modernised their fleets. In 1935, the first new Red & White double deck delivered to Stroud was no. 254, a Bristol Bus Works GO6G with Northern Counties 48 seat body. Built to a higher standard than any previously seen in the town, it came with a silver roof, red rear dome, red lower panels, white window surrounds and upper panels. It included a fine painted advertisement for Red &

From its earlier "National" days, Western National offered tours and excursions from Stroud using early charabancs and up to 10 motor coaches. One of seven Leyland Tigers with Duple 31 seat bodies at Stroud was 3353, dating from 1932. *Johnson collection*

White coaches on its sides. Red & White also saw the delivery of new single deck buses and coaches from 1937, all of which were Albion PVs, PWs or CX13s.

Tilling Group subsidiary Western National, on the other hand, was increasing the number of vehicles manufactured by fellow subsidiary Bristol, with the purchase for Stroud by 1939 of at least five new Bristol Ks with Beadle bodywork and, earlier, seven Bristol H single decks with Bristol bodies and five Bristol J single decks. Western National had not become exclusively Bristol, however. The company liked the little 14 to 20 seat Dennis Aces with either Brush or Mumford bodies, there being six at Stroud from the mid-thirties, including one coach and four bought new for the town. The Mumford bodied example was seven feet wide with perimeter seats on both sides, for 14 passengers and was used on the Ruscombe service 230A, a route which passed from Red & White in 1934. In addition to the Aces, Western National operated a slightly larger 26 seat Dennis Mace. Western National coaches in the town tended to be Leyland TS2s with Duple bodywork.

In addition to its new London Road premises, built in 1927 and extended in 1936, three buses were still parked overnight at the GWR station, as had been the case when GWR directly operated services. National also maintained a number of outstations in nearby towns and villages. All but those at Framilode and Dursley were established by National in the twenties. This was a sensible arrangement, as there was no traffic between the picture house returners from Stroud in the evening to the first bus to Stroud the following morning. It also enabled the recruitment of local drivers and conductors. Most outstationed buses were taken in to Stroud by the end of the thirties or during the early forties. Western National's outstations were at:

Framilode: Darrell Arms 1934 to 1942.
Frampton-on-Severn: Bell Inn to 1937 and Mr Hazel's shed to 1940.
Minchinhampton: Ogden's Yard to 1934 and Minchinhampton
     Motor Co to 1940.
Miserden: Post Office to 1933.
Nailsworth: Britannia Square to 1931 and Cossack Square to 1936.
Uley: Frank Smith's shed to 1938.

A further outstation was maintained at Dursley Hunger Hill during 1938 only.

Both Red & White and Western National continued to operate coaches as well as buses during this period. In fact, coaching activities continued to be popular and proved to be most profitable, virtually every excursion leaving fully booked and often over-subscribed. Roads in Britain were of a reasonable standard throughout the thirties, excepting those on the tours beyond Kington and Rhaeadr, in mid-Wales. Such longer trips to Aberystwyth and others proved long and tiring for drivers with vehicles without power steering. Both companies extended and improved their ranges of day and half-day summer excursions and expanded the private hire side of their businesses, including works outings. By this time, Stroud's drivers had a considerable route knowledge and experience and they and their vehicles would regularly duplicate express coach workings from Gloucester and Cheltenham to many parts of the country. Men on the six driver Western National summer coach roster would invariably find themselves on summer Saturday Black & White express duplicates to Southsea and London. It was rarer to see Red & White vehicles on express duplicates, other than with vehicles from Chepstow. The use of the general bus service for leisure activities continued to prove popular, as well, this being boosted by the increasing numbers travelling from the midlands to holiday in the Stroud Valleys.

Delivered to Stroud in 1939 was Red & White 419, an Albion CX19 with Weyman 56 seat body. *Johnson collection*

In spite of diminished opportunities for growth, the decade was one of reasonable prosperity for Stroud's bus companies. In 20 years, the bus service had matured from scattered services to a vital part of the social and economic fabric of the area, something that the Stroud Valleys could no longer do without. The decade was also quite literally a colourful era on Stroud's buses. Bus liveries of Western National's green (replacing an earlier grey), Red & White's red and Bristol Tramways' blue were the only colour on the streets. Such cars as there were came in sombre blacks. Yet, at the end of the decade, times were about to change. With much debate as to when (not whether) the country would go to war, local public transport was to suffer most.

CHAPTER 4

1940–1949
CONFLICT AND CLIMAX

If Stroud's bus network saw a certain stability and co-existence emerge during the thirties, as compared to the decade beforehand, things were about to change completely. The Second World War was as difficult a time for Stroud's public transport as it was for every other facet of life. War with Germany began in September 1939 and immediately there were reductions in bus services, in an effort to conserve what were now precious fuel supplies. Stroud's operators were effectively under the war time control of the Traffic Commissioners as it was these government appointed overseers who dictated which services should run and which could be sacrificed in the national interest.

From 16 September, after just 10 days public notice, many of the usual duplicates on Fridays and Saturdays were withdrawn. The trunk service between Nailsworth, Stroud, Painswick and Cheltenham was cut by approximately half and this was exacerbated by the complete withdrawal of services from Stroud to Gloucester via Painswick. Evening services began to suffer and there were reductions of between a quarter and a half on the more frequent Sunday services.

By 1940, the Minchinhampton via Amberley service was operating at hourly intervals, although the pre-war half-hourly service was maintained on Saturdays. Consequently, passengers for Minchinhampton had to put up with overwhelming overcrowding, right through the afternoon and early evening, and would often have to queue for the next bus. Double decks were deemed unsuitable for the route because of the potential drop at Butterow (although this consideration was to change some 40 years later). From 1940, when later buses were introduced, the problem continued during the evening with passengers becoming stranded. The Minchinhampton situation was somewhat alleviated by 1943 with the introduction of a half-hourly service on

46

Fridays, in addition to that on Saturdays.

Kingscourt and Rodborough services were reduced by a quarter and Sunday journeys withdrawn. In addition to some Monday to Friday reductions, Randwick via Cashes Green saw a third fewer buses on Saturdays and the Sunday service was halved. Whiteshill's Sunday service was similarly cut. Sunday buses to Ruscombe were withdrawn entirely and the Saturday service cut by a third.

In deeper rural areas, where departures were infrequent, there was often a reduction of one or two buses per day, including Sundays, while any extra Saturday journeys were often withdrawn. Examples included the Stroud to Dursley service via Selsley which was halved from five to three journeys on weekdays and from five to two on Sundays; a reduction of five to three journeys between Stroud and Frampton-on-Severn on Mondays to Fridays and from six to four on Saturdays; two fewer journeys between Nailsworth and Wickwar on Mondays to Fridays and one less on each of Saturdays and Sundays; two fewer buses to France Lynch on Saturdays and one less on Sundays; a reduction by one to

A high proportion of Red & White's double deck fleet was at Stroud during the Second World War. No fewer than seven Albion CX19s with Duple 56 seat bodies were delivered in 1941, one being 437, seen here. *Peckham's of Stroud*

Oakridge on Saturdays and from five to two on Sundays; and between Stroud and Cirencester, there were reductions from four to three on Mondays to Fridays and five to three on Saturdays.

However, aside from the withdrawal of duplicates, services between Nailsworth, Stroud and Gloucester were largely maintained, even on Sundays, though during the war, Red & White took over entirely on what had otherwise been a joint route. Monday to Saturday buses to Minchinhampton via Brimscombe remained intact, although Sunday services were halved. Weekday and Saturday scheduled buses from Stroud to Chalford actually saw a modest increase in journeys while those in the opposite direction to Stonehouse saw a 10 per cent reduction on Mondays to Fridays, largely during the evenings. Buses to Kings Stanley were unaltered, as were buses between Stroud and Whiteway. Even so, passengers were unable to board buses travelling along the Slad valley to Whiteway – something previously unheard of.

With the changes imposed on Stroud's travelling public, it is hardly surprising that as the months progressed, overcrowding became something of a serious problem. This may have been at its most acute where workers' duplicates were withdrawn but even the unchanged service to Whiteway, not the busiest service before the war, saw severe problems. There was much acrimony on the entire network regarding short-distance passengers who took up spaces at the expense of those travelling further. Yet, with longer wartime work hours and increasingly difficult employment conditions, who would deny such people a ride home? In any case, how could road staff be expected to differentiate between such passengers? There were further problems: as buses filled to bursting, so punctuality suffered.

By 1940, taking these pluses and minuses together, Stroud saw a reduction of some 15 per cent of its pre-war scheduled bus mileage. In this respect, Stroud actually faired well when compared with reductions in other parts of the country. The local Red & White manager at the time was moved to comment that wartime Stroud remained the best served area anywhere in Red & White's extensive territory. Many parts of Britain were suffering far more. Stroud's wartime public transport problems were related more to increased demand than decreased supply.

It was the strategic industries along the valley bottoms and the constant need to supply them with labour that ensured Stroud was spared the considerable reductions seen elsewhere. Local mills and factories were converted to munitions manufacturing while woollen mills produced uniforms, battle fatigues and even shell packing. Then there were the needs of the military and civil personnel at Aston Down airfield, near Minchinhampton.

In order to cope with the demands of war and the increased output required of Stroud's converted munitions factories, Stroud's industry needed a larger workforce than before. People, especially housewives but also retired men, who would not normally have used the bus service day-in-day-out, were now turning up in large numbers to do so.

Added to this was petrol rationing, introduced for private motoring on 16 September 1939, at the start of hostilities. In the early days of the war, there were still supplies for urgent and essential journeys, although all private motoring was to stop altogether, in 1942. Nevertheless, increasingly motorists from 1939 were laying up their cars owing to rationing or the problems of driving in the blackouts.

A further burden was placed on the system by the arrival from Birmingham of child evacuees, in some cases with their mothers, not so much relating to the actual arrivals in large numbers themselves but the additional day-to-day traffic they generated. Upon arrival at Stroud rail stations, child evacuees were transported to their reception areas largely by coach. Coaching had otherwise began to be run down at the outbreak of war, whether for excursions, express services or private hires. Express services were not to emerge again until 1946.

And not just children – Stroud's urban and rural areas had seen nothing short of an influx of people both to work in the munitions factories but also eager to seek an alternative to the dangers of larger urban areas. They all needed transport to and from Stroud for work or shopping. Being used to different travelling practices, some of these new passengers took it upon themselves to ring the buses' bells, something left entirely to conductors in Stroud at the time, and this led to concerns over safety, especially on double decks.

The bus companies were doing all they could in a difficult situation and it was clear that local managers of all three concerns – Red & White, Bristol Tramways and Western National – wanted to do more but simply could not. While there was some satisfaction for Painswick to Gloucester passengers who were able to use the Gloucester – Cranham service which was extended to Painswick, managers were powerless to overcome much of the overloading now so common on Stroud's buses.

Timetable changes were not simply imposed by restricted fuel supplies. Staffing remained a problem for Stroud operators. These difficulties increased as any surplus drivers (following the reduction in mileage) and conductors (whether surplus or not) were being called to the Colours. The matter was eased somewhat with the employment for

The role of the bus service during the Second World War is typified in this shot of five Red & White double decks at Hoffman's, Oldends Lane. As the first loads, the rear four are already full. Note the "Workmen" designation on the destination indicator and the wartime hooded headlamps and white tipped wheel arches. *Peckham's of Stroud*

the first time of female conductors, from February 1940. Their numbers increased steadily throughout the war although, in Stroud, women never got behind the wheel. This last fact was perhaps surprising as services were being cancelled as a result of the dearth of drivers, which resulted in the Ruscombe service being cancelled in its entirety for a whole week in February 1940!

Local conductresses were joined by others from Western National's Devon operations, notably from Plymouth and Bideford but also from Penzance in Cornwall, where seasonal and recreational demand had obviously dried up. Such staff were offered a choice of working in factories in their home areas (or sometimes some distance away) or conducting at Stroud. While in Stroud, they often lodged with families already connected with Western National.

In coping with periodic shortages of conductors, Red & White had by the early 1940s acquired some unusual working practices. At times of need, a conductor from Cirencester might alight at either Chalford or Brimscombe Corner to conduct a Chalford to Stroud service. Then, the same conductor might alight at Bowbridge to conduct an incoming

Red & White company staff at Stroud line up in c.1945. Note that of the 39 uniformed road staff, 22 are conductresses, the use of women for this role being a wartime innovation. *Peckham's of Stroud*

bus from Minchinhampton. In this way, although not all fares were taken, at least most people were seen by a conductor. Of course, the system relied heavily upon the honesty of passengers.

As the war progressed, there was also the difficulty in keeping older vehicles on the road. With spare levels low, Stroud's fitters managed to extend every last mile of life out of their pre-war vehicles, some of which were old even in 1939. In fact, in order to prop up its vital wartime service, Red & White at Stroud received two double decks from London and three from Oldham. In spite of this, not a day passed in Stroud during the war without a breakdown.

It was rare to see brand new buses on Britain's roads during this time. Only operators who could make a case for them could secure them. Yet Stroud actually received an unusually high number of new vehicles and this was a further recognition of the importance of the town to the wartime economy and the need to transport its workers back and forth. Between 1941 and 1943, Red & White received no fewer than 10 new double deck Albion Venturer CX19s with pre-war specification lowbridge Duple 56 seat bodies, these being nos. 432 to 437 and 439 to 443. This meant that almost the entire Red & White double deck fleet at Stroud was no more than 10 years old at the end of the war. The first seven were actually finished by a firm with close links to Red & White, Lydney Bodybuilders, while the last three were constructed there using components prepared by Duple. Rather than appearing in the usual wartime grey, these vehicles arrived in Red & White's standard red with white upper and lower deck window surrounds. The exception to this was the first of the batch, which was delivered in reversed livery, although this was subsequently modified soon after. In addition, the roofs of all ten were painted khaki and the front wheel arch tips and the skirt rails were picked out in white in a rather vain attempt to improve their visibility in the blackout. Wartime Stroud, up to 1943, actually operated most of Red & White's entire stock of double decks.

Western National, on the other hand, saw just four new double decks, nos. 313, 314 and 315 in 1940 and 348 in 1942. They were Bristol Ks with 56 seat lowbridge ECW wartime "utility" bodywork, to a much lower build specification than the standard of vehicle arriving at Red & White. Like the Red & White arrivals, all were powered by diesel, being among the first at Stroud to have these engines.

Between 1940 and 1943, Western National re-bodied seven of its Stroud Bristol H single decks with 35 seat bodies of Bristol Bus Works manufacture. These had been new in 1933 and 1934. At the same time, its six-cylinder Bristol petrol engines were replaced with five-cylinder Gardner 5LWs. These vehicles survived as buses at Stroud until 1950 and 1951 and were demoted to driver training vehicles before being either resold or scrapped in 1952 and 1953.

At this point, it is worth recording problems that were associated with the first diesel engines. On some, it took three to crank start the engines, one on the handle and two with ropes. It was not uncommon to see buses being tow-started around the King Street, George Street and Russell Street triangle. Some required a flame up the intake to get them started while for others trolley batteries were available. During extremely cold weather, engines would be left running all night with the night cleaner keeping them going. Such engines were reliable starters when warm.

During 1940 and 1941, enemy bombers passed over Stroud from bases in France and Germany on their way to Bristol, South Wales, the Midlands and Plymouth. By day, enemy aircraft would use Bisley steeple as a navigation mark. Aside from two deaths in Painswick in June 1941, such bombs falling on the locality as there were caused few problems, destroying some property and killing livestock. There were no direct hits on either of Stroud's bus garages. Nevertheless, in

4 March 1947 saw rapidly worsening winter weather. Driver Jack Ireland became stuck at Stancombe near Bisley that day and after waiting five hours for assistance, abandoned the vehicle but not before seeing a disabled passenger safely to shelter. The vehicle, Western National Bristol H 113, was only able to be dug out on 7 March, by A Ryland, H Morris, W Hill, C Larner and V Watkins. *Jack Ireland collection*

October 1940, a Stroud Leyland 26 seat coach with Duple bodywork was damaged by flying shrapnel – in Weymouth! July 1941 saw the end of enemy action over the Stroud area. In something of an own goal, Western National's London Road garage was damaged in 1943 by an unrestrained barrage balloon. The Western National garage was one of six local out-of-hours rallying points in the event of an emergency for the Ministry of Labour's Emergency Repair Squads plus others from firms not engaged directly in munitions work.

Throughout the war years, there were timetable adjustments. By 1943, services between Nailsworth, Stroud and Cheltenham returned to their pre-war hourly frequency. On the other hand, weekday services to Gloucester, previously unaffected, were reduced from 16 to 13 departures per day but Sundays increased from five to eight. Minchinhampton's buses via Brimscombe and those to Whiteshill and Randwick were reduced marginally across the week and Kings Stanley's service actually increased slightly. The timetable for the Stroud to Dursley via Eastington service saw the publication of a considerable number of "workmen's" buses, augmenting the service between Stroud, Cainscross, Ebley and Stonehouse (LMS Station and Oldends Lane).

Largely unchanged in 1943 when compared to 1940 were services to Whiteway, Trowbridge, Cirencester, France Lynch, Oakridge, Frampton-on-Severn, Kingscourt and Dursley via Selsley.

When compared to the 1939 and 1940 situation, by 1943, the Chalford to Stonehouse via Stroud route saw a reduction in Saturday afternoon and early evening quarter-hourly frequency to Monday to Friday half-hourly levels. This was remedied first in 1944 with the introduction of a twenty minute frequency during the Monday to Saturday afternoon peak period and, a year later, a twenty minute service throughout, paving the way for a service at this frequency for the next 35 years. Passengers might have expected the luxury of more space in which to travel but in reality there was still plenty of standing. Numbers were so great at peak times that whenever possible Red & White (though not Western National) would employ one conductress per deck. Some passengers who had forsaken the bus for the parallel local rail service, which if nothing else offered more standing room (the trains known as "pram trains" because of wide doors and gangways), would have been tempted back by a more frequent bus service.

As the war progressed, there was no abatement in passengers. In fact, matters were getting worse. This was in spite of most single deck vehicles now offering "perimeter seating". On a number of single decks, Stroud's operators stripped out the usual arrangement of double rows of forward facing seats and replaced them with side facing seating, though it was more common in Stroud to see vehicles with such an arrangement on the nearside only. This increased the passenger reservoir space and regulations were slackened to increase the number of standing passengers in the centre of the vehicle in ratio to the number of seats along the perimeter. In practice, this was relaxed still further by conductresses to ensure that the maximum number travelled. If these conditions were arduous for passengers, it is a wonder that the conductors coped at all, especially the women. Manners in such cramped and harsh on board conditions were not always their most refined and conductresses found it difficult to deal with passengers in these situations. Nevertheless, there was much praise for the way in which they undertook their duties in such harsh conditions. Road staff received a war time bonus owing to the exceptional conditions and long shifts expected of them.

In spite of Stroud being well placed when compared to many – if not most – areas of Britain, there was much criticism of Stroud's wartime bus service. Aside from the problems of over-crowding, capacity for workers, workmen's buses (which, as the war progressed, were increasingly taken up by women, not men!), spaces required for season ticket holders and the rights – or otherwise – of short distance travellers, there were concerns that children in the more rural areas could not get to and from their schools at reasonable times.

As queues built up on Stroud's streets, there were problems over the public's safety, particularly at the Subscription Rooms, as passengers pushed and shoved to find spaces on buses. The creation in 1942 of new stops at London Road for Minchinhampton, Malmesbury, France Lynch and Oakridge helped. This was further solved in 1942 with the erection of barriers at town centre stops, which had a remarkable effect on discipline. In addition to workers and pupils, the period between 1630 hrs and 1830 hrs was also worsened by shoppers and returning cinema-goers. Shoppers were asked to keep the peak periods clear for others, if at all possible. On the other hand, weekend buses were affected by overcrowding whatever the time of day.

Gloucester buses were so full that the rear platforms of the Red & White Albion double decks would actually ground as they passed through the junction at St. Barnabas Church on the outskirts of Gloucester. Loadings on otherwise quite normal routes would also cause grounding. The judicious use of speed and third gear along King Street Parade to George Street in Stroud would cause the rear platform of a full bus to scrape and sparks to fly! Meanwhile, those passengers who had been unable to find any space within the body of the vehicle hung on to the rear platform for grim death. It was also not unknown for passengers on single decks to sneak up the rear ladder to the roof top luggage pen on vehicles so fitted!

Staff and passengers had to acclimatise themselves to the wartime night blackouts. The poor forward vision associated with the necessary hooded headlamps of this time considerably slowed buses and caused not a few accidents. In an early example of road safety education, Western National periodically ran local advertisements under the banner "Look Out in the Blackout", warning people to be wary of buses, look where they were going and wear light coloured clothing at night. Evening travel within buses was depressingly gloomy, adding more to the miseries of war. Red & White experimented with lamps fitted over luggage racks shining up to the ceiling to give a subdued light which was more natural than the bluish lights otherwise used, which were said to give people an anaemic disposition and even were thought to be the cause of headaches.

It was particularly hard for conductors to read, punch and issue tickets in these situations, let alone ensure that correct fares were paid.

This Red & White Albion CX13 with Lydney 35 seat body, new to Stroud in 1948 as no. 869 and part of a batch of six, is seen after transfer from Stroud to Red & White's heartland as no. S848. *Photobus*

The conductors occasionally received foreign coins in these situations but had insufficient light to distinguish them. Western National introduced a novel system. Some buses were fitted with a 11/2 inch wide lath along the vehicles' ceilings to which a copper wire was attached. Connected to it was a single light that the conductor could draw up and down the length of the vehicle. This gave reasonable light at the point the conductor most required it but the connection would invariably be lost if the vehicle jolted or hit a pothole.

A further sacrifice in the cause of the national emergency was the last bus home. At the outbreak of the war in 1939, there was little initial change to last departures. However, this was to deteriorate as the war progressed. The last buses before the war from Stroud to Stonehouse and Chalford had been 2215 hrs. Although these were retarded to 2230 and 2220 respectively in 1941, they remained at 2100 hrs in both directions from 1942 and throughout the war. The last bus from Stroud to Nailsworth at 2230 hrs in 1939 became 2205 hrs in 1940 but was cut back variously to 2105 hrs (in 1942), 2050 hrs (1943) and 2140 hrs (1944 and 1945). Other routes suffered similarly with last buses from Stroud generally between 2100 hrs and 2130 hrs in 1942, and between 2030 hrs and 2120 hrs in 1944. With the scrapping of the 2130 hrs departure to Minchinhampton in 1942 (henceforward to be 2030 via Amberley or 2055 via Brimscombe), the issue of short- and long-distance passenger difficulties resurfaced as return ticket holders were sometimes stranded at Stroud. Although evening services terminated by 2140 hours, there were also a handful of "ghost buses" for permit holding workers whose occupations meant that they had to travel later than was otherwise allowed. There was, of course, a general curfew at 2300 hrs.

While it is true to say that things improved at the end of the Second World War in 1945, it would perhaps be more correct to say that, for the first year or so, they eased. No longer was the area outside the Subscription Rooms and King Street Parade quite so swamped with waiting passengers. Munitions work ceased, factories returned to normal working and the demand for labour, though buoyant, was no longer quite so pressing. Petrol rationing for private motorists after the war was actually to get worse before it got better and it was with some relief that duplicates began operating again.

The war had taken its toll on the older of Stroud's buses, though the fleet was in reasonable shape compared to some areas and cities. Aside from those delivered new, second hand or rebodied during the war, vehicles were old and in poor condition. It took a couple of years to see replacements for some of these veterans. Red & White received six Albion CX13 single decks with Lydney 35 seat bodies and a Bedford

One of the most unusual buses to operate at Stroud arrived at Western National in 1948. It was 2015, a "Chassisless Bedford" with a Beadle 35 seats bus body. The vehicle was constructed by Beadle using Bedford parts. The vehicle is seen after passing to a Cornish operator. *C L Caddy*

OB 29 seat coach with a Duple body in 1948. Red & White's double deck stock was actually quite up-to-date, having received the 10 between 1941 and 1943. An eleventh of this type, numbered 438, joined Stroud in 1948. Between 1946 and 1950, Western National received eight Bristol Ks with ECW 55 seat bodies. In 1949, Western National also received five 30 seat Duple bodied Bedford OWB single decks (nos. 450, 452, 454, 457 and 459), built in 1943 to Ministry of Supplies' wartime specification, including wooden seats and without the usual rear or side destination displays.

The re-bodying trend continued after the war when in 1948 and 1949 Western National rebodied six Stroud Bristol J type single decks, replacing the original Mumford bodies with 36 seat Beadle examples. All but one of this batch was new to Stroud in 1936 and, apart from one whose body went on to a further J in 1952, saw service at Stroud until withdrawal and sale in 1958.

During the Second World War, the nation had been urged to save. This now resulted in sometimes significant bank balances and while not every one was wealthy by any means, the population as a whole had some money behind it. There was actually very little upon which to spend this cash as the austerity of the war years was to continue for some time. Undeterred, there were two outlets for expenditure and these often went hand-in-hand. One was the local cinemas. This included the Ritz, which had opened in August 1939 together with the Picture House and Palace at Stroud and a cinema at Stonehouse. The second was travel.

Thus began the real golden age of the bus service, when drivers and conductors would know their passengers and when road staff often became well known local personalities in their own right. By 1948, vehicles long overdue for replacement were exchanged for new or newer ones, the oppressive operating conditions associated with the war had gone and passenger demand was high. But the golden age was short lived – petrol rationing for private motorists remained in force to 1950 – and thereafter, starting with the rural population around Stroud, people began to forsake the bus for the car. Yet, in the post war years, things were looking good for Stroud's bus services, even if the conditions were somewhat artificially created. In time, the television would kill the evening cinema trade so that, by the early seventies, Stroud would have no cinema at all.

Nevertheless, it was after the Second World War that Stroud, as elsewhere in Britain, saw a leisure-driven resurgence in bus travel. When excursions and tours started again, they proved more popular than ever. It was not unknown for tours over the bank holiday period to be fully booked within hours of destinations and dates being released. At its height, Western National operated no less than 29 vehicles from Stroud during the August bank holiday weekend of 1948, including duplicate coaches hired in. On this particular occasion, upon hearing that tours destinations were published, 400 people queued at the company offices in George Street and all seats were sold within four hours. Both companies extended their selection of tour destinations while remaining committed to the more local evening tours at half a crown each, including the mystery tour.

For the most part, tours drivers tended to be picked from the most experienced and longest serving drivers and were on separate rosters. Consequently, it was difficult to get on this roster and the only way to do so was to become a "second driver", taking a duplicate coach and following the senior driver. No overtaking was allowed. Tours drivers at Western National were issued with smart white peaked caps and white smocks.

After the last cinema shows, it was not uncommon to see queues waiting for buses stretching from the cinema in London Road to the rail station and round the corner to King Street. Similarly, queues started from Montague Burton near the Ritz. To serve the needs of returning cinema goers, Red & White and Western National laid on "palace buses", so called because of the Palace Cinema in the town. Essentially, the departure of the last bus would be dictated not by the timetable but by the end of cinema performances. There was always a further duplicate for Stonehouse standing by. Buses would await their passengers and then leave when loaded. A double deck would leave each evening from Stroud for Aston Down airfield and this, too, would be duplicated at weekends.

Neither did rural areas miss out. Both operators on their respective routes introduced evening services on one, two or three nights a week timed around the conclusion of cinema performances. These first appeared from October 1946. Often, these were the first late buses operating to rural districts off the trunk routes, other than on Saturdays. In this way, France Lynch via Eastcombe and Bussage, Oakridge via Bisley, Randwick via Cashes Green, Frampton-on-Severn via the Stanleys and Eastington and Whiteway via Slad, Sheepscombe and Miserden all benefitted.

There was more! Stroud's coaches were in demand at weekends in the late forties as express duplicates. Stroud drivers for both Western National and Red & White would book on at between 0530 and 0600

3136, a 1931 Duple bodied Leyland Western National coach, waits outside the Western National's offices at George Street with driver Valder King in Western National's smart uniform. Excursions and tours were invariably well booked at this time. *Jack Ireland collection*

and operate from Cheltenham – then the hub of the Associated Motorways express pool, which included the express coaching arm of Western National, known as "Royal Blue", and Bristol Tramways' "Bristol Greyhound" coaches. They might travel as far as Paington or Brighton without a break and then return. To operate tours, private hires and excursions, Stroud had a coach fleet of Red & White Albions and Western National Leyland Tigers.

And more! Double shifts were the norm during the late forties and early fifties when it was not uncommon to work 80 or 90 hours a week. Fathers would be away from home for long periods, seeing little of wife or child. To overcome some of these difficulties, Red & White drafted in some drivers from the Forest of Dean, who were encouraged to move because of better working conditions in Stroud. Western National conductors were expected to carry with them a fair amount of baggage in the shape of a large ticket machine and ticket rack, or sometimes two for longer or busier journeys. Each rack measured some 18 x 9 inches. Red & White's ticket system was more compact but did involve writing a ticket by hand, with the counterfoil looping back into the machine for later analysis.

Actual bus services also improved over this period. Passenger numbers ensured that there would be duplicates between Stroud and Gloucester all day on Saturdays. In 1947, the seasonal service between Stroud, Nailsworth, Bristol and Weston-super-Mare was reintroduced for the first time since the war. Sunday buses from Chalford to Stonehouse via Stroud operated at 20 rather than 40 minute intervals from June 1948. In April 1948, passenger loadings meant that double decks substituted for singles between Stroud and Frampton and the same applied on the Oakridge and Whiteshill routes in 1950, and trees along each of the routes were duly lopped. October 1948 saw further improvements to Sunday buses to Kings Stanley and Whiteshill plus the introduction of hourly weekday services for the first time over the short, steeply rising route to Uplands and the re-establishment of the otherwise aborted weekday service to Summer Crescent, again hourly.

A further though small scale boost to bus services came in June 1947 with the closure of the Dudbridge Donkey rail services between Nailsworth and Stonehouse which had opened to passenger traffic in 1867 with an extension from Dudbridge to Wallbridge near Stroud in 1886. In truth, few passengers had used this former Midland Railway service in its latter years. The line remained open for limited passenger traffic in the form of excursions but these ceased by the early fifties. The line was also used for occasional coal freight traffic which ceased in 1966 amid much local concern that Nailsworth coal prices would escalate.

As the forties concluded, although general traffic was increasing, the good times were set to roll just a little longer. The fifties were already around the corner and this would be yet another decisive decade of change.

CHAPTER 5

1950–1959
RISE & FALL

The 1950s government statisticians working away with their ledgers and adding machines recorded an unprecedented event. It was in the year 1953 that bus passenger kilometers in the UK fell for the first time ever, from 93 to 92 billion. A significant trigger had been the final lifting in 1950 of war-time petrol rationing.

Of course, 92 billion passenger kilometers were still rather a great deal! The bus accounted for a 41 per cent of market share at this time, compared to 29 and 17 per cent for the motor car and rail respectively. Throughout the country, this equated to over 13,000 million local bus passenger journeys. About 15 per cent of homes owned a car but by the end of the fifties, this was to increase to 27 per cent while the corresponding number of passenger kilometers would fall by over 10 per cent. The long period of decline had begun.

Even so, life went on pretty much as usual on Stroud's buses. Buses were full and the optimism of the latter half of the previous decade was to continue a little longer. The bus was still a most important part of community life, for work, for shopping and for leisure. In the early 1950s, duplicates were still required at peak times to and from Chalford, Nailsworth and Stonehouse, with up to three required at certain times for valley industries towards Stonehouse. It is surprising to record that two double deck football specials were required for each of Stonehouse football club's home games, something that declined with both the increase in car use and changes in the club's performance. Evening buses coinciding with films at Stroud's two main picture houses were still crowded and would also require duplicates for Stonehouse standing by. The only means of guaranteeing a seat to Cheltenham during Cheltenham Cricket Week was to travel first in the opposite direction to Nailsworth and come back on the through bus to

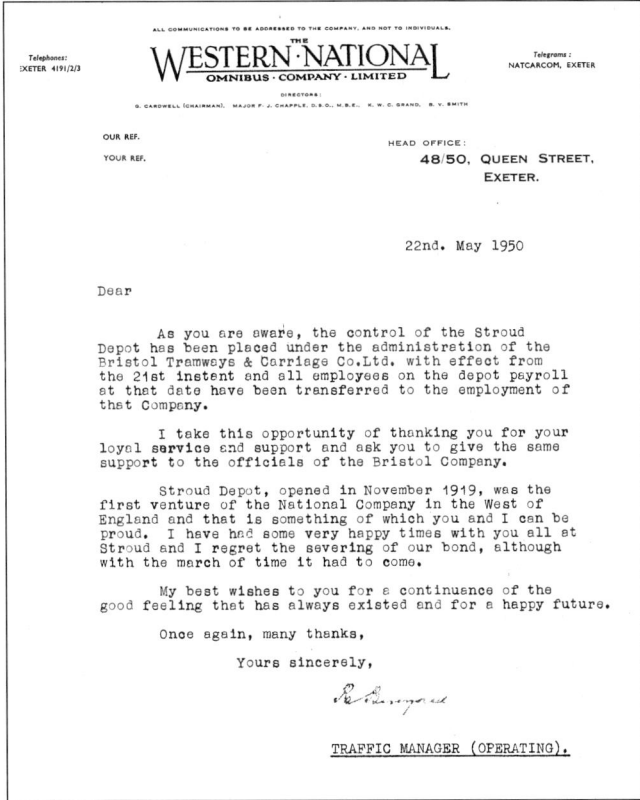

Received by all those working at Western National at the transfer to Bristol Tramways was a letter of thanks and good wishes from Exeter headquarters

Cheltenham. The bus service continued to offer reliable employment, within an industry well regarded at the time.

Yet even in 1950, things were changing significantly in Stroud, though few understood the reasons why and fewer cared, judging by the lack of comment at the time. Outwardly, all it meant were fewer red buses and more green ones.

In fact, Stroud was lying on one of the major transport fault lines of the time. Politics was playing out its part on the streets of Stroud. At the close of the 1940s, two operators predominated in the town: the red buses of Red & White and the green of Western National. The giant Bristol Tramways & Carriage Company, marketing themselves as Bristol Omnibus Services, were minor players entering the town as they did from Gloucester and Cheltenham. Stroud's lack of importance

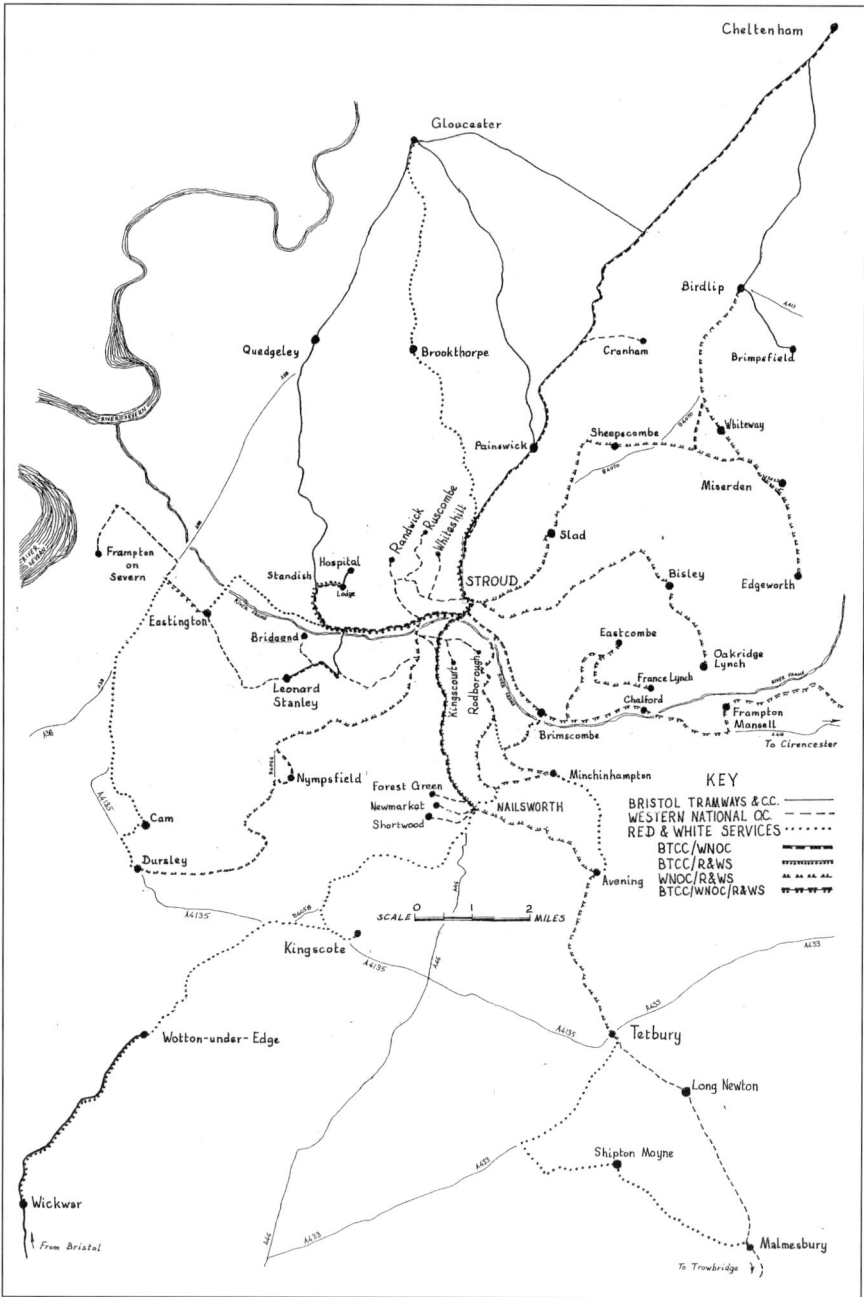

The position before the 1950 merger can best be illustrated by a sketch map of the area, showing the routes operated by the respective companies, many of which are shared

to the Bristol company was graphically illustrated on the front cover of its timetable books that failed to show the town at all or any routes going near it. All three companies had co-operated since the 1930s but the position was somewhat perverse as Stroud's local Red & White and Western National operations were landlocked within Tramway's territory. Yet, Western National's origins were strongly linked to Stroud as the town chosen in 1919 by the National Steam Car Company as its pioneering outpost in the west.

The Bristol company, by contrast, had opened branches at Cheltenham and Gloucester somewhat earlier in 1912 and 1913 respectively. That company rapidly developed services in and around both towns and later, in conjunction with the city council, on Gloucester city services. As was typical of the times, the Bristol company as territorial operator became dominant in Gloucester while the situation in Cheltenham was complicated by other operators. For example, Cheltenham town services were operated by a Red & White subsidiary, these also being landlocked.

Both the Western National and Bristol companies came into public ownership following the sale of the Tilling Group to the state in September 1948. The Tilling board had in fact been in discussions with the government since the Second World War. The post-war Labour government took a strongly pro-nationalisation stance and, in terms of transport, had created the British Transport Commission in January 1948 following the assent of the Transport Act 1947. The privately owned regional rail companies with, in Western National's case, their bus interests, and the fragmented road haulage industry passed to the Commission but the government had made no requirement for the Commission to take control of bus operating companies, only to prepare area schemes for consideration by ministers.

This caused uncertainly among Britain's provincial bus operators. However, a great deal of this was removed at the aforementioned sale of Tilling to the state. Following its transfer, the Commission continued to negotiate with and purchase other companies and this included independent Red & White United Transport, the parent company controlling bus operations in Basingstoke, Newbury and Oxford as well as the Red & White Services of Chepstow, the operator directly responsible for Stroud's red buses. The Red & White directors had seen the writing on the wall, so to speak, and although it is clear that the sale of the business was tinged with regret, the board consisted of astute businessmen who saw an opportunity to sell at the peak of their business.

It was at the sale of Red & White in February 1950 that all three of Stroud's stage carriage bus operators found themselves under state control. Like Bristol Tramways and Western National, Red & White was managed under the Commission as part of the newly acquired Tilling Group and plans were swiftly accelerated to reorganise transport in the Stroud Valleys.

The territorial anomaly that was Stroud was resolved on 21 May 1950 when the Bristol Tramways & Carriage Company took over the administrative control of routes, premises and responsibilities of both the Western National Omnibus Company and Red & White Services. It had taken the establishment of the BTC to do what Bristol Tramways had wanted since the coming of the National to Stroud and the emergence of Red & White in the town. From an efficiency and organisational perspective, this was an eminently sensible move. It was therefore surprising that a resolution to the other land locked Western National operation at Trowbridge, Wiltshire, took a further 20 years to be absorbed by the Bristol company! May 1950 also saw Red & White's Cheltenham District Traction town routes pass to the Bristol company. Unlike in Stroud, Cheltenham's town buses were to retain a distinctive red livery in one form or another for some 25 years, even though control rested with Tramways throughout that period.

In a rather absurd move, Red & White had issued a complete timetable book for its South Wales and Stroud services dated 1 May 1950, just three weeks prior to the route exchange! Even the cover of its 1951 timetable showed a network of Red & White routes fanning from Stroud, though on this occasion there were no Stroud details within.

The Bristol Tramways "take-over" was not completed for many months. Outwardly, passengers would have assumed that it was business as usual. In fact, the Bristol company began by managing operations in their present condition, acting as a kind of holding company. Tramways issued its own Stroud timetable in June 1950, replacing the need for three separate publications to gain a comprehensive view of all Stroud's buses. Not only that, it was to a Tilling standard and consequently, easier to read than Red & White's. The timetable referred without distinction to the services operated by all three companies as separate entities with each of the existing Bristol, Red & White or Western National companies retaining their own services and route numbers. Even the small number of remaining ticket interavailability rules was kept intact. The network was therefore run as if it was still three separate businesses. In spite of bad weather over the following

Of the seven 1933 and 1934 Bristol Hs which passed from Western National to Tramways in 1950, 2490 seen here and 2487 survived the longest, to November 1951. 2490 was rebodied by Bristol Bus Works in 1942. Having transferred to Tramways, the painted out "Western National" name is just visible on the side. It was later to be repainted in Tramways' style. The pod on the roof rear was an integrally panelled roof luggage locker accessible by ladder. Note the dual aperture destination display favoured by Western National at the time. *Brian Ellison-Ward collection*

Whitsun week in 1950, tours booked up well in advance under either the Red & White or Western National names carried on as before.

Red & White's public office at Russell Street closed immediately. Yet, throughout the remainder of 1950, repaints from red into Bristol's Tilling green with cream livery, adopted in 1944 instead of dark blue and white, were rare and vehicles continued to operate in the traditional fleet livery, with standard Red & White gold filenames. Western National's green buses continued in a similar fashion. The only telltale signs before repaints were the application on each vehicle of Bristol Tramways legal lettering – the requirement for each bus operator to include a small company name and address identifier on the nearside.

Tramways began the process of transferring the necessary stage carriage route licenses from both Red & White and Western National as late as October and November 1950. All had been granted by the

Traffic Commissioners by January 1951. Country service timetables issued by Tramways on 28 May 1950 and 1 October 1950 showed only those Tramways services that had served Stroud from the 1920s onwards. It was not until the 1951 editions of Bristol Tramways' timetable that all Stroud's services were included and by this time there were no references to Red & White or Western National, save on the joint route to Trowbridge. It was from 1951 that the services became truly integrated and even then, some buses still required repainting.

Most of Stroud's red buses had disappeared by January 1951, either repainted, withdrawn or, as was more likely, transferred back to Red & White. There were those who lamented the passing of Stroud's red buses yet otherwise, the changeover was remarkable for its lack of response from the Stroud travelling public. This was for a number of reasons.

First and most importantly, the conductors themselves had a reputation in Stroud for their customer care and drivers and inspectors for the swiftness in resolving problems. There was never anything such as lost mileage in those days and local reliability, punctuality and courtesy were second to none, something that would later earn the road staff the appellation "gentlemen (and later ladies) of the Northern Division", throughout the Bristol years.

Secondly, customers had been used to a variety of red and green buses operating odd shifts and patterns and often they did not know – let alone particularly care – which colour bus would turn up. As buses

Upon transfer to Bristol Tramways, only one ex-Red & White Albion single deck was painted green, this being 2606 which is seen at Bristol awaiting a return to Stroud on the 400 service, introduced in 1950. *R Mack*

The remainder of Stroud's Albion single decks retained the livery and fleet name of Red & White while being allocated Bristol Tramways fleet numbers. All returned to the Red & White heartland in January 1951. Renumbered as 2609 in the Bristol Tramways fleet is this Albion CX13 with Duple bus body, seen on London Road while still operating at Stroud. *Bristol Vintage Bus Group*

did not go the green of the Bristol company overnight, the only outward sign might be a red bus operating on a green route or at a green time, or vice versa. This is graphically illustrated by Crawley & Simpson (1990), who state "After the transfer, one observant passenger, who was travelling from Cheltenham to Stroud over the former Bristol/Western National joint route, found himself riding in a former Red & White bus manned by a conductor wearing Western National uniform with a Bristol cap badge who issued a ticket bearing the name Ralph's Garages, a Red & White subsidiary based in Abertillery!" Truly integrated transport ahead of its time!

If the public were ambivalent, under the surface things were very different. The new management had to grapple with three sets of working conditions, two of which – in the case of Red & White and Western National – theoretically became obsolete over night. In practice, bits and pieces lingered from both for some time.

The manager appointed to oversee this transition was Hubert Sollars who a month earlier had been Red & White's man at Stroud, having taken over from Les Grimmit. The Western National manager based from 1943 at Stroud (but who also had responsibility for Trowbridge) was Mr A G Biles, who had begun to consider other possibilities as news of an amalgamation was considered in 1949 prior to Red & White's sale to the state. He returned to his native Weymouth in February 1950, where he continued to work within the management of sister company Southern National, with eight depots under his control. Such was the regard for Biles in Stroud that 13 staff travelled south for his retirement in 1966. Mr H G Lee succeeded Biles at Stroud in February 1950 for the short period to the transfer.

In spite of crews of different companies getting along well with each other before the transfer, during the first months, the merger itself was not wholly amicable. Not only were there differences over working conditions, practices and pay rates, even the different arrangements for such things as employees' and their families' free travel passes caused concern. Red & White had operated more split shifts – where the drivers' or conductors' eight hour stint would comprise a long day of morning and afternoon peak work with a considerable break in between, usually between about 0930 and 1430. Some Western National drivers were not prepared to accept this situation. Staff at Red & White felt that their company's reputation in terms of uniform, appearance of vehicles and maintenance was superior; those at Western National felt the opposite, and this caused some friction. Western National road staff refused to undertake overtime on former Red & White services and vice versa.

However, this was nothing compared to the apparent abhorrence felt by both sets of employees towards Bristol Tramways. The Bristol company operated a third set of conditions, rostering crews in a different way. Whereas, for example, Red & White had promised suitable conductors that they could be made up to driver at the legal minimum age of 21, Tramways insisted that its own age limit of 23 should apply. The Transport & General Workers Union regional group secretary, Mr A J Coxwell, walked into the Stroud situation at boiling point. For one thing, the road staff at both Red & White and Western National were against the merger. For another, Red & White was TGWU while the Western National crews were represented by the National Union of Railwaymen, a legacy of Western National's rail heritage. The NUR later vanished in Stroud as the TGWU already represented Bristol road staff. Of course, the unions had to concede that there was no alternative to the merger but were successful in negotiating concessions through give and take.

Unlike later years when two or three concerns reorganised into one, there were no redundancies of road, inspectorate, engineering or clerical staff. This was in spite of the Bristol company inheriting more

All but three of the ex-Red & White Albion double decks were repainted green by Tramways. They lasted longer than the single decks and this one, L4143 in the Bristol numbering series, was withdrawn in January 1953 prior to the chassis being sent back a month later to Red & White for spares. The body was immediately transferred to L3644, a Bristol K6A which operated at Stroud to 1956. *Roy Marshall collection*

vehicles and property than it needed. The Red & White premises at Russell Street was closed at the merger in favour of the former Western National premises at 8A George Street, passengers henceforward bene-fitting from one inquiry office for all service, tour and private hire inquiries and bookings. In the early months, Bristol arranged its serv-ices so that each of the two garages was responsible for particular routes, rather than perpetuate the system of joint operation as before-hand. Red & White's Dudbridge depot remained open throughout the decade but was gradually downgraded to a parking area only, latterly for coaches. Nevertheless, to be as efficient as possible, extra space was required at London Road and the Bristol company began parking vehi-cles at the LMS stables at adjacent Midland House until it was able to extend the parking area in 1963 by demolishing the adjoining building. It is worthy of note that in spite of the takeover of 1950, the London Road premises continued to be owned by Western National until the site's transfer to Bristol in 1954 simply because, until then, there appeared to be no mechanism within the British Transport Commission to reassign it. During this period, Western National leased the site to Bristol for £480 per annum.

When things had settled a little, the Bristol company at Stroud found itself with excessive vehicles. From Western National, it inherited a number of vehicle types that were familiar to the Bristol operating company. It had been the practice for many years for Tilling Group member companies to purchase vehicles of Bristol Bus Works manufacture and since Western National had been one such company, the Bristol chassis held sway at Stroud, even if it was not totally dominant. Furthermore, Western National vehicles were liveried in a similar green to Tramways' own, a shade known as Tilling green, and these of course did not require initial repainting and a couple of Bristol K double decks lasted to their withdrawal in 1955 in the Western National version of this green and cream livery.

Western National vehicles at Stroud transferred to Tramways included 10 coaches, 24 single deck and 13 double deck buses. These comprised of two Bedford small coaches with Duple bodywork, seven Leyland Tiger coaches also bodied by Duple, one Dennis Ace coach with a Brush body, five further Dennis Ace single deck buses, a Dennis Mace, five Bedford WTB buses of Duple wartime utility construction, seven rebodied Bristol Hs, six rebodied Bristol Js and, representing double decks, 11 Bristol Ks and a Leyland Titan, the Beadle body of which returned to Stroud on a Tramways Bristol K following the Titan chassis being scrapped.

Ten of the 11 transferred ex-Western National Bristol K double decks carried ECW bodywork familiar to Tramways although all were to the lowbridge design with sunken upper deck gangways, which where hitherto unusual in the Bristol fleet. The oldest, dating from 1939, carried a Beadle body. Two of the ten ECW bodied Ks were new to Stroud in 1940, one in 1946 and another in 1947. Six were delivered new to Stroud in 1949 and 1950. As a consequence, most of the Ks were young and five survived at Stroud until 1966, the last, L4134 (formerly Western National 950), being withdrawn in November that year. In actual fact, this was the very last example of the Bristol K chassis on the entire Bristol operating company. Bristol K L4137, a 1947 example, exchanged its Gardner five cylinder for an unusual AEC 7.7 litre engine in 1954. There was also a twelfth double deck from Western National, this being a 1931 Leyland Titan TD1 which passed to Western National from Exeter Corporation in 1945 and was rebodied by Beadle in 1947. While the chassis was scrapped in 1950, the body was transferred for further service. Some of these Ks had initially operated on loan to London Transport when new to cover a severe shortage of serviceable vehicles in the late 1940s. Another of the Ks was interesting in that it had been ordered by Caledonian Omnibus Company of Dumfries. Caledonian had been the only Tilling company in Scotland and was absorbed by the local Scottish Motor Transport company, Western, when both groups were nationalised in 1948. The four Caledonian K5Gs on order at the time were not required by the new owners and two were delivered to Southern Vectis and one each to Western and Southern National. It is also perhaps interesting to note that L4136 carried an LTA registration, and twenty years later three more vehicles in the LTA series, in the form of KSWs L4155 and L4156 and LS 2412, joined the Bristol fleet with the Trowbridge operations which were acquired in 1970.

Tramways began withdrawing some Western National single decks from September 1950. Bedford OBs replaced the similar though substandard wartime Bedford OWBs and the Dennises. The OWBs' seating pitch meant that they had been authorised for wartime use only and if not withdrawn, more space between the seats was required. The Dennises were withdrawn between September 1950 and February 1951. These measures effectively halved Stroud's number of small, narrower rural buses. Seven elderly Bristol H single decks were replaced by standard Bristol Js and Ls from the Bristol Tramways fleet. These early casualties had generally gained the Bristol city arms but were not repainted. One of Western National's Bedford OB coaches which was to be retained till 1954 appeared in Tramways all over cream coach livery with green flash and wings. The rebodied Bristol J buses were repainted to Tramways' choosing but five of the seven Hs remained in Western National style with Bristol coats of arms.

Additionally, the ex-Western National Leyland Tiger coaches, all of which were in handsome full Western National coach livery with sunshine sliding roofs and all of which tended to spend the winter in store and on bricks, were withdrawn completely in September 1950, after summer service. Replacements found were recently rebodied Bristol Js with coach seats in standard bus bodies but some of these appear to have been replaced by rather more luxurious pre-war Bristol L coaches. For a short period, Stroud also operated two unusual secondhand coaches which had been acquired in May 1950 from Henry Russett after his large fleet of lorries had been acquired by the Road Haulage Executive. These were 281, a Duple bodied Bedford WTL dating from 1935, and 2200, a 1948 Plaxton bodied Foden PVSC5.

By contrast, Red & White's vehicles were anything but standard when measured against a Tramways fleet of approaching 100 per cent

Bristol H 2496, new to Western National at Stroud in 1936 but rebodied in 1948, is here seen with the Bristol crest but with Western National route number, at the GWR station. *Bristol Vintage Bus Group*

Bristol chassis. Save for one Bedford OB coach and a solitary and elderly 1935 Bristol GO double deck, the Red & White fleet was entirely Albion, consisting of eight coaches, a further nine single deck buses and 12 double decks. 11 of the single decks were Albion CX13s, six of which carried Lydney bodywork and were new to Stroud in 1948, along with the Bedford OB. The remainder were all pre-war buses or coaches, bodied by Duple.

All of the Stroud single deck Albions were transferred back to Red & White's stronghold in January 1951. Between May 1950 and January 1951, they operated with Tramways legal lettering and fleet numbers but retained their red livery, the "Red & White" fleetname and route blinds. The exception was a solitary vehicle, numbered 2606 by Tramways, which was painted green and cream primarily for use on new route 400 to Bristol. Red & White's solitary Bedford stayed until September 1954 and this, too, was painted green by Tramways but without the standard Bristol coat of arms as the only readily visible outward sign of Bristol ownership applied to its vehicles at the time. One of the returned Albions, a 1932 PMB28, rebodied by Duple in 1938, came with a confusing reverse action handbrake and a twin gearstick arrangement. Seven of the eight Albion coaches to go back featured powerful

Gardner 6 cylinder engines, five had roof luggage compartments accessible by a short ladder at the centre rear and one had originally carried a 1½ deck body before being replaced with a standard coach body. This was reported to have been used by Joe Loss and consequently named the "band bus".

The transfer in January 1951 coincided with a further swap of Bristol Tramways Forest of Dean routes at that time. The Tramways depot at Coleford was in a position similar to Stroud's, only it was the Bristol company's operations that were landlocked by Red & White's, 22 Tramways vehicles being based there in 1949. Coleford depot came with an outstation at Cinderford where vehicles were actually garaged at the Red & White premises in the town. Red & White received back Albions, the type with which it was most familiar and, in exchange, lost the vehicles based at Coleford. Those at Cinderford largely transferred to Red and White but most subsequently were transferred back to Bristol Tramways.

The 12 double deck Albion CX19s with Duple bodies, new between

The oldest vehicle which transferred from the Red & White fleet was 3782, the first new vehicle brought in by Red & White to Stroud, in 1935. It was a Bristol GO6G featuring a Northern Counties body and it lasted on Tramways service till October 1950 when it was withdrawn and scrapped. It is seen here at the Subscription Rooms. *Bristol Vintage Bus Group*

1939 and 1942, lasted longer. Two were swapped for Bristol Ks in the January 1951 exchange and returned to Red & White along with Stroud's Albion single decks at that time. The oldest example from 1939 was withdrawn in December 1951 in spite of receiving green paint. A further six were returned to Red & White or neighbouring United Welsh in 1952 having been replaced by a batch of lowbridge KSWs. Only one of these KSWs actually came to Stroud. However, the remainder displaced Bristol Ks and GOs, which were subsequently moved to Stroud. Two were withdrawn from service in January 1953, and the last was withdrawn in October 1953. The bodies were removed from these three vehicles and returned to Stroud on wartime Bristol K chassis. The utility bodies from the Bristol Ks were fitted to the Albion chassis and the resultant combinations were then sent back to Red and White who dismantled them for spares. All those Albions lasting beyond January 1951 – 10 in total – were repainted green and cream. Like the single decks, vehicles carried the "Red & White" fleet-name but Tramways legal lettering until repainting. The elderly native Bristol GO double deck, Red & White's first new double deck at Stroud (from 1935) was withdrawn in October 1950, retaining its exquisitely painted red livery till the end. The replacement incoming Tramways GO double decks lasted until March 1955.

Like the Albion single decks, the double decks were highly regarded by crews. All were in fine condition externally, offered a comfortable ride to passengers, were fitted with six-cylinder 9.6 litre Albion diesel engines and, as a consequence, were fast. Nine of the examples remaining after January 1951 carried either bodywork by Duple finished by Lydney or constructed at Lydney using Duple parts. L4139 (former Red & White 432) was delivered in reverse livery and lined out in gold.

The Stroud Coleford swap balanced the books nicely between Red & White and Bristol; there were no such measures in Western National's case and this, apart from Bristol Tramways paying the asset value of vehicles and machinery, led to a considerably less rate of return on Western National's 1930s shareholding in Tramways.

If there were no redundancies and only minimal loss of mileage from a small route reorganisation, was the merger anything other than a grand tidying up exercise? Did the merger offer significant financial savings? The answer is that, yes, it did.

Sources suggest that the total number of vehicles transferred to Bristol Omnibus from Red & White and Western National was between 74 and 78. This was the number required during summer months. The total for winter operation was lower, at about 67. Of the

L4128 was a 1940 Bristol K5G with ECW body delivered new to Western National at Stroud in 1940. It transferred to Tramways before withdrawal in 1955 and like sister vehicle L4129, it retained Western National style livery throughout. It is seen here at King Street, outside Lewis & Godfrey. *Brian ward-Ellison collection*

summer complement, 19 were coaches and all but two were withdrawn by the end of the 1950 season. However, Red & White frequently used its nine coaches on stage carriage services. This meant that some 66 vehicles were available for stage carriage, works and school services, including duplicates. The total number of buses required to fulfill Stroud's regular, non-coaching requirements before the merger, including engineering spares, was 58, the number in the town following the January 1951 vehicle swaps. This meant that the merger of Red & White and Western National saved eight vehicles for normal traffic duties. The vehicles of the forties required a higher ratio of spares and with a combined operation, this need was further reduced. Basically, the sum of the 1950 parts was greater than the 1951 whole. What other bus operation could save over 12 per cent of its semi-fixed assets without sacrificing mileage?

To compensate for the vehicle withdrawals and transfers out of the early 1950s, Stroud received a number of transfers including 16 Bristol JOs and three Bristol Ls, all but two of which were rebodied between 1946 and 1950 by Bristol Bus Works or in two cases each by ECW and Longwell Green. It is probable that at least 13 of the JO buses, a JO dual-purpose vehicle and one L arrived as a direct exchange from Coleford. Most of the JOs were allocated to Dudbridge.

All the JOs were 35 seat buses with the exception of a solitary 31 seat dual-purpose vehicle. Three more rebodied bus examples were to arrive between 1958 and 1959, this time with Beadle bodies.

In spite of being rebodied, the JOs dated back to between 1933 and 1937 and were powered by five cylinder Gardner engines which were no match for the withdrawn Albions and offered less passenger comfort. They were generally inferior vehicles to the Albions they replaced and few, unlike the Albions, had heaters, (although the Albions themselves had no heaters for drivers who were obliged to wear gloves and over-coats). Road staff at Stroud were unhappy at the loss of what were pretty decent Albions, some of which were only a few years old, and their replacement by elderly Bristols. This was in spite of the Lydney bodied Albions having bodies that tended to rattle and be drafty. The unease among crews was undoubtedly a consideration in the JO's early replacement. Most had left by November 1951, seven replaced by newer Bristol Ls dating from 1949 and 1950, all with metal rather than wooden body frames. Further examples had been replaced by Bristol K double decks by November 1951. Even so, four of the JOs were to donate bodies to other vehicles when withdrawn by Bristol between 1957 and 1959.

2370 was one of several Bristol Js drafted in to Stroud by Tramways to replace non-standard or older buses. It started life as a Greyhound coach, passing to Tramways upon takeover of Greyhound in 1936. Its body was destroyed by enemy action in 1941 and it received a second hand coach body but was later rebodied with a new Bristol Bus Works bus body in 1951, as seen in this picture at Dudbridge. It was converted from petrol to diesel in 1948, prior to arrival at Stroud. *David Johnson*

For the time being Tramways also allocated coaches to Stroud, although these tended to be more seasonal than the dual purposes and would therefore come and go. Superior among these were three 25 seat Bristol LWL6Bs each with a striking ECW body and a similar Bristol LL6B. These full coaches operated largely in cream livery with either the "Bristol Greyhound" and motif or just the motif on the sides and from 1957 onwards, with "Bristol Omnibus Co." on the rear luggage door. Other coaches from the mid to late 1950s included two 39 seat ECW bodied LSs to full coach specification, again liveried in cream and with green window surrounds.

A single deck Bristol L with ECW 35 seat body arrived in August 1950. Two more followed in 1951, one with dual door Bristol Bus Works 32 seat body (although the front entrance was sealed before arrival) and another, with ECW 35 seat bodywork, new to Tramways in 1949 and withdrawn as late as 1966. The fifties saw quite an influx of other Bristol Ls, all with rear entrance 35 seat ECW bodies except one with 33 seats and dual doors. All were first manufactured between 1949 and 1950 except one, new in 1939 and all arrived at various points throughout the fifties. The last was withdrawn in September 1966 and this tended to work between Rodborough, Stroud and Minchinhampton (429). By January 1958, 23 J and L types were based at Stroud and this

New in 1937, 2060 was another drafted-in Bristol JO5G. It was rebodied by Bristol Bus Works in May 1950 to a dual purpose standard, although the trim was only marginally better than that on standard buses. It is seen here in 1958 with standard bus seats and following a repaint out of its cream and green dual purpose livery. *David Johnson*

Dating back to 1935 but rebodied by ECW in 1949, 2195 was another elderly Bristol JO5G which found its way to Stroud, albeit not until 1959 when it operated for six months prior to withdrawal. It is seen climbing Rowcroft towards King Street. *David Johnson*

The service between Nailsworth and Minchinhampton was the first to be numbered in the 400 series, in June 1950, when "4" was prefixed to the old service number 67. It is seen waiting at the Nailsworth terminus on the area adjacent to today's bus station. *Bristol Vintage Bus Group*

was reduced to 11 by the end of the decade.

From December 1950, the first of a number of Bedford OBs arrived for use on routes formerly operated by the Dennises. The routes included services to Ruscombe, Kingscourt, Cranham and the "Nailsworth Outstations", local services in and around Nailsworth. Buses working the Nailsworth routes were not outstationed in the usual sense – a vehicle remaining overnight away from its parent garage – but travelled out and back from Stroud each day, spending its time away from base on Nailsworth local services. Mid-shift crew changes required a journey on a service bus to and from Stroud. All the Bedfords, new in 1949 and 1950 before arriving at Stroud, were initially fitted with Bedford petrol engines though progressively converted to diesel between December 1957 and March 1958. Three arrived in December 1950 and another two in January 1951.

The Bedfords were converted to one-man operation from December 1957, this being the year when the company and union agreed that selected services could be single manned. Western National and Red & White between them had operated one man vehicles before the 1950 merger and these included the Dennis vehicles once used on the Bedford OB routes and it is interesting that such routes were actually converted to crew operation under Tramways. One-man buses had otherwise been in operation in the Stroud Valleys since the introduction of the GWR routes at the turn of the 20th century.

From 1954, Stroud received its first Bristol LS single deck buses. LS stood for "Light Saloon" and, with their front entrance ECW bodies and under floor engines, were thoroughly modern, even down to some being fitted with heaters from new. The overall body width on these (and subsequent) vehicles was increased to eight feet, thereby offering more comfortable passenger accommodation. The driver was reminded of this fact by a white or cream rather than black steering wheel. Not only was the driver now in direct control of the passenger door (rather then in a separate cab next to the engine), the additional length which resulted from an underfloor engine gave a 45 seat capacity vehicle, significantly above the 35 seat norm of an older half-cab Bristol L. 13 LSs were in use by the end of the fifties. Most were converted for one-man operation between September and December 1958 but two were altered earlier, in April and May that year.

Two examples arrived with dual purpose 41 seat ECW bodies rather than the standard 45 bus seat variant. They were initially numbered in the LS series and painted as if standard buses but were renumbered in

During the early fifties, Tramways brought some newer Bristol L single decks to Stroud, typified by 2463, a 1950 example which arrived at Stroud in June 1951. Its destination shows "GAC Brockworth". Factories in Brockworth had been destinations for contract hires to 1989. *David Johnson*

March 1961 into a dual-purpose number sequence, having gained cream roofs in November and December 1959 to mark them out.

Stroud had generally operated low rather than highbridge double decks. This had been both Red & White's and Western National's custom, though not Tramways'. Highbridge vehicles could actually squeeze under the pessimistically posted height restriction at Rowcroft railway bridge, if technically unlawfully. Even the air vents of some double decks would just scrape Rowcroft bridge, until the road beneath was lowered. There were other bridges in the area for which only lowbridge vehicles were suitable, including two railway bridges at Stonehouse. Red & White did, in fact, operate two highbridge vehicles at Stroud, including the Bristol GO with Northern Counties bodywork and an Albion CX19 with a Weymann body. Both could negotiate the Stonehouse LMS railway by first stopping, giving way to all other traffic and proceeding centrally and with caution. Even so, both frequently suffered roof damage, from trees as well as bridges.

A further pressing reason for the use of lowbridge vehicles at Stroud was in fact the London Road depot height and doorways, which prevented the use of highbridge examples reaching the pits! This had been no problem for Western National with lowbridge vehicles. One rather absent minded driver did, in fact, attempt to get a highbridge double deck in the depot, managed to get the vehicle trapped and had to deflate the tyres to back it out again!

Tramways had chosen the 400 series for its newly acquired Stroud routes. Nevertheless, even though Red & White had not displayed its numbers on vehicles, Tramways carried on using the established Red & White and Western National dual route numbering system until late 1951, following both applications to license services under Tramways and the progressive modification of Western National's more complicated bus destination indicators to carry Tramways style blinds, although some Western National vehicles received Tramways blinds prior to alteration. The last to be converted were actually in 1953! This resulted in a dual numbering system such that, at times, certain buses would display a 200 series number while others on the same route would show a number in the 400 series. There was, however, one exception to this: the 67 between Nailsworth, Box and Minchinhampton was renumbered 467 in June 1950. The 1951 renumbering shown in Table 1 largely mirrored the Western National 200 series.

Aside from the renumbering, there were some route developments. The Bristol company operated service 63 between Cheltenham, Birdlip and Brimpsfield. Red & White had operated between Stroud and Birdlip and also, jointly with Western National, between Stroud and Dursley via Uley. Bristol amalgamated all three as through service 63 between Dursley, Uley, Stroud, Birdlip and Cheltenham. The journey for Dursley residents to Cheltenham was a frustrating one of country twists and turns lasting about two hours. It was actually some 30 minutes quicker for Cheltenham bound Dursley passengers to change at Gloucester!

Another significant development was a new service between Stroud and Bristol via Wotton-under-Edge. There had been political pressure during the late forties for such a service as travel by rail from Stroud to Bristol had become more difficult with the cessation in 1947 of the connecting Nailsworth to Stonehouse branch line passenger trains. An announcement was made by Tramways in February 1950, well before the May amalgamation, that the firm hoped to introduce such a service in the near future.

In the event, a service numbered 400 started on 2 July 1950, with a return fare to Bristol of 4/9, 1d less than the fare on Western National's regular Bristol excursions. The stage carriage service offered far more flexibility, however, with six round trips on weekdays and four on Sundays, something that was not to alter substantially until almost exactly 30 years later. 400 was indeed warmly welcomed and the Bristol

Table 1. 1950 Stroud bus network before merger

No.	Route	Operator/s	Number of trips		
			Mon–Fri	Saturday	Sunday
46/220	Nailsworth – Cheltenham via Stroud, Painswick	BT/WN	Joint hourly	Joint hourly	Joint hourly
51	Stroud – Gloucester via Stonehouse	BT	7	7	4
54	Painswick – Gloucester via Cranham, Brockworth	BT	10	10	5
56	Nailsworth – Gloucester via Stroud, Edge	RW	At least hourly	At least hourly	At least hourly
62/225	Stroud – Dursley via Uley	RW/WN	6	6	4
63	Brimpsfield/Birdlip – Cheltenham	BT	10	11	6
57/221	Chalford – Standish Lodge via Stroud	RW/WN	3 per hour	3 per hour	3 per hour
58	Nailsworth – Gloucester via Stroud, Painswick	BT	7	7	4
58/228	Stroud – Minchinhampton via Amberley	RW/WN	Half-hourly	Half-hourly	Hourly
59	Nailsworth – Avening	RW	12	12	5
61	Stroud – Dursley via Eastington	RW	14	19	6
64/226	Stroud – France Lynch	RW/WN	14	14	4
65/226A	Stroud – Oakridge	RW/WN	13	13	5
66/222	Stroud – Cirencester via Chalford	RW/WN	7	7	3
67	Nailsworth – Minchinhampton	RW	5	5	3
117	Leonard Stanley – Gloucester via Stonehouse	BT	3	3	3
160/225A	Stroud – Birdlip via Slad	RW/WN	10	11	4
223	Stroud – Trowbridge via Nailsworth, Tetbury, Malmesbury	WN	5	5	2
224	Stroud – Nailsworth	WN	Hourly	Hourly	Hourly

227	Stroud – Frampton-on-Severn via the Stanleys	WN	6	8	2
229	Stroud – Minchinhampton via Brimscombe	WN	Hourly	Hourly	Hourly
230	Stroud – Whiteshill	WN	Half-hourly	Half-hourly	7
230A	Stroud – Ruscombe	WN	14	14	4
231	Stroud – Randwick	WN	Every 40 minutes	Every 40 minutes	Hourly
231A	Stroud – Foxmoor Lane	WN	Hourly	Hourly	None
233	Stroud – Bridgend Estate via King Stanley	WN	24	26	9
250	Stroud – Summer Crescent	WN	Hourly	Hourly	None
250A	Stroud – Kilminster Road	WN	Hourly	Hourly	None
251	Stroud – Uplands	WN	Hourly	Hourly	None
252	Stroud – Cranham via Painswick	WN	14	14	None
253	Stroud – Kingscourt	WN	16	16	4
253A	Stroud – Rodborough	WN	Half-hourly	Half-hourly	4
255	Nailsworth – Shortwood	WN	Hourly	Hourly	None
256	Nailsworth – Newmarket	WN	Hourly	Hourly	None

company was congratulated in starting the service so soon after the takeover.

The curious thing about the 400 was that it was initially marketed as a joint Tramways and Red & White service. Generally, two vehicles were required, one from Bristol and one from Stroud, and Stroud had few buses available at the time with the "Bristol" fleetname. The service was introduced during the period immediately after takeover, when Tramways was portraying a three company public image. The choice of Red & White was logical as, under the old regime, it alone operated from Nailsworth to Wickwar via Wotton, the local route replaced by 400. Previously, the connections between Red & White and Tramways, at Wotton, had been far from satisfactory. The vehicle used in the early days of 400 often tended to be 2606, the only Albion painted green, plus the Bristol L which came to Stroud in August 1950.

The July date also saw other improvements. Bristol Tramways introduced a 2220 departure between Stroud and Sapperton via Aston Down and Frampton Mansell, and an 0630 Stroud to Oakridge, returning at 0700. Relatively minor changes to services through Painswick were not so well received.

Regarding other routes, there were very few changes in the fifties, till later in the decade. The early and mid fifties were a time when passenger numbers, though starting to decline, were still buoyant. During the period 1950 to 1956, services 46, 422, 423, 424, 426, 426A, 427, 428, 429, 430, 431, 434, 452, 453, 454, 455, 456, 459 and 461 remained unchanged. Of the remainder, services 56, 58 and 63 saw minor changes.

More significant route changes did occur during this period, usually for the better. Services between Gloucester and Stroud via Stonehouse were supplemented on Saturdays and Sundays with a journey to Cashes Green Hospital. The Chalford – Stroud – Stonehouse service 421 increased in frequency on Saturdays from every 20 to every 10 minutes. Three Sunday journeys and one evening journey were introduced on 431A to Foxmoor Lane. The 433 between Stroud, the Stanleys and Bridgend Estate was extended to and from Stonehouse's Park Estate, although the Sunday service was reduced. The 450/450A between Stroud and either Summer Crescent or Kilminster Road benefitted from a Sunday service and a 2115 departure between Stroud and Tetbury on 470 was introduced.

The Summer 257, renumbered as 457, between Stroud, Nailsworth, Tetbury, Bristol and Weston-super-Mare, reintroduced after the war, was extended in Western National days to Minehead via Highbridge,

Note the police constable on point duty, once a common sight at or near the Holloway statue. When this shot of 2191 was taken, the Bristol L had already been downgraded from a dual purpose vehicle to a standard bus. It originally operated express services from Bristol and upon arrival at Stroud, sported a six cylinder Bristol engine, although this was replaced by a Gardner five cylinder in 1956. The bus is heading from King Street towards Rowcroft. *David Johnson*

Bridgwater and Watchet but operated on Saturdays only and high summer weekdays, with the introduction of the 400. Tramways introduced a new route between Stroud and Highfields with five journeys on weekdays and a new service from Nailsworth to Tiltups End, offering four return journeys on Tuesdays and Fridays, while other Nailsworth local services 449 to Windsoredge and 467 to Minchinhampton saw respectively an additional journey and extension on Tuesdays, Fridays and Saturdays to Cherrington.

However, things were about to change. Rural bus service operators were beginning to become concerned at the loss of revenue following a decline in passenger numbers. Fares, static beforehand, had begun to rise after the war in an effort to compensate for the tail-off in demand.

The UK wide fall in passenger journeys masked very real concerns in rural areas, where the drop was most acute. The Stroud of the mid to late 1950s was slightly different for, although there were routes causing considerable concern, numbers travelling along the more profitable trunk corridors still remained buoyant, enabling cross-subsidy.

Towards the end of 1956, the Suez Expedition brought with it cuts in the supply of crude oil. During this national emergency, each of the

1950 Bristol L 2453 arrived in 1958 for a stay of about six months. It is pictured at the former Red & White Dudbridge depot now the site of a super-market but which remained open as a bus garage throughout the fifties, although it was used progressively less as the decade progressed. *David Johnson*

Traffic Commissioners required operators to make cuts of 10 per cent in mileage owing to a pro rata cut in fuel. Stroud was no exception, though its own reductions totalled less than 10 per cent of its mileage.

General petrol rationing for private motorists did account for some increases in bus patronage at this time, particularly on busy routes and especially during the morning and afternoon peak periods. Consequently, some adults and school children were left stranded. On 22 January 1957, the 1900 Stroud to Stonehouse was heavily loaded owing to a troop of some 30 Brownies travelling to their regular meeting at Ebley! Arrangements were made in future to accommodate the children on the following 1905 Stroud to Dursley departure, also via Ebley.

With such overcrowding and restrictions continuing after the national emergency had abated, passengers were actually discouraged from travel and the downward trend in passenger journeys continued. Bristol Tramways' statement that "the Company regrets the necessity of these restrictions but hopes that they will be accepted in the national interest" was of little comfort to the travelling public of the time, even though the company itself had no option but to accede to the Commissioner's directive and, wherever possible, withdrew only off-peak mileage or services that were little used.

Stroud's Suez Crisis measures came into force on 16 December 1956 and affected the following routes:

51 Stroud – Gloucester via Stonehouse. The Stroud – Stonehouse section withdrawn while other journeys were retimed, becoming irregular in nature rather than clockface.

63 Dursley – Cheltenham via Stroud. Some journeys curtailed or operated direct, thereby missing out villages at certain times.

421 Chalford – Stonehouse via Stroud. Monday to Thursday evening service cut from every 20 to every 40 minutes.

426 Stroud – France Lynch. 1030 and 1430 journeys from Stroud to Brownshill and the 2215 to France Lynch withdrawn.

427 Stroud – Framilode. 2215 Mondays to Saturdays terminated short at Leonard Stanley rather than Eastington.

431 Stroud – Randwick. 1115, 1150, 1225 and 1440 Westrip Turning journeys withdrawn.

433 Stroud – Stonehouse (Park Estate). 1120, 1320 and 1945 on weekdays and 1615 and 1946 journeys on Sundays from Stroud to Park Estate curtailed at Bridgend Estate.

451 Stroud – Uplands. One Sunday journey withdrawn.

452 Stroud – Cranham. 0720 and 1413 Stroud – Painswick withdrawn.

456 Nailsworth – Newmarket. Outer terminus to become the George Inn rather than Hillier's factory.

461 Stroud – Dursley. One Sunday journey withdrawn.

Because of falling revenue, it was perhaps with some relief that the company was able to make these cuts. A number became permanent even upon normalisation, notably changes to services 51, 431 and 456 and as such became the first ever bus service cuts in the Stroud area of any significance, signalling as it did events that were to follow in the sixties and beyond. Other services reverting to their pre-emergency timetable did so in the late spring.

Perhaps the most significant Suez-related cut back – another that became permanent – occurred on 27 January 1957. This was the curtailment at Malmesbury of the Stroud to Trowbridge service 423 which, at the 1950 merger, had become a joint Bristol and Western National

Meanwhile, London Road garage became the more important of the two at Stroud, even though it could not accommodate highbridge vehicles, the last of which was withdrawn in 1953. Lowbridge Bristol K L4113, transferred that year though new in 1947, stands next to Bristol L 2431, which was transferred to the town in 1950. *David Johnson*

operation. The service was also thinned from five on Mondays to Saturdays to three on Mondays to Fridays, and five on Saturdays, with the two Sunday services unaltered, although these measures proved only temporary during the emergency. Before 1950, it was the one route linking the two landlocked Western National outposts and over the years had seen crew swaps between buses including at Hullavington's "pretty chimneys" and buses garaged overnight at opposite depots. Its withdrawal as a through service signalled the very end of Western National involvement in Stroud.

Worse was to come in Stroud in February. Following a dispute over a local appointment of a driver to the post of inspector, supposedly over the heads of longer serving men, crews were set to strike on Saturday 2 February 1957, in the midst of petrol rationing. Coxwell of the TGWU again found himself at Stroud. The company maintained that applications had been sought in the usual manner, the successful applicant had been the best man and Coxwell actually doubted the validity of the crews' claims. The company conceded that it should re-examine the facts and the strike was postponed accordingly. However,

Similar Bristol K L4104 was allocated to Stroud as a direct replacement for one of Red & White's Albions. Like L4113, its ECW body was of wooden frame construction and it was powered by a Bristol engine. After L4104 became surplus in 1959, it was sold to operator Thames Valley for further stage carriage use. It is seen here working its way up Rowcroft towards the town centre. Note the pre 1968 "No Waiting" lollipop on the left. *David Johnson*

negotiations broke down the following week and local drivers ignored Coxwell's request that no action be taken that might prejudice the case pending a further meeting the week after.

Saturday 9 February was Stroud's first ever all-out stoppage. The only bus that entered service that day was to allow visitors to reach Standish Hospital, being the 1340 421 Stroud to Standish Lodge returning at 1620. On-bus pickets ensured that passengers carried were for Standish Hospital only. Other pickets on the outskirts of the valleys at, for example, Nailsworth and Painswick, prevented buses from other depots entering the town. Although there were threats of further Saturday strikes, the stoppage lasted for one day only. Coxwell had been accurate in his view that the appointment was carried out correctly, interest in strike action fizzled out among the crews and the newly appointed inspector carried on working at Stroud, although he did transfer some months later to Bristol.

Meanwhile, on 30 May 1957, the Bristol Tramways & Carriage Company Ltd, incorporated in 1887 upon the amalgamation of the

L4115, arriving 1953, was a further Bristol K replacing an Albion. It was one of a number of similar vehicles which received a six cylinder Albion engine in exchange for its original Gardner unit. As such, the technology would have been familiar to ex-Red & White fitters at Stroud. It is seen on the 424, the hourly short working between Stroud and Nailsworth via Cainscross, outside what was Lewis & Godfrey on King Street. *David Johnson*

Tramways Company Ltd and the Bristol Cab Company Ltd, modernised its name, becoming the Bristol Omnibus Company Ltd. Trams had not operated since their withdrawal in Bristol in 1941, following enemy action. Two years previously, the motor construction works became a stand-alone company within the British Transport Commission, known as Bristol Commercial Vehicles.

The remainder of 1957 was to be a harsh one for the newly named Bristol Omnibus Company and if it felt that with the resumption of its proper timetable from late Spring onwards would see a return to normality in Stroud, it was mistaken. There loomed in July a national bus strike, sponsored by six unions including the TGWU who claimed increases in pay of £1 per week were necessary. 100,000 provincial bus workers would be affected, it was claimed. 100 per cent support was pledged for the action.

The main problem on the nationally chosen strike period was that it coincided with Stroud Show day. The Show was already suffering losses and any withdrawal of transport would affect it further. The

Some 11 Bedford OBs with Duple 30 seat bodies were operated by Bristol at Stroud, although not all at the same time, the first of which arrived in December 1950. They tended to see service on Nailsworth locals, to Uplands, to Ruscombe, certain journeys to Cranham and, seen here at the GWR station, to Kingscourt. The Kingscourt service was successor to one of the GWR routes and terminated at the station as it had from the beginning. OB no. 217 arrived at Stroud in 1957 and received a Perkins diesel engine in place of a Bedford petrol unit at the same time. The vehicle was equipped for one-man operation in June 1958. *David Johnson*

union at Stroud recognised the additional burden a strike would place on both Stroud's travelling public and the Stroud Show committee and gave due consideration to operating buses especially for the show. The problem was that in order to operate from every corner of the Stroud Valleys, virtually all buses would be required. In the event, no buses operated for the second Saturday in 1957 and the strike was to continue the following week, affecting the usual business of the area including schools and factories. The following week saw schools and some factories close for the summer or annual breaks but the buses were back on the road in any case.

During the latter part of the fifties, more LS single decks arrived, making inroads into the Js and Ls. From 1957, agreement with the union was reached to commence one-man operation. There were no redundancies at this point as any surplus conductors who wished to be trained as drivers began to counter Stroud's driver shortage in a period of full employment in the area. Nevertheless, Stroud's fleet was still largely crew operated.

Fares increased throughout the fifties in a bid to balance the company's accounts. Those applied immediately before and during the 1957 fuel crisis to return fares continued after the situation eased. However, the company reduced about three-quarters of its single fares by 1/2d or 1d while the remainder stayed as they were or went up. The fares increases beforehand were to offset additional labour costs and this was a pattern of wage-related rises already established at this time. However, in 1957, it had got to a point where fares were already thought to be excessively high. The Chancellor of the Exchequer's reduction by 1d per gallon on fuel motivated people to ask why bus fares were not actually coming down. There was a further outcry when the company rounded its child fares not to the nearest half-penny but to the nearest penny upwards. It was clear that Sollars had something of an uphill task in explaining that twist in events!

A new breed of modern double deck arrived in Stroud from 1955 in the shape of L8249, L8255, L8260, L8262 and L8280. These were Bristol Commercial Vehicles LDs, or "Lodekkas" as they were better known,

More modern single deck Bristol LSs, with engines mounted underfloor rather than at the front, began to arrive from 1954. One such was 2849 seen at the former Stroud Brewery site while heading for Stroud from Bristol. The vehicle was converted for one-man operation in 1958 but at the date of the photograph was conductor operated. Note the white steering wheel to denote an 8ft wide body. *David Johnson*

Coaches at Stroud during the fifties tended to fluctuate with seasonal requirements. Bristol LS6G SHT 349, variously numbered 2876 and 2098, is seen in
full Bristol Greyhound livery in 1958. This picture demonstrates the importance of Rowcroft as a through route at the time. In addition to the two cars
and two buses, two bicyclists can be seen descending the hill at a time when
cycling was still a popular and essential travel mode. *David Johnson*

with 58 seat ECW bodies. Stroud's were among the first production
LDs delivered to Bristol Tramways. The Lodekka was to a very radical
design for its time. It was the first double deck low bridge bus to
feature a central upper gangway between two rows of double seats
rather than the sunken side gangway and one row of four seats as hitherto, known as "skittle alleys". The continuous row of four seats on the
older low bridge double deck Bristol Ks was disliked by passengers,
who had to squeeze past each other, and conductors, who had to lean
over passengers to reach the furthest fare. They also featured rear platform passenger doors, quite an innovation on double decks at the time,
which otherwise offered only an open platform (although Stroud's
couple of lowbridge KSWs were the first to have these). Five more new
examples arrived in 1956, one in 1958 and five in 1959, together with
second hand examples transferred in to Stroud during the fifties and
sixties to replace older double decks. The first LDs, either directly or
indirectly by bringing later lowbridge Ks to Stroud, enabled the Bristol
GOs and a number of the more elderly Ks either to be withdrawn or
transferred to less demanding duties elsewhere. Bristol Omnibus' last

Bristol LS 2897, new in 1958 but arriving in Stroud the following year, is seen waiting at King Street Parade in front of F W Woolworth with what amounts to a reasonable load for the deep rural route to Cheltenham via Slad, Miserden, Whiteway and Birdlip. Through running from Dursley on service 63 was achieved as a result of the 1950 merger between companies. Behind the LS and heading for Gloucester on the 56 is one of the new breed of Bristol LD "Lodekka" double decks. *David Johnson*

LD, L8546, came to Stroud new at the end of 1959.

At the close of the decade, in spite of a merger that brought forth obvious economies, investment in newer and more comfortable vehicles and thinning of the weakest services following Suez, the state of the local bus network was far less healthy than 10 years earlier. Passenger numbers had started a natural decline but it was the two strikes of 1957 that signalled what amounted to a sea change. Had these done more harm than good?

It was evident that, in spite of speculation to the contrary, much of the Stroud Valleys carried on as normal during February's and July's strikes. True, there were fewer shoppers in the town during the February strike but those people who had no choice whether they travelled – shop assistants – virtually all managed to be at their posts by 0900. Of the 82 assistants at F W Woolworth, only nine had not arrived by 0900. Boots and Lewis & Godfrey reported 100 per cent attendance in spite of some staff living some distance from the town centre. Neither was Stroud totally empty as had been predicted. The

Considerably more modern Bristol LD "Lodekka" double decks began to appear at Stroud from 1955. They offered new standards of passenger accommodation, especially on the upper deck. L8395, allocated from new in 1956 to 1958, shows the original 36 ft x 11 ft destination indictor box. Behind is an ex-MOD Ford lorry acquired after the Second World War. *David Johnson*

Bristol MW single decks began to arrive from 1959 and were to last in operation till the late seventies. One of the first at Stroud was 2943 which, in common with the Bristol operating company's first batches, featured cream window pillars and came without the waistband associated with later models. *David Johnson*

Road staff assembled at London Road, c.1957. From left, Stan Cooke, Frank Washbourne, Percy Clarke, Mr Jamieson, Lawrence Harding, Mervin Bennett, John Nottingham, Inspector Hall, Ken Shelley, Martin Hyde, Dave Cruickshank, Reg Mansfield, Eric Bridges, Doris Phillips, possibly Ken Oakey, Nat Hammond with unidentified member of staff behind, John Shipton, Vic Watkins, Inspector Ireland and Roy Adams. *Jack Ireland collection*

people of the area had used their resourcefulness to find alternatives, even during February's strike amidst the Suez fuel crisis.

In July, the local railcar was often full to bursting, bicycles again came out of sheds and, worryingly, the practice of offering lifts in the more rural areas had further developed. This last fact must have been much to the dismay of the local management as it would have longer-term consequences throughout the sixties. Factory and school absenteeism was reported as practically nil with some firms even laying on private transport. Only two pupils at Stroud High School for Girls were reported off school owing to the strike. The Rotary Club and Round Table between them ensured people could reach Standish Hospital from Stonehouse rail station. Hospital visiting at Stroud was not seriously affected. The earlier February strike cost Tramways lucrative private hire business from Stroud High School for Girls as, at the time, the company was to provide transport for exchange students

In order to ease congestion in the town centre, buses to Frampton-on-Severn, Randwick, Foxmoor Lane, Stonehouse (Park Estate) and Dursley terminated at the old LMS station yard for a short period in 1952, where Bristol K L4136 and Bristol L 4263 are seen. *Jack Ireland collection*

from Duderstadt. In the event, the work went to and stayed with F Hand (Rover Coaches).

Even those in outlying communities who could find no alternative benefitted from the recent increase in village shop deep freezes and, of course, mobile shops were still common place at this time.

The real test came with the Stroud Show. Attendance was hardly different from the year before. The Stroud Valleys were no longer totally reliant on the bus service. In July 1957, the Stroud News & Journal summed it up rather well. "If the local busmen... imagined that their absence from work was going to dislocate the life of the district, they were sadly mistaken".

CHAPTER 6

1960–1969
EASIER TO GET
TO THE MOON?

The Stroud public's determination to overcome the bus strikes and service withdrawals of 1957 signalled a considerable change in the fortunes of Bristol Omnibus, one that increasing car ownership would perpetuate throughout the sixties. No longer was the bus service the only means of travel. There was suddenly an alternative for many ordinary families as the car began to alter the pattern of life in the Stroud Valleys.

Up to this time, Stroud had been the principal focus of valley life. 89 drivers, 72 conductors, five inspectors plus some 16 clerical staff worked for Bristol Omnibus. Most other employment in the Stroud Valleys was local in nature, in textiles, engineering or in chemicals along the valley floors or in town centre shops and offices, all of which were readily accessible from Stroud by bus. This was amply demonstrated by the hiatus caused in April 1960 following significant adjustments in shop and factory hours. Because of the lack of adequate consultation, Stroud's transport manager, Mr H R Sollars, struggled to cope with the changes, which affected thousands of passengers and every bus and crew. He called it "the biggest upheaval in our services since we came here ten years ago".

Local shopping was the norm, too, at this time with trips to Cheltenham and Gloucester also of importance. Car ownership was low and bus frequencies high. Even villages away from the valleys on the Cotswold Hills enjoyed at least a reasonable service to Stroud.

Coinciding with a time when petrol again became freely available, increased disposable income led to the widespread use of the motor car. This speeded up dramatically during the sixties. Separating work and home, many of the village settlements became attractive to new occupants who commuted by car, not any more to Stroud (as was possible by bus) but to Gloucester, Cheltenham, Cirencester, Swindon and even Bristol. This was supported by improved road access. In short, the car changed village life, the expectations of its residents and brought with it migrants who could afford to commute longer distances.

During the sixties, Bristol Omnibus reacted accordingly with the speeding up of one man operation resulting, for the first time ever, in conductor redundancies. In spite of a decline in passengers, it was to the company's credit that it was able to protect many of its Stroud services throughout the sixties with a drop in departures of just five per cent in 1970 when compared to the position ten years earlier. This it did in a number of ways. While seeking to contain costs by increasing productivity and withdrawing marginal journeys, the company sought to raise fares above inflation, now on an annual basis. Stroud's urban-rural mix ensured that the more profitable services cross-subsidised the more marginal, a tool the company was able to use in Stroud throughout the decade, though things would change later. Even though Bristol Omnibus declared in 1963 that 65 per cent of all its services were making a loss, Stroud's were relatively healthy.

The gradual withdrawal of bus services first seen in 1957 following Suez had begun. However, perception was to be different to the actual situation on the ground and complaints began to surface. At the annual Eastington parish council of 1960, one observer living near the village felt moved to comment that "we try to go to the moon but we cannot even go to Gloucester by bus". It must also be remembered that in spite of the ascendancy of the motor car, there were still full buses throughout the first half of the sixties. Friday afternoons and Saturdays were particularly busy, the former because early finishing workers would coincide with returning shoppers. Friday was a significant shopping day as workers had been paid their weekly wage that day or the day before. In an era before supermarkets, non-working housewives would come into the town for basic shopping. Saturdays were also bustling because whole families would travel together. It was still common to see regulars travelling during the evening to local pubs for a pint even though the cinema had by now given way to the television, with a consequent further reduction in demand.

In spite of this now established steady down turn in passenger traffic, the sixties started optimistically enough in Stroud both for the Bristol Omnibus Company and its customers, with the opening on 3 July 1960 of a new bus station at Merrywalks, the first departure being

1960 was about to see the end of on-street running. Bristol K L4125 awaits by the queue rails at the Subscription Rooms, on of the busiest town centre stops before the Bus Station's completion and one used after the Bus Station's completion as a dropping off point on services from Stonehouse to Chalford. *David Johnson*

the 1056 hrs service 400 from Stroud to Bristol.

For the first time, this brought together all of Stroud's services in one place. The new terminus became fully equipped for both passengers and employees. Road staff and inspectors particularly benefited from these improvements, not least of which were mess and lavatory facilities close at hand and, with the consequent closure of the Company's inherited offices at 8A George Street, improved working conditions for the significant numbers of clerical staff.

In spite of the aforementioned decline in passenger numbers, in the still relatively confident public transport world of the late 1950s, the company had begun a programme of terminus improvements. Wells bus station opened in 1955 followed in 1958 by bus stations at both Bath and Bristol. A year later, Weston-super-Mare's pre-war bus station was considerably refurbished. Gloucester's new bus station at Market Parade opened in 1962, replacing what was designed as a temporary site at King's Square. This trend was to continue with the completion of a "temporary" bus station at Swindon in 1967, used for 17 years. Nailsworth gained its own bus station in 1966, on land adjacent to the parking ground used up till them for buses. Cirencester saw its bus station completed in 1973.

The street pattern in Stroud did not lend itself particularly well to on street running. Prior to the bus station, buses were scattered on relatively narrow roads at a number of locations. At the close of the fifties, these points were Russell Street, George Street, Cheapside, London Road, Badbrook, King Street and from February 1956, Lansdown adjacent to Bank Gardens. The result was somewhat chaotic for a number of reasons. First, at busy times, some pavements could not adequately cope with the number of people queuing for buses. Secondly, passengers requiring to change buses would not always be able to walk from one point to another without missing their intended connection. In any case, the scattered nature of stops caused some confusion. Thirdly, supervisory staff inevitably found difficulty in attempting to cover buses and crews at times of need (for example, because of vehicle breakdown or driver illness).

Added to that, some traders in the town were vociferous in their campaign to rid the streets of buses. They felt that the increasing traffic problems of the late 1950s were directly attributable to public rather than private transport. They felt that buses simply took up too much space, clogged the town and prevented cars parking.

The first bus using Stroud Bus Station was on Sunday 3 July 1960, with the departure of the 1056 service to Bristol. Here, the unofficial "opening" is marked by the crew of driver and conductor standing next to their bus, MW no. 2961, with an inspector looking on. Between the crew is Mrs Johnson, wife of the photographer, David. Note that the bus station is far from complete. Although the vehicle was based at Stroud some ten years later, at the time it was one of Bristol's, as the first Sunday departure at that time was a Bristol working. *David Johnson*

Although the idea of a bus station in Stroud was first mooted as early as 1933, the idea came to prominence during the late 1940s and early 1950s. Congestion was the prime reason for the debate at this time – streets clogged by buses and passengers, and motorists ignoring queuing and crossing pedestrians. The police were taking action against bus crews who failed to prevent passengers alighting at town centre stops already occupied by a bus waiting to depart. Waiting restrictions placed upon general traffic in 1950 did ease the situation as did queue rails during the war. Yet it was not until 1952 that a solution was found, albeit a temporary one. For no more than a couple of months, buses to Frampton-on-Severn, Randwick, Foxmoor Lane, Stonehouse (Park Estate) and Dursley all terminated at the former LMS yard rather than King Street but reverted to their old stops following concerns that this was too far from the town centre.

It was pursued again from the mid-1950s. This followed the election on to Stroud Urban District Council of regular bus user Mrs Pat

The early days of Merrywalks Bus Station were somewhat chaotic. The road itself was of sub-standard width and the site was not fully finished-off. Bristol K L4121 heads for Standish Lodge, the infrequent terminus beyond Stonehouse's Horsemarling Lane for visitors to Standish Hospital and behind it is a Bristol L on the works service to Oldends Lane. Note the young boy on the right with contemporary school uniform, including cap. *Brian Ward-Ellison collection*

Parker, then a young mother with a child in pushchair, who found great difficulty in transferring from bus service to bus service in the town. With senior councillor Walter Preston, Mrs Parker was prominent in both setting the agenda for the bus station and ensuring its reality. Similarly, Bristol Omnibus had for some time been keen to centralise its activities.

After some debate, the site chosen was the old Armoury in Stroud, which throughout the early 50s had been the site of the Territorial Army Drill Hall. Bristol Omnibus had favoured this location as a bus station for a couple of years. It was also on this site that periodically voluntary chest screening would take place, tuberculosis still being something of a scourge at the time. In fact, the former rural sanatoria at Standish, Cashes Green and Cranham were for this purpose.

Stroud Urban District Council had progressively been purchasing the somewhat poor terraced housing along Merrywalks and with the passing of the Armoury site first to the council and then to Bristol Omnibus, all obstacles had been removed from the path of a new terminus.

Building work commenced in 1959 and further demolition contin-

Soon after the bus station was built, the adjacent Ritz Cinema burnt down. This 1966 shot just shows the scaffolding erected to hold up one of the cinema's walls. The double deck is Ex-Western National long serving Bristol K no. L4133. *David Johnson*

L4131 was another long serving former Western National vehicle, new in 1949 and withdrawn in January 1966 prior to being sold the following month. Note the Bristol scroll under the lower deck windows, used by Bristol Omnibus from 1965, and the contemporary advertisement urging the population to use the bus service. *David Johnson*

ued, the principal contractor being H W Tily & Son. Various office functions moved into the new bus station building in 1960 ahead of its general use. From late 1959, private hires and tours were bookable at what amounted to a large garden shed affair on the incomplete station concourse. Surrounded as it was by builders' sand, it would often blow into the hair and teeth of the clerks. The Slade Brook ran through the site and was duly culverted, though this procedure was to cause concerns in later years. The total cost of the new bus station was put at over £20,000.

The contractors, Urban District Council and Bristol Omnibus Company staff rushed to complete the terminus in time for its first day of operation in July 1960. Work was still on going on the very day of first use. Nevertheless, all town centre stops were duly closed that day and with only a little public confusion, the bus station became operational.

Bus passengers appeared to welcome the new facilities and the ease of transfer between buses that the new terminus provided. A minority was concerned at its distance from the town centre shops and the descent from the town via steps in Bath Street adjacent to Tuck's Premiere Hall. However, immediately upon the completion of the bus station, some traders were calling for the re-establishment of town centre bus stops. A number of them, especially to the east of the town centre around Sims Clock and London Road, stated that they had been particularly hit because passengers now forsook these local streets. This was in spite of a setting down stop at the Gaumont Cinema near Sims Clock for inbound services arriving along London Road from, for example, Minchinhampton and Chalford. A further setting down stop was later introduced at the Subscription Rooms for buses from Stonehouse crossing the town towards Chalford. What was bad news for London Road, however, was good for Gloucester Street as traders progressively opened the backs of their shops onto Bath Street so that passengers walking between bus station and town might be attracted to these outlets.

At the time of the bus station's opening, Merrywalks itself was little more than a lane. It proved impossible to widen the road before the

This view shows life as it would have been throughout the sixties before work commenced in 1970 on the Merrywalks Shopping Centre. The buildings at the back of the Bus Station are those on Bath Street. Bristol K L4132 was another ex-Western National vehicle which saw service to 1966. The Ks tended to frequent "The Track", service 421 between Chalford, Stroud and Stonehouse. Next to it is 2964, a Bristol MW. *Photobus*

opening of the bus station and there followed considerable disagreement between the highways authority, district council and the former Amoury site owner, the Ministry of Defence. This took some time to resolve and, indeed, it was not until after a series of improvements later during the sixties and seventies that the road was to be considered as satisfactory. Congestion along Merrywalks eased considerably, however, with the construction of a separate exit from the bus station in 1968. Up to this point, buses entering and leaving the site were compelled to use just one access. With the construction of the egress, buses were no longer required to reverse on to stands and from this point onwards, buses pulled up nose first, to the considerable benefit of passengers, the majority of whom now travelled on front entrance buses.

Potential disaster struck a year later in 1961. A huge fire razed the neighbouring Ritz cinema to the ground. Buses were hurriedly moved out of danger from the bus station to any location throughout the town that could be found, including Beeches Green. Staff cars were also at risk. Crowds watched in disbelief as this proud symbol of the modern age was destroyed. All that was left of the cinema erected in 1939 was a solitary wall precariously hanging over the drivers' canteen, which stayed in this state for some years. The resultant need to fill the gap in

The last Bristol K double deck on the entire Bristol Omnibus Company was Stroud's L4134, appropriately an ex-Western National vehicle, new to Stroud in 1950. *Bristol Vintage Bus Group*

the town following the fire would spawn the Merrywalks Shopping Centre eleven years later, with its associated bus station improvements and multi-storey car park.

As near as can be determined, Stroud's bus fleet at January 1960 comprised of four single deck small capacity Bedford OBs, 14 half-cab Bristol L single decks, 10 single deck underfloor engined Bristol LSs, nine single deck MWs, three Bristol MWs, 12 double deck Bristol Ks, 15 double deck Bristol LDs and a solitary double deck Bristol KSW. In addition, there was also at least one Bristol LL for coach work.

The trend towards higher capacity single decks suitable for one man operation, which began in the mid fifties, continued apace in the 1960s. There arrived from 1959, the first of some 60 Bristol MW single deck vehicles which were used throughout the sixties and seventies at Stroud, though not all at the same time, the later examples arriving ready for one man operation. Seating 45 but sometimes modified later to 43, they were similar in length and looks to the preceding Bristol LSs of the 1950s but with a more modern and less plain looking Eastern Coach Works body featuring an attractive raked front windscreen. Indeed, the MW was a symbol of Britain's rural bus services of the sixties.

Usually with Gardner five cylinder engines, the MWs plied many of the rural bus routes in Stroud. Early examples largely replaced older half-cab JOs, although one here and there would replace a double deck. The continued arrival of MWs, like the LSs before them, facilitated the conversion of more routes from crew to one man operation so that by 1963, for example, the only services operating consistently with conductors were the 46 Avening – Cheltenham via Stroud, 56 Nailsworth – Gloucester via Stroud, 421 Stonehouse – Chalford, 429 Rodborough – Minchinhampton via Stroud via Stroud, and services from Stroud to France Lynch (426), Minchinhampton via Amberley (428), Whiteshill (430), Randwick (431), Foxmoor Lane (431A), Westrip Turning (431B), Stonehouse (Park Estate) (433), Oldends Lane (434), Thrupp Lane (448), and Dursley (461). Of these, the 426, 428, 429, 431, 431A, 431B, 434 and 448 were single deck operations, the remainder generally double deck although the 430 was more mixed. The routes to France Lynch (426) and Minchinhampton via Amberley (428) were at this time deemed unsuitable for double deck operation owing to the drops at Toadsmoor and Butterow, respectively.

Like the preceding Ls and LSs, the MWs would struggle on Stroud's steep ascents. In fact, the MWs were slightly heavier. This was unfortunate as, of course, all of the rural routes upon which the MWs found

Lasting longer than the Bristol Ks was one of two Bristol KSWs allocated to Stroud. L8093, new in 1952 but only allocated to Stroud between February 1966 and June 1968, it is seen parked up at London Road depot. Also dating from 1952 was sister vehicle L8092, the first new bus allocated to Stroud by Bristol Tramways and Stroud's first 8 ft wide vehicle. It lasted till December 1960. *David Johnson*

themselves saw considerable climbs. First gear was common in a number of situations and the hills took their toll. Stroud's fitters were particularly skilled at keeping these vehicles going in spite of differential and prop shaft failure and inspectors wherever possible would schedule buses wisely to ensure that the few better six cylinder vehicles would find themselves on the steepest ascents, especially the Rodborough to Minchinhampton service 429. The punishing operating conditions associated with Stroud's hilly terrain often meant new engines and gearboxes. The driver of five cylinder versions would need first gear for Rodborough and the pitch towards the bottom of Burleigh Hill at Brimscombe bridge whereas those with a sixth cylinder could cope in second. MWs would crawl over the steep twists before and after the railway bridge at Butterow and beyond upwards towards the Bear Inn almost 700 feet above sea level, making slow progress. It was only at Amberley Ridge that the driver was able to make a dash along the common either to Tom Long's Post or Amberley Memorial, depending on the route.

In spite of its shortcomings, there is no doubt that the MW was highly successful at Stroud. By the time of the last new MW delivery to Bristol Omnibus in 1966, it was firmly established as the backbone of the single deck bus fleet, Stroud having around 20. As double decks routes were converted to one man operation throughout the 70s, this was to rise to some 27 in 1974. By June 1972, the last four of the earlier LS type delivered from the mid-fifties had been withdrawn at Stroud. Even MW numbers rapidly declined after 1974, the last two at Stroud being among the final on the company and withdrawn in October 1979, 20 years after the first arrived in the town. In addition to buses, Stroud operated MW coaches and dual purpose vehicles. Three 39 seat coaches operated at Stroud at various times during the early to mid sixties and these were joined by 41 seat dual purpose examples. In 1971 and 1974, Stroud also received two demoted MW 39 seat coaches which were used as dual purposes, each with a single line destination indictor without route numbers.

One MW left the road in April 1967 at Rockstowes Hill, Uley on service 415 from Stroud to Dursley and narrowly escaped plunging down a steep bank into a stream. Eight people were taken to Gloucester hospital for treatment but allowed home afterwards.

It was time in 1962 to retire the Bedford OBs, some of which had been almost new to the town in the early fifties. Stroud's remaining three at this time were all that were left of this type on the entire company and lasted because their narrow bodies were well suited to the confined spaces of certain of Stroud routes upon which they were used. There was no surprise that the Bedfords' chosen replacements were of Bristol Commercial Vehicles manufacture. Classed as SUS4A for "Small-capacity, Underfloor, Short", with narrow 30 seat Eastern Coach Works bodies and four cylinder Albion engines, the three replacements demonstrated that Bristol Omnibus was keen to invest in what were clearly low volume and uneconomic Stroud bus routes.

SUS nos. 300 to 302 arrived at Stroud in November. They were part of a batch of only nine new to Bristol Omnibus. Whereas Western and Southern National between them operated over 130 similar though usually longer examples, the SUS was not to catch on elsewhere. Nevertheless, throughout their working lives at Stroud, these rather quaint, dwarfish vehicles were dependable on their lazy and unhurried home routes to Ruscombe, to Cranham, to Uplands, to Cheltenham via Birdlip and on the Nailsworth outstations, although a Bristol LS single deck operated half of the Nailsworth services for a time. Even in the late sixties, a number of Nailsworth journeys could have easily been operated with little more than a motor cycle and side car! An SUS might occasionally deputise for a MW on other routes and this would usually result in the diminutive SUS earning its keep with peak time

Bristol LD 8259 arrived in 1966 as the Bristol Ks were going. It sports a conversion to a four track "T" style destination and route number indicator. Buses pulled in nose-first on to the Bus Station platform from 1968. The advertisement on the side for HTV shows the television company's logo at that time. *David Johnson*

6007, a 1960 vehicle arriving in September 1961 from Gloucester depot, was the second of two Bristol FSFs to be based at Stroud. Both FSFs would invariably be used on the 56 between Nailsworth, Stroud and Gloucester and both were transferred out in February 1965. They were somewhat non-standard as they seated 60 passengers, compared to the longer FLF's 70 which were coming into service by then. *David Johnson*

standing passengers. As an indication of the steep pitches of Stroud, one SUS found itself substituting for a larger bus towards Summer Street, the driver having to reverse it up Hollow Lane which, for those who know that stretch of road, is not surprising.

Conductor-operated routes continued to have a future at this point as Bristol Omnibus persisted in buying half-cab double decks, which required a two-man crew. From 1960 in fact, there was a new breed of such vehicles in the shape of the second generation Bristol Lodekka F type and two variants were seen at Stroud: the FSF and the FLF. Bristol Omnibus was to buy FLFs in large numbers. As was usual with Bristol chassis, both were bodied by Eastern Coach Works with a similar though more upright frontal appearance than earlier LDs and although a few at Stroud had the rather under powered, sometimes temperamental yet "torquey" Bristol derived engine, most came with highly regarded and more consistent six cylinder Gardner units.

FLF stood for "Flat-floor, Long, Forward entrance" which meant that the passenger entrance was situated directly behind the front wheel rather than at the rear as had been the case to date, and that the chassis length was 30 feet. This meant that the vehicles could carry more seated passengers than had ever been possible on buses before. Drivers in some parts of the company's territory referred to the FLFs as "Seventies", a reference to their seating capacity, although in Stroud they were known simply as Lodekkas. Typical Bristol K, KSW and LD double decks used at the time of the arrival of the FLFs carried between 54 and 60 passengers only.

Although Stroud operated a significant number of FLFs, the first F types to arrive were the only two of the shorter 60 seat FSF derivatives, one, no. 6035, new in April 1961 and the other, 6007, arriving five months later. Both saw service usually on the 56 between Nailsworth and Gloucester where new stock tended to be used but also on other routes including more significantly the 427 (Framilode) before leaving the town in April 1965 for Swindon. The next Fs were of the larger FLF type and these, too, saw service on the 56. In 1966, no fewer than 19 operated at Stroud and this was to drop by only one at the end of the decade. Naturally, they tended to be used on Stroud's trunk routes and replaced older Bristol Ks and by then a solitary KSW, including the double decks transferred to Bristol Omnibus from Western National at the merger of 1950. In fact, the last Bristol K to operate on the entire Bristol Omnibus network was one such Stroud vehicle, being ex-Western National L4134, replaced by Lodekka 7282 in November 1966. The Chalford-Stonehouse service (421) tended to be either K-or LD-

The 433 to Stonehouse Park Estate was a route to see a mixture of double and single deck vehicles. 7239 arrived when new in 1965 and was one of the five double deck FLFs which lasted until the type was withdrawn at Stroud in 1979. *David Johnson*

rather than FLF-operated.

The chassis and body combination on the FLF was actually quite revolutionary. Air suspension at the rear improved the passenger ride and the lower saloon floor was such that passengers could mount directly from the pavement to the bus without an internal step. In the current era of low floor easy access buses, available in single deck form since about 1996, it is often forgotten that the FLF was perhaps the first ever mass market, high volume low floor bus, yet this had been available since 1960! Another feature on all FLFs plus FSF 6035 was fluorescent tube interior lamps rather than the filament lighting standard up to this time.

The drawback with these vehicles was that a crew of two was needed to operate the bus. However, this did not present a problem at the time as regulatory and operational conditions were not right for one-man operated double decks, even had they been available to Bristol Omnibus. Even towards the end of the sixties, Bristol Omnibus felt that double deck routes should remain crew operated, even in country districts. In the seventies, Bristol Omnibus did briefly consider converting some of Stroud's FLFs to one man operation in a similar fashion to those altered by Eastern National by modifying the driver's bulkhead. Unlike Eastern National's FLFs, Stroud's, and indeed all Bristol Omnibus' featured manual transmission and the idea was dropped even before a prototype could be converted. This was as well

114

FLF 7053 had arrived by 1964. Note the advertisement for Hilliers pies and sausages. Hilliers of Newmarket, Nailsworth were sausage and other pork meat product manufacturers and often advertised on local bus sides throughout the region. The Bristol scroll to identify the operator was in use from 1965. *David Johnson*

because of the intensive nature of some of the work still usual on Stroud's busier routes at the time.

Meanwhile, events on the railway were bound up with Stroud's bus services. Following a reprieve, it was on 2 November 1964 that British Railways finally closed its local Chalford to Stonehouse railmotor service, calling as it did at 11 halts, with approximately every other journey extended to Gloucester. The railmotor service had started in 1903 with innovative single steam railmotors as a means of stifling potential road competition. It operated hourly and, by 1922, this was supplemented by extra trains at busier periods. In 1938, the hourly service saw alternate trains running through to Gloucester but by 1957 the pattern of service had become somewhat irregular. At the time of their demise, the railmotors had long since become push-pull autotrains, with a tank engine fixed at one end alternately pulling and pushing either one or two passenger cars.

Although many of its passengers remained indifferent to the railmotors' fate, supporters mounted a vigorous campaign to keep the service. Stroud Urban District and Chalford Parish Councils were the most vociferous. The chief advantage of the railmotor was that there was room for prams and bicycles. They also had the potential to accommodate many standing passengers though this need rarely arose. None of this was possible on the bus service.

FLFs were longer than the FSFs as can be seen by the additional window bays on both decks. One of Stroud's first Bristol FLF "Lodekkas" was 7063 which operated at Stroud from 1962. It is on the Whiteshill service when numbered 430. Although this was latterly a traditional FLF route, in previous years it was frequented by single decks. Note the operator name in block letters under the second lower deck window, in common use between 1961 and 1965. *Andrew Fruscher collection*

Supporters cited the inadequacy of the bus service as a justification for keeping the rail service alive. This was only true in part. As a result of the Suez Crisis fuel shortage, one return bus journey on service 51 between Gloucester, Stonehouse and Stroud was withdrawn in December 1956 and all other journeys were curtailed at Stonehouse. These cuts were never reinstated. Nevertheless, with parallel service 117 between Gloucester, Stonehouse and Leonard Stanley, there were still sufficient journeys from Stonehouse to Gloucester for work, leisure and shopping, even if from December 1956 passengers from Cainscross and Ebley were required to change buses for Gloucester at either Stroud or Stonehouse.

However, it was precisely because of the quality of the bus service that BR was able to make the decision it did. With a service 421 bus every 20 minutes paralleling the entire route between Chalford and Stonehouse from 0600 to after 2200, with a 10 minute service on Saturday daytimes and the added utility of 26 bus stops rather than 11 halts, the rail service was viewed as somewhat superfluous. Campaigners were optimistic in their assessment of actual railmotor passenger numbers and the 421 service required no extra capacity at all to cater for the rather residual rail demand. Bristol Omnibus did lay on one extra journey as a direct rail replacement, this being the 0555 Mondays to Saturdays service from Chalford to Stroud, which then operated the existing 0615 onwards to Stonehouse.

Horrified campaigners watched as that very month BR began demolishing the halts along the route. In spite of crusades to see the re-establishment of the service in 1987 and again at the reopening in 1995 of Coaley station, once the halts were removed the chances of reinstatement had faded and the more flexible road public transport, as so feared by the GWR at the turn of the century, had won the day. But it was the private motor car that was the real victor, with the public's predilection towards it now strong.

A curious thing happened in 1966. On 9 September, the Stroud to Dursley via Uley service was extended to and from Chepstow! This followed the completion that year of the Severn Bridge. Stroud had, in

Bristol LS single decks dating from the mid-fifties continued operating throughout the sixties and a number survived at Stroud as late as 1972. 2849, which dated from 1954 and was converted to one-man operating in November 1958, is seen on the "Nylon Run", the long standing contract from Stroud and Stonehouse which operated three times a day to what became the ICI Fibres factory at Brockworth. *David Johnson*

Bristol LS single deck 2893 travels along the upper end of Russell Street near Sims Clock, the base of which is visible on the left, in the mid-sixties. For many years, BMC dealers Wycliffe Motors occupied the spot before moving to Cainscross. The shop with the name "Elizabeth" marks the premises formerly occupied by Red & White. Peckhams next door is still trading. *R Mack*

The mainstay of the 1960s single deck fleet at Stroud was the Bristol MW. Stroud's first arrived in 1959. One such 1959 example was 2960 seen at Cheltenham while loading passengers before returning to Dursley via Stroud on rural ramble 63. The Stroud Building Society, who's simple publicity may be seen on the vehicle, was another frequent advertiser.

fact, contributed to the opening celebrations the day before by sending coaches for the inaugural run in formation across the bridge plus at least one double deck of sightseers which remained on the English side. These departed the Stroud area at 0830 and were due to return from the bridge between 1300 and 1400, the fare being 5/- from Stroud and 6/- from Painswick.

Regular bus services to Chepstow via the Severn Bridge were something else altogether. To do this, Bristol Omnibus took apart the through service 63 between Dursley, Stroud and Cheltenham. Created as one benefit of the 1950 merger, the Stroud to Cheltenham via Slad leg remained as 63 while the Stroud, and Dursley and Chepstow element became 415. So it was that Stroud-based Bristol Omnibus vehicles operated into the heart of Red & White territory in a remarkable turn of events when compared to the situation in Stroud just 16 years earlier.

The new 415 was an odd service in the tradition of the Stroud to

In this scene taken in c.1964, the bus on the left is MW 2998, which operated in Stroud when delivered new in 1960 and remained for 10 years. That on the right is a Bristol K no. L4126, fitted with "T" style destination and route number boxes. Rootes Group car dealers Steel's occupied the site in Russell Street until the Stroud Building Society built on the site, moving from Rowcroft. Next to Steel's, on its left, is the former Gaumont Cinema, by now called the Odeon and visible between the two buses at the start of London Road is J H Wilkes, furnishers. *R Mack*

MW 2589 is seen with driver, complete with peaked cap, preparing to load for Randwick. During the sixties, the 441 to Randwick and the 442 to Foxmoor Lane between them operated about every 35 minutes in what must have been a confusing timetable for the public. The schedule was constructed more for the benefit of the company, so that only one bus was required. Randwick's route number changed from 431 to 441 in 1967. *David Johnson*

MW 2630 arrived at Stroud in 1967. Service 425 to Oakridge (previously 426A) offered a small number of short trips to Bisley. The MW was the favoured vehicle on most 425 trips but the route was actually one of the last deep rural routes to see conductor operated double decks, as late as the mid-seventies. Like services to Randwick, services have been drastically cut in recent years. *David Johnson*

Seen in 1966 approaching Stroud Bus Station along a much improved Merrywalks, MW 2611 arrives from Cheltenham on service 63. It is one-man operated and the vehicle displays a sign in the front nearside passenger window to this effect. Such signs were hinged so that they could easily be either visible to passengers waiting to board or hidden from their view. *David Johnson*

Trowbridge and Malmesbury – Stroud – Gloucester services operating before it. Apart from Severn Bridge sightseers, just who wished to travel between Stroud and Chepstow? Not even the attraction of connections at Chepstow via Red & White's service to and from Newport and Cardiff could muster any trade, not that the 415 was particularly well timed for a Cardiff visit. Initially, there were five round trips between Stroud and Chepstow on weekdays and four on Sundays but this was cut to two on Sundays to Fridays and four on Saturdays. Drivers at the time often reported making the round trips to Chepstow without any passengers at all. What was even more bizarre was that the service survived in this form till 1972, when it was curtailed at Berkeley.

The Severn Bridge could be problematic on stormy days. One trick drivers used on such occasions was to wedge their empty ticket box in the door well to stop the doors blowing open. This was more of a problem into Wales than from it, owing to the prevailing wind. Occasionally, the bus would need to cross in convoy with other vehicles.

Stroud's bus services saw a major renumbering on 25 June 1967, the first since the merger of 1950. This converted the five remaining two-digit and eight remaining four-digit numbers to three, thereby removing the A and B suffixes. With the exception of the SUs delivered in 1962, buses up to this point had been capable of indicating a four-digit number. The renumbering coincided with the arrival of new vehicles with three track route displays only. Even so, there remained many similarities to the numbering scheme adopted by Western National 40 years before.

With routes such as 461 becoming 416 and the recycling of numbers such as 430 (previously to Whiteshill and now to Minchinhampton), there must initially have been some passenger confusion. The renumbering in full, including those not affected, was as follows:

46	Avening/Forest Green – Nailsworth – Painswick – Cheltenham became 564
56	Nailsworth – Stroud – Pitchcombe – Gloucester became 556
58	Stroud – Painswick – Gloucester became 558
59	Stroud – Cranham – Gloucester became 559
63	Stroud – Slad – Cheltenham became 563
400	Stroud – Bristol was unchanged
415	Stroud – Chepstow was unchanged
421	Chalford – Stroud – Stonehouse was unchanged
422	Stroud – Cirencester was unchanged
422A	Stroud – Aston Down became 420
423	Stroud – Avening – Tetbury – Malmesbury was unchanged
423A	Stroud – Tiltups End – Tetbury – Malmesbury became 424
426	Stroud – France Lynch was unchanged
426A	Stroud – Oakridge became 425
427	Stroud Framilode was unchanged
428/428A	Stroud – Amberley – Minchinhampton became 430/431
429	Rodborough – Stroud – Brimscombe – Minchinhampton was unchanged
430	Stroud – Whiteshill became 435
430A	Stroud – Ruscombe became 436
431	Stroud – Randwick became 441
431A	Stroud – Foxmoor Lane became 442
431B	Stroud – Westrip Turning became 443

433	Stroud – Stonehouse Park Estate was unchanged
434	Stroud – Oldends Lane was unchanged
447	Nailsworth – Tiltups End was withdrawn
448	Stroud – Thrupp Lane was withdrawn
449	Nailsworth – Windsoredge became 401
450	Stroud – Kilminster Road became 439
450A	Stroud – Summer Crescent became 440
451	Stroud – Uplands was unchanged
453	Stroud – Kingscourt was unchanged
454	Nailsworth – Forest Green became 404
455	Nailsworth – Shortwood became 402
456	Nailsworth – Newmarket became 403
461	Stroud – Eastington – Dursley became 416
470	Stroud – Minchinhampton – Tetbury – Malmesbury became 428

Another significant turn of events occurred in 1967 with the

From 1968, Bristol Omnibus increased the amount of cream on vehicles operated without conductors as a better way of marking them out for the general public. This gave the vehicles so treated a far more modern and brighter appearance. MW 2622 displays the broad cream band nicely while on the 424 between Stroud and Malmesbury. Note the cash dispenser, designed to make one man operation easier, visible to the driver's left. *Bristol Vintage Bus Group*

Meanwhile, the last of the Bristol L single decks, in use at Stroud since 1950, were being withdrawn. What was to have been the last, 2408, had departed in September 1965 before being resold a month later. However, 2455, pictured here, arrived later that month after all others were withdrawn, and stayed till June 1966. It was invariably used on the 429 between Minchinhampton, Stroud and Rodborough and had been fitted with a single line destination aperture front and rear. *David Johnson*

delivery in July of Stroud's first 36-ft single deck bus. This was fleet number 1017, was brand new to Stroud and was a Bristol Commercial Vehicles built RELL6L with 53 seat ECW body. RELL stood for "Rear Engine, Long, Low" and it came not with the expected Gardner engine, as was usual with Bristol chassis, but with a Leyland six-cylinder, 11 litre 0.680 unit. Preceding this arrival had been the loan for a short while of United RE CHN 336C for evaluation and trials, though the bus did not enter revenue earning service.

The vehicle was unlike anything based at Stroud at the time. This was first because of its sheer size. Passengers noticed and, indeed, commented upon the length of the Eastern Coach Works body. It directly replaced L8280, a 1955 Bristol LD double deck which seated only five passengers more than the new RE. In fact, the single deck seating capacity was only two seats less than the last Bristol K double deck (no. L4134) withdrawn only eight months beforehand. Secondly, the modern vehicle design caught the eye. Thirdly, to drivers more used to single deck 45 seat MWs with under powered, five cylinder Gardners, the RE with its eleven litre engine was a powerful bus, if somewhat noisy for passengers, with the rich and thundering engine

The tiny Bristol SUS4A was well suited to Stroud's narrow lanes. Three arrived in 1962, no. 300 being the first numerically. This vehicle was replaced at Stroud by 307 after ten years. 300 is seen on the Ruscombe service 430A, a number used till 1967, a regular haunt for such vehicles. Note that the three track route number indicator cannot actually accommodate a four digit service! *Brian Ward-Ellison collection*

and at speed, a high pitched gearbox whine. Fourthly, its semi-automatic transmission, new to drivers, helped them considerably. Fifthly, in spite of early examples being delivered with a dark green interior, 1017 looked considerably spacious, light and airy when compared to the late 50s design of the MW. One problem, however, was that the RELL exceeded the automatic bus washes at Stroud by 0.5m and had to be hand washed.

After a substantial period on driver training, 1017 set about operating service 564 shorts between Stroud and Nailsworth. These shorts were something of a bus driver's dream, with a 20 minute running time starting at 05 past each hour from Stroud and 35 from Nailsworth, added to which no agreement had yet been reach with the union to convert the vehicle to one man operation. The driver's duty thus comprised forty minutes driving in every sixty with no fares to collect.

When a second full length RELL no.1081 arrived in June 1968, it invariably saw service on the 416 between Stroud and Dursley. Like 1017, it started as a crew operated vehicle and would operate all day on the route which, during the off-peak, had a requirement for one vehicle with a 90 minute round trip time. The vehicle working at the time was typical of Stroud's pattern, one that satisfied the scheduler rather than the passenger. Other examples of "busman's' workings" included the Randwick and Foxmoor Lane services with odd vehicle workings of every 35 minutes at the time. A double deck FLF or LD joined the RELL on 416 at peak times to infill between the RE's duties.

With more RELLs arriving, the 416 was the first Stroud route to see high capacity, full length RELL buses, which replaced the double deck workings on this route. This was further strengthened by the arrival in December 1969 of RELL no. 1007 and in July 1970 by RELL 1097.

As REs were capable of one man operation, a timely agreement was reached with the Transport & General Workers Union throughout Bristol Omnibus in 1969 for the use of 36 feet REs without conductors. Up to this point, it had been the lighter loaded rural routes operated by smaller MW or LS single decks that had been converted to one man operation and, in truth, these were the ones the company could not keep going without such a conversion. The agreement of 1969 paved the way for the conversion of trunk routes to one man operation and the first to be so treated was 416. It also sparked further conductor

Two of the SUSs arrived in November 1962, replaced the remaining Bedford OBs that month. 213 was one of the two last OBs, new in 1950 and in service at Stroud since November 1951. *R Mack*

redundancies at Stroud depot, which had begun only a couple of years earlier with the conversion of shorter single deck routes to one man operation. They were the first redundancies at Stroud since the introduction of the motor bus in 1905. Up to this point, conductors had either left voluntarily or been trained as one man drivers to cover for the periodic driver shortages of the time.

The spread of one man operated services was now widespread throughout the company. It is interesting to note that further conversions to single manning were to spark a significant fares increase in the summer of 1968. Although Bristol Omnibus was to benefit in the longer term, it needed the extra revenue to pay bonus payments to drivers. While the union was generally against the thought of conductor redundancies and indeed initially against one man operations, it conceded that drivers should be compensated for taking fares. Drivers who at first had been opposed to job losses began to think twice about their own rate of pay and this resulted in a quiet acceptance of one man operation. The fares rises at this time did, however, see the welcome reintroduction of return fares while the company withdrew its proposals to raise the shortest distance fares by 25 per cent in exchange for a general agreement from the complainants that they should withdraw all other objections.

A special livery was adopted to mark out such one man operated vehicles from those still running with conductors. Rather than the post war single deck livery of all Tilling green with a single cream stripe under the window, from 1968 one man single decks now began appearing with an attractive broad cream band extending from the lower window line to the beading above the skirt. The Bristol city crest used on all Bristol Omnibus vehicles until 1961 had already been replaced outside the city itself first by the term BRISTOL in block letters and then from 1965 with the Bristol scroll as used by the bus chassis manufacturer.

Meanwhile, three more REs in the shape of 500 to 502 arrived in June 1969. These were of the shorter RESL variety seating 43 rather than 53. They were initially used on the Minchinhampton routes. It was felt that long RELLs were unsuitable for the 430 and 431 for fear of grounding at the top of Theescombe at Pinfarthings, something that proved to be unfounded. When 500 was replaced by 53 seat 1007 in December, the remaining two could be seen on a variety of duties, although the RESLs would still feature in Minchinhampton, being inter-worked with MWs.

There was a further significant arrival in 1969. This was in the shape

Among the large cohort of MWs operated at Stroud over the years have been a number of dual purpose examples capable of both bus and coach operation. 39 seat 2036 was one such vehicle which commenced service in the town from new in 1966. It offered forced air ventilation. It is seen here wearing smart dual purpose livery of cream above the window line and green below. It survived at Stroud till 1979, although it was downgraded to bus work as 2424, carrying 43 bus seats. *David Johnson*

of a Bristol RELH6L no. 2050 and it followed similar 2041, in use at Stroud for just three months in 1967 on summer express work to and from London. Unlike the lower floor (low frame) RELLs and RESLs delivered to date, 2050 was a high floor example of the RE chassis, RELH standing for "Rear Engine, Long, High Floor". Basically, this was an RE with a coach body, 47 luxury rather than 53 bus seats on the same chassis length as the RELL and with forced air ventilation rather than sliding ventilators or hoppers. It could accommodate luggage under the main seating area. It boasted a five rather than four speed gear box and high speed axle.

This was the beginning of a popular new breed of updated country dual-purpose vehicles which could be used on stage carriage, tours and motorway express work and it is something that in the age of both the low floor bus and minibus is no longer now available at Stroud. When not required for coach duties, it was also available to speed the conversion of routes to one man operation when the need arose. Painted initially in Bristol Omnibus' attractive and distinguished dual-purpose livery of half Tilling green and half cream, it joined the three existing MW dual-purpose vehicles for use on Stroud's extensive seasonal tours programme of the time and clearly out-performed them in terms of

Although dual purpose vehicles predominated at Stroud from the mid-sixties, a number of full coaches were also operated, including NHY 941, a 1951 Bristol LWL6B seen at Dudbridge depot. Coaches were occasionally used on school or works contracts. During the years to 1962, Dudbridge's role had been very much downgraded and latterly stored only coaches. *David Johnson*

speed and passenger comfort, although like the RELL buses, the gearbox was somewhat whiny at speed and the Leyland engine raucous.

Before the MW dual purpose vehicles but also overlapping with them, Stroud operated up to three LS coaches from 1953, each with 39 seat bodies and up to five 41 seat LS dual-purpose vehicles, with a sixth arriving in 1970. The dual purposes were new in bus livery in 1957 but had roofs painted cream in 1959 to mark them out as different. The last two of these were withdrawn from Stroud in April and June 1972. The early sixties also saw the continued use of a small number of ECW bodied 39 seat Bristol LL and LWL coaches, new to Bristol Omnibus in the early fifties. Four saw service in Stroud at various times to the early sixties and, like the LS coaches, were in full Bristol Greyhound livery. All such vehicles saw service on private hires, summer express duplicates and tours. It was in about 1962 that a number of tour licenses for those heading south from Stroud transferred to Black & White Motorways of Cheltenham, leaving Stroud with mostly excursions to the north and to Wales.

Unaccompanied parcels were still carried on buses throughout the sixties. Although never a significant part of Bristol's business, it nonetheless contributed to the company's bottom line. The practice dwindled with the gradual reduction in conductors and with the

Another coach at Stroud was 2058, a Bristol LL6B, again from 1951, with similar ECW 35 coach seat body to the LWL. *R Mack*

introduction and later widespread use of the light van. Even so, parcel tickets were available from one man drivers in the sixties. Nevertheless, both daily and evening newspapers continued to be delivered to villages by bus as late as the seventies. Marriott's newsagent at the top of Stroud High Street would take papers down to the bus station for onward distribution by bus. This practice continued throughout the seventies to such places as Oakridge, Bisley (for the then bottom shop), Miserden, Whiteway and Frampton.

The bus service had a larger role to play in the dissemination of Stroud's local news, however, and it is this that demonstrates the local bus industry's specific usefulness to local business. The method used by the weekly Stroud News & Journal newspaper to ensure that its printers in Dursley would receive editorial copy was the bus service. Before the age of electronic delivery, the process was quite cumbersome. Not only would reporters use the bus regularly to go from site to site or meeting to meeting, once articles had been typed and amended, they would be placed on the 461 Stroud to Dursley service (later, 416) for collection. On occasions, no one would be waiting and the package would go back to Stroud, only to return later. The shuttle of news between Stroud and Dursley occurred each working day as lino operators built up each edition of the paper progressively on frames. While this process extended deadlines, there was never an occasion when the paper failed to appear on the streets. The bus' role in news was therefore pivotal: from reporter, to printing and delivery of newspaper.

As the sixties closed, the pattern of services was beginning to change. With some notable exceptions in terms of marginal increases in service to Kingscourt (453) and Kilminster Road (450A) plus significant extra mileage to Chepstow as noted above, the late 1960s saw withdrawals. However, withdrawals did lag behind the decline in passenger numbers. By 1967, the Chalford section of the 421 saw a 20 minute weekday service whereas the Stonehouse section continued to enjoy its Saturday 10 minute frequency. Sunday and weekday evening services on this route were reduced from every 20 to every 30 minutes, cutting the Sunday service by one third. Sunday services on 433 were reduced first from Stonehouse to Leonard Stanley and later by withdrawing one journey, leaving seven return trips only. A similar situation

The era of the truly modern bus began at Stroud in 1967 with the arrival of 1017, a Bristol RELL single deck capable of seating 53. Note its length when compared to the adjacent FLF double deck and the long overhang over the passenger platform. In its early days, it was used almost exclusively on short Stroud – Nailsworth journeys on the 564. The picture is taken shortly after delivery when the vehicle operated with a conductor. With a high seating capacity and capability to be operated by a driver only, life would not be the same on the buses following the emergence of the RE. *Bristol Vintage Bus Group*

occurred on the Oakridge route (426A).

Deeply rural services were to fair poorly. Services on 452 to Cranham saw approximately a 25 per cent cut in the number of departures on Mondays to Fridays and a 40 per cent cut on Saturdays. Similarly, the overall number of departures on the 63 to Slad, Sheepscombe, and Cheltenham fell some 40 per cent on Mondays to Fridays, some 25 per cent on Saturdays and was halved from six to three buses on Sundays. Nailsworth local services were reduced from about 40 journeys per day Mondays to Saturdays at the beginning of the sixties to just 26 while the Sunday timetable was withdrawn completely.

Whatever the scale of cuts, all this was nothing as to what was around the corner in the early and mid seventies. In the words of Bachman-Turner Overdrive's hit single of the time, "You Ain't Seen Nothin' Yet".

CHAPTER 7

1970–1979
BLAME THE BUS
SERVICE

In spite of changes in car ownership, it was Stroud's curious mix of urban and rural population types that maintained a good bus service in the area during the sixties. The Bristol Omnibus Company had managed to retain much of its local service network by reducing costs, improving productivity, cross-subsidy and increasing bus fares. This approach became increasingly difficult to sustain in the seventies. Had Stroud been more urban in nature, it is likely that the area's bus services in the seventies would have faired better. However, though not entirely rural, neither were the Stroud Valleys entirely urban and the Cotswold scarp settlements certainly were not. In the seventies, therefore, events were finally to catch up with Stroud's bus network.

The Bristol Omnibus Company found itself in a worsening financial position throughout the seventies. It became increasingly reliant upon Gloucestershire County Council's rural bus grant, introduced from May 1971, which included significant central government and district council contributions. Even so, costs were rising during the inflationary seventies even before the oil crisis. The 1973 OPEC oil embargo resulted in significant overnight crude oil rises in October 1973 and January 1974 and the UK saw the inflation rate peak at 28 per cent at that time.

Yet, the deepening national economic situation and fuel price increases barely dented the rise in car ownership. For the first time, heavy traffic was now causing significant problems on Stroud's roads, especially at peak periods. Not only were Stroud people able to afford more cars during the seventies, the affect of their decisions were now felt in ways otherwise only seen on the congested routes to

Following planning permission granted in 1970, work began on the Merrywalks Shopping Centre behind Stroud Bus Station and the associated multi-storey car park adjacent to it. During the construction phase, which constricted the Bus Station, buses parked at the bottom of Rowcroft Retreat where no. 300, a Bristol SUS4A now wearing Bristol Omnibus' OMO livery, is seen. *Bristol Vintage Bus Group*

Cheltenham, Gloucester and Bristol.

The Transport Act 1968 also had a part to play. From 1 January 1969, it saw the passing of Transport Holding Company (British Transport Commission's 1963 successor) subsidiary Bristol Omnibus Company along with its Stroud operations to the National Bus Company, Bristol being one of its largest components. Henceforward, Britain's two territorial bus groupings, including THC, found themselves under one, centrally managed, state controlled holding company. This move and its subsequent first outward signs – the adoption from 1972 of a lighter corporate National leaf green livery with a single white waistband and "double N" logo – seemed almost a cosmetic irrelevance in the face of the increasingly unhealthy state of Stroud's bus service. Yet, the Transport Act 1968 was highly relevant for two reasons.

On the one hand, under the Act, each National Bus subsidiary was obliged to break even year on year – by this time, quite a tall order. Municipal bus undertakings and those under the newly created metropolitan Passenger Transport Executives had no such restrictions. On the other, Section 34 of the Act gave local authorities and central government the powers to give financial assistance to maintain socially necessary bus services in rural areas. Powers were further consolidated with the passing of the Local Government Act 1972, which enabled transport authorities such as the county council to use Section 203 to subsidise an entire network rather than specific services.

Bristol Omnibus reacted in several ways to the crisis ahead of it in Stroud. During these years, Stroud's network became almost exclusively one man operated. Double decks were largely phased out as no longer required for the smaller number of passengers now travelling. The company began to "revise" its fares (as it euphemistically put it) well ahead of inflation and with alarming regularity, often more than once a year. Not only was this the company's preferred approach in a bid to safeguard as many jobs as possible, it was far easier to apply to the Traffic Commissioners for blanket fare increases that would instantly garner many thousands of pounds than to justify and fight for withdrawals before the same Traffic Commissioners but in the face of much local opposition. However, in spite of Bristol Omnibus always being reasonably confident in winning the Traffic Commissioners' support for such increases, there was one occasion in Gloucestershire when the County Council persuaded the Commissioners not to grant an increase. This resulted in the company destroying revised faretables already printed in advance of the Commissioners' inquiry!

The cycle of events – increasing costs, rising fares, withdrawals that all resulted in fewer passengers – became self-fulfilling and something of a crisis by the end of the decade. By 1975, 20 per cent of departures at Stroud had been withdrawn when compared to the 1960 level of service and by 1979, about one third had gone. This resulted in passenger resentment at the worsening bus service but also some understanding that significant steps needed to be taken.

The company attracted much negative attention in Stroud throughout the seventies. The bus service was even blamed for the most unlikely of situations. Commenting upon the decline in the number of books lent out at Stroud Branch Library, one councillor during the September 1972 County Council Library and Archives Committee suggested that "The increase in bus fares has meant that many people from outside the town cannot get to the library". Was the bus service really to take the blame for fewer borrowings? It would seem so!

The troubles that beset Stroud's bus managers were temporarily put aside when an unlikely film star emerged. This was in shape of 862 RAE, no. 301, one of Stroud's 30 seat Bristol SUSs. With Driver Stan

300 was replaced in 1972 by further SUS 307. From 1972, Bristol Omnibus began adopting the standard National Bus Company leaf green livery with single white waistband, as depicted by 307 on Nailsworth local service 404 to Forest Green, although the number was reused later for the route to Minchinhampton. The use of "Service" as a destination was quite common on the Nailsworth routes. *Andrew Fruscher collection*

Boud, the vehicle appeared three times in the 1971 EMI film *Dulcima*. Aside from the SU, the film also starred Carol White as Dulcima, a discontented and scheming young woman who played off two admirers against each other, one of which was acted by John Mills. Much of the film was shot in and around Minchinhampton, Avening and Tetbury. During one clip, Stroud's SU was observed with "Forest Green 8" for about 115 seconds at various locations including several in Minchinhampton and on Minchinhampton and Burleigh commons. At one point, it passed a dark blue, bonnetted BMC delivery van of the erstwhile pork meat manufacturer Hilliers, once of Newmarket near Nailsworth. Special dispensation was granted to use false registration 752 REA during the filming and it is said that on its journey home to Stroud depot one day, a police constable noticed that the front number plate had slipped and stopped the vehicle to get something of a surprise!

The director made good use of one of the vehicle's rear longitudinal seats as "Albert", Dulcima's younger admirer, was seen at right angles glancing affectionately across to her during the journey. There was even an actor playing the part of a conductor, complete with Setright ticket machine, cash bag, crossover straps and Bristol Omnibus summer khaki uniform. There are those who believed that the vehicle in the film was sourced from another operating company and not from Stroud depot. However, the attention to detail, even down to the use of Stroud fleet plates, indicates that the vehicle was genuine and Stroud company staff, including the driver, have always maintained that it was "one of theirs".

It was also fitting that Stroud's Driver Stan Boud together with other long serving Driver Alf Chambers, should be chosen two years later to feature with a youthful John Craven during a *Newsround* report on rural bus services. The fact that the BBC chose Stroud seemed fitting, given its problems at the time, and the programme concentrated on service 563 along the Slad Valley and towards Birdlip and Cheltenham.

In fact, service 563 was one of the routes of considerable concern to the company and Gloucestershire County Council. The company had sought grants from Gloucestershire under Section 34 as soon as it could from May 1971. Up to this point, profitable routes cross-subsidised the unremunerative. Yet, declining passengers had begun to reduce the robustness even of these profitable core routes and the company's ability to balance the books in Stroud was subsequently reduced.

During the financial year 1971/72, the 563's annual loss was £6,200 or nearly half of Stroud's total deficit. At this time, it was one of only five Stroud area routes declared to the Council as loss making. In addition to the 563, these were 415 Stroud to Chepstow via Selsley, Dursley and Berkeley, 423/4 Stroud to Malmesbury via Nailsworth, Avening and Tetbury, 551-3 Gloucester to Leonard Stanley or Dursley via Stonehouse and 568 Gloucester to Frampton-on-Severn. Of the total grant of £38,382 required by Bristol Omnibus, routes in the Stroud area, including 551-3 and 568 for which Gloucester depot was responsible, accounted for £15,104.

The continued inability of the company to cross-subsidise routes to the same extent as was possible during the sixties produced an alarming increase in losses for 1972/73. The complete list of loss making routes so far as Stroud's buses was concerned was:

415	Stroud – Berkeley via Selsley, Uley, Dursley
422	Stroud – Cirencester via Chalford, Sapperton, Daglingworth

423/4	Stroud – Malmesbury via Nailsworth, Avening, Tetbury
425	Stroud – Oakridge via Bisley
427	Stroud – Framilode via the Stanleys, Frocester, Frampton-on-Severn, Saul
428/9	Stroud – Malmesbury via Nailsworth, Minchinhampton, Avening, Tetbury
447-9	Stroud – Minchinhampton via Brimscombe
452	Stroud – Cranham via Painswick
551-3	Gloucester – Leonard Stanley/Dursley via Stonehouse
563	Stroud – Cheltenham via Slad, Miserden, Whiteway, Birdlip

Bristol Omnibus believed that by making "rationalisations" (cuts, basically), the loss on these services for the financial year would be an estimated £9,823 p.a. Again, service 563 accounted for nearly half of this. Action had already been taken to wipe out the loss on service 568 (Gloucester to Frampton) but this again became loss making a year later. In fact, the figure was to rise to £28,031 in 1974/75 with the grant required for 563 overtaken by that needed for the 551-3.

Occasionally, the SUSs would stray off their regular routes and operate to other destinations. Displaying BRISTOL logo in block letters with the National Bus Company "double N" is 307, now parked at London Road having last worked a 430 from Minchinhampton. Because of their size, SUSs when used at peak times on the 430, often had to cope with standing passengers. *David Johnson*

In order to balance the books, few Stroud services were unaffected by the changes. Even profitable routes saw cuts, to ensure a continued and strengthened contribution to the network. Bus service withdrawals at Stroud during the seventies tended to be by stealth. With each timetable – or often in between – there would be a gradual erosion of services.

1971 was the year of decimalisation. The conversion went well at Stroud, in spite of public transport thriving on small change. There were a few mistakes caused by confusion but these did not last. 1971 saw the splitting of the through Rodborough to Minchinhampton service 429 into two. Minchinhampton departures via Brimscombe formerly numbered 429 became 447-9 and saw a reduction of one return journey per day. The 449s made the small but steep diversion via Thrupp Lane, withdrawn as a stand alone service in 1967 while the 448 made a steeper and shorter detour via Highfields, previously served by the Cirencester service (422). Meanwhile, the Rodborough end was amalgamated with the Kingscourt service to become 453 (direct to Kingscourt) or 454 (Kingscourt via Rodborough), thereby reducing 37 departures per day on the former routes to just 20. This change made sense of what was, in fact, a legacy of the GWR in 1926. The 453/4 was reduced further and by 1978 stood at 15 round trips. In 1971, buses between Stroud and Uplands reduced from 11 to 10 round trips, while the 441 and 442 to Randwick and Foxmoor Lane saw minor changes.

The 558 through journeys between Gloucester, Painswick, Stroud, Minchinhampton and Malmesbury were withdrawn in 1971 to be replaced by separate services between Stroud and Malmesbury (428/9) and Stroud and Gloucester (558). The through service was something of an anachronism with a two-hour end-to-end running time, hardly conducive to travel. Nevertheless, the Stroud – Malmesbury section (428/9) remained intact, albeit with ever-increasing public subsidy, performing as it did a range of useful middle-to-middle links. A year later, both sections saw withdrawals, the Malmesbury section being cut from seven to six per day and the Gloucester section being near enough halved from seven to four buses.

Also in 1971, Cirencester buses (422) were thinned from seven to six per day but the service was to end the decade with four departures only. The Ruscombe route was reduced first from 13 to 11 journeys in 1971 and the following year to just six a day.

The year 1972 saw further withdrawals. Direct buses to Dursley via Eastington were cut by one bus per day on Mondays to Fridays and four on Saturdays. Uplands saw 10 rather than 11 buses each day. The

Although the OMO livery of green with a broad cream band hung on at Bristol longer than the National Bus Company intended, efforts were made to repaint vehicles into leaf green. Former Greyhound MW coach 2433 which operated as a downgraded bus during its time at Stroud from 1974, did see service in the town in OMO livery. Although technically a "bus", the vehicle retained its 39 coach seats. Note the single line destination display. *David Johnson*

service between Stroud, Uley, Dursley and Chepstow (415) was truncated at Berkeley while the 430/1 to Minchinhampton saw reductions on weekday mornings.

Reductions to the 430/1 Minchinhampton service via Amberley sparked some public concern in 1972 with the replacement each weekday morning of the established half-hourly service by one at hourly intervals. Afternoons continued as half-hourly until this, too, was reduced to hourly in 1975. At the time of these first cuts, the service was not one declared as overtly loss making.

Service 430 to Minchinhampton is a clear example of the changes having taken place on rural services in the Stroud area. Minchinhampton had been a wealthy town during the 19th century thanks to the wool trade. As wool production shifted in search of water and the greater accessibility of the valley floors at the turn of the 20th century, so Minchinhampton's fortunes declined, in no small measure because there was no possibility of a rail connection to a settlement some 700 feet above sea level. The equally prosperous Painswick was

MWs remained active during the seventies, 10 surviving until 1979, one of which was 2630, withdrawn in February that year. Note the route number is that occasionally used for the ICI Fibbers contract. *David Johnson*

in a similar situation but benefitted not only from being on the Stroud to Cheltenham road but from early GWR motor buses from 1905, which connected with trains at Stroud GWR station.

The result in Minchinhampton was a town that was considered by some to have ebbed during the first half of the 20th century, rather like the settlement at Bisley on the opposite hill. However, like other Cotswold villages, changes brought about by the private car from the late-1950s meant that such communities became accessible to all. The car brought incomers with new money and increased affluence. They had no need of the bus service. Later, housing in these settlements was to become much sought after, the resultant high prices again attracting residents that were more affluent. Thus began the serious decline in bus usage of the late sixties and seventies.

With some notable exceptions, such a story is replicated throughout Stroud's immediate Cotswold edge settlements, all of which once saw at least reasonable levels of service. These included Avening, Bisley, Box, Miserden, Nympsfield, Oakridge, Randwick, Ruscombe, Sapperton, Slad, Sheepscombe and, until lately, Tetbury.

Other significant changes in 1972 were reserved for Saturdays and this more than anything reflected the changing travel habits of the time. Saturday enhancements had resulted from more people travel-

Stroud depot operated its annual Carol Bus each Christmas from 1969 to 1993. During the early 1970s, the vehicle would double as an entry for Stroud Carnival and Show. The garage's first Carol Bus was former Bristol Joint Services KSW C8108 seen here at the 1970 Stroud Show. It may have been a little optimistic at this time to state that "It's a Great Life On The Buses in Stroud" but staff at the garage were renowned for the way in which they operated more or less as a large family. *Chris Blick collection*

ling, including whole families together. After the Second World War, there were often Saturday duplicates or extra journeys. Now the car, which during the working week was parked at the head of the household's place of work, was suddenly available on Saturdays to transport the whole family for outings and shopping.

It was on Saturdays that the 556 between Nailsworth, Stroud and Gloucester had been enhanced to half-hourly rather than hourly. In 1972, the Nailsworth section reverted to an hourly service. Similarly, the section of the 421 between Stonehouse and Stroud was doubled in frequency to every 10 minutes but from 1972 was cut back Monday to Friday to 20 minute intervals. By contrast, Chalford had not seen a 10-

minute Saturday service since 1967.

The 421 was to see thinning in 1973, in the evenings. Evenings had already been reduced from a 20 to 30 minute service in 1967. Also in 1973, there were marginal withdrawals on 426 (France Lynch), 427 (Framilode) and 439 (Kilminster Road). Given its financial performance, it is not surprising that the Stroud to Cheltenham service via Birdlip was reduced from 10 journeys (including shorts) on Mondays to Fridays and 11 on Saturdays to seven.

It is interesting that the overall policy of the County Council at this time was to seek major economies by reducing the number of buses required at peak times. While this had a considerable affect on required subsidy levels, it did mean that works journeys were affected. Such an approach is rarely taken today, except in extreme circumstances. Nevertheless, in conjunction with the Council, the company tried to withdraw services carrying the fewest passengers. This meant that Sunday services were hit hard. Those to Minchinhampton via Brimscombe or Amberley were halved in 1971 from a total of 18 to nine. Sunday services to Rodborough and Kingscourt were amalgamated in the same way as the daytime services, with an overall reduction in departures from nine to four. A year later, Sunday services on Leonard Stanley (433), Whiteshill (435), Summer Crescent (440), Randwick (441), Foxmoor Lane (442), Nailsworth – Gloucester (556), Stroud –

The cast of Stroud's *On The Buses* parodied the popular seventies television sitcom of the same name, starring Reg Varney and Stephen Lewis. Stroud's own "staff" from the "Town & District" were, from left to right, Mike Thompson as Arthur, Graham Jackson (sic) as Olive, Chris Bailey, Lynne Clements, Millie, Jack Ireland as Blakey and Fred Bennett as Jack. Many others were involved in the preparation. *Chris Blick collection*

The 1972 Stroud Show entry featured St Trinians. This picture features two of Stroud's most well known staff. The first on the left and under a wig is well-respected Senior Inspector John Holmes who, having retired once, is back part time at the time of writing. The second is the late Evelyn Gardiner, eighth right, who started work for Red & White and who as a condustress for over 35 years was well known to passengers . *Chris Blick collection*

Gloucester via Painswick (558) and Nailsworth area – Cheltenham (564) were reduced, some by up to 50 per cent, while those to Ruscombe were withdrawn entirely.

Not surprisingly, 1973 saw yet further Sunday withdrawals. On the trunk Chalford to Stonehouse route (421), the frequency stepped down from every 30 to every 40 minutes, thereby withdrawing a quarter of Sunday mileage. Sunday services to Dursley via Uley (415), Cirencester (422), Framilode (427), Foxmoor Lane (442), Kilminster Road (439), Summer Crescent (440), Kingscourt (454) and Cheltenham via Birdlip (563) were withdrawn completely while Sunday services to Dursley via Eastington (416) saw some withdrawals and those to France Lynch (426) were halved from four to two round trips.

In fact, by 1975, Sunday departures from Stroud were half their 1970 levels and 40 per cent of their 1960 levels. This followed the axing of

Even though many were second hand to Stroud, the arrival of more RELL buses during the seventies meant that Stroud depot amassed a considerable number of them and they became the backbone of the town's fleet. Wearing standard National Bus Company leaf green is 1038, an example of the original ECW bus body available to Bristol Omnibus with its flat front and "T" style destination indicators. 1038 was a 1968 bus in service at Stroud for the four years to 1981, when this shot was taken at Frampton-on-Severn. *Geoff Gould*

Sunday services to Gloucester via Painswick (558) in 1974, thinning the same year on the Whiteshill (435) and Randwick (441) services and a year later reductions on the direct Gloucester and Cheltenham services 556 and 564. The net result, at the mid point of the decade, was that Sunday services operated only on the following routes:

400	Stroud – Bristol
416	Stroud – Eastington
421	Chalford – Stonehouse/Standish Lodge via Stroud
429	Stroud – Malmesbury
430	Stroud – Minchinhampton via Amberley
433	Stroud – Leonard Stanley
435	Stroud – Whiteshill
441	Stroud – Randwick
447	Stroud – Minchinhampton via Brimscombe
556	Nailsworth – Gloucester via Stroud
564	Forest Green – Cheltenham, although by this time the

Sunday service had been split at Stroud into separate services, offering a usable connection between the two only in the northerly direction.

Among this gloom, there were a few positive notes. Following the opening of the M5 between Stroudwater and Almondsbury in December, Bristol Omnibus began operating that month a Saturday limited stop stage carriage service between Stroud and Bristol via the M5, M4 and part completed M32 motorways. Numbered 702, and offering two return trips each Saturday, it stopped at Cainscross, Ebley and Stonehouse. The end-to-end journey time was 75 minutes compared to 127 minutes on a typical 400 Stroud-Bristol journey of the time. This welcome development was set to become increasingly popular during the seventies and early eighties. Renumbered 830 in 1976, it was extended to and from Weston-super-Mare, operated daily during the high summer, even saw duplicates and in the early 1980s, it was double decked.

Of particular note was the completion and official opening on 25 July 1972 of Merrywalks Shopping Centre with 34 units and the associated improvements to Stroud bus station beneath it. After much public debate during the late sixties, planning permission for "the precinct", as it was known, was granted in 1970. The centre was to fill the gap left

One of the first Bristol RELL buses with a revised front body style and side-by-side route number and destination was 1972 vehicle 1294, which arrived in September that year, seen when almost new in OMO livery at Gloucester Bus Station on a short working of the trunk Gloucester service. *David Johnson*

after fire had destroyed the Ritz Cinema and included a multi-storey car park. Although it seems odd today, at the time, the bus station was seen as integral to the success of the shopping centre just as much as the car park. During the 15 month construction period, a temporary wooden passenger platform with canopy had been constructed by shrinking the 1960 bus station. This structure was perilously slippery underfoot when wet.

The 'new' bus station opened ahead of the shops in the spring of 1972 and brought with it better passenger facilities. In fact, Bristol Omnibus called it "one of the most up to date in the country". The passenger platform was enlarged to give more reservoir space for queuing. A larger canopy replaced the inadequate shelter accommodation associated with the 1960 design and this came complete with better lighting and illuminated stand indicators. Stroud's management revised the stand allocations so that departures going broadly in the same direction were grouped together. Buses at most stands now pulled up at a slight angle, helping in the reversing out of buses in the more confined space. The works also cured the problems relating to six springs which ran from the bank above the 'old' bus station and would cause mud and cracking of the concrete concourse, necessitating patching.

Pricerite in Russell Street, near the Sims Clock setting down stop, was the first 'modern' supermarket to arrive in the town, opening till 1900 on Fridays. As Stroud further entered the modern age with a covered precinct, the close proximity of a range of new shops within easy access of the bus station was expected to have an impact on bus usage. Such optimism was exaggerated but at least bus passengers had a shorter distance to walk with groceries. The shopping centre itself, officially opened on 25 July 1972, boasted two anchor food retailers, Key Markets and Fine Fare. Fine Fare, opened by Ronnie Corbett, moved from smaller premises in Kendrick Street. Key Markets became Gateway and then Somerfield, although Fine Fare closed, leaving a considerable gap for many years until Argos appeared. Some of the other known names attracted to the precinct in 1972 were Atkinson, then a large electrical retailer, Dorothy Perkins, Hodges, H Samuel, Granada and regional bakers and confectioners, the Lite Bite and a second bread shop, The Baker's Oven, from which the smell of fresh bread would waft around the precinct, always attracting large crowds. Woolworths cut an entrance into the centre from its King Street Parade premises. For many years, The Gorge café proved popular at the top of the bus station escalator.

While vehicles were away for major accident repair or major rebuilds, Bristol Omnibus' Central Repair Works would allocate a traffic pool vehicle as temporary replacement. One such vehicle was used to cover for the absence of RELLs 1100 and 1105 and this was RELL 1306. *David Johnson*

As important, five of the six small shop units on the bus station concourse itself were occupied by newsagent E M Merrett until the late-eighties, with the sixth being taken by a wool shop, perhaps in the hope that the predominance of female passengers might knit on their homeward journeys. In subsequent years, from the mid-eighties in fact, a sharp decline in passenger numbers, the renaissance of the High Street itself and reported high unit rents between them took their toll on the precinct.

One further positive side to Stroud's life on the buses was its closely-knit community. This was especially apparent at smaller Bristol garages but particularly so at Stroud. The depth and range of outside activities actually caused some problems in finding adequate numbers of staff to cover overtime. The best example of this was the Carol Bus which operated each Christmas between 1969 and 1993. Among others, this had been the idea of Stroud Congregational minister Revd Gerald Gossage. Each Christmas, a team of Stroud employees would prepare and then drive around the district in a decorated and brightly-lit double deck, raising many thousands of pounds for local charities. This became an eagerly awaited feature of Christmases locally, including in areas unserved by double decks. During the seventies, on the Saturday before Christmas, it would park in Stroud bus station, where Nailsworth Brass Band would assist Father Christmas in collecting

This 1974 shot of Merrywalks Bus Station typifies operations at Stroud in the early to mid-seventies. In view are two Bristol RELLs, one in attractive OMO livery and the other in newer leaf green, three MW single deck buses, one in OMO livery and two in leaf green and a conductor operated Bristol FLF double deck, also in leaf green. The OMO liveried Bristol RELL single deck moving across the apron is an unusual vehicle on the Saturdays only limited stop 702 to Bristol, the service normally being reserved for a dual purpose vehicle. *Geoff Gould*

money by playing carols during the morning, under the escalator. In addition, during the seventies, the vehicle would also double as the employees' entry to the annual Stroud Show and Carnival.

Coinciding with the bus service withdrawals of the early seventies came the remainder of Stroud's 36 foot Bristol/ECW RELL6L single decks, each of which was capable of one man operation. This saw the speedy conversion of routes from crew double deck to driver operated single deck, with consequent savings in labour costs. Three had been delivered between 1967 and 1969 including 1007, which was transferred to Stroud in December 1969. Then came no.1097 in July 1970, replacing 58 seat Bristol LD double deck L8481which moved to Trowbridge. 1097 was itself swapped for 1105 of Marlborough Street in October 1970.

Similar examples followed. 1216 arrived new in February 1971, 1070

Contrast this with a view one year later of Sunday parking at Merrywalks. All OMO vehicles have been painted out of OMO livery in favour of leaf green and in addition there are now Bristol LH6Ls in view. The duty cleaner/shunter had his work cut out to ensure that all vehicles required for Sunday operation were fuelled, accessible and on the correct stands! *Chris Blick*

and 1093 were transferred to Stroud in February 1972 and 1100 in September 1973, all of which save 1216 replacing double decks, 1959 LD L8499 being withdrawn from service and FLFs 7107 and 7282 being transferred.

The RELLs were delivered with two distinct though similar bus body styles. All the RELLs at Stroud numbered up to 1100 inclusive had 53 seat bodies with a flat front and route number and destination equipment in a "T" formation above the front windscreen. The others were all delivered with 50 seat bodies, in-line route and destination displays and an attractive curved or bowed rather than flat front. The opportunity was taken on these later arrivals to lighten the interior, with the use of creams, whites and an attractive Wearite finish with a gold leaf effect. On the earlier 53 seat examples, it was possible for passengers to convert the long, near side longitudinal seat adjacent to the entrance into a luggage rack by folding down the seat back. In addition, they came with overhead luggage racks on both sides.

Henceforward, vehicles arrived with a single overhead luggage rack and a permanent luggage pen immediately behind the driver, reducing the seating capacity by three. The newer vehicles came complete with "reversing" horns and rear indicators, which flashed when reverse gear was engaged. The earlier 53 seat variants were modified to include this feature.

No. 1105 was something of a transition. It retained the flat front of earlier models but came with a deeper front windscreen and destination equipment in-line across the front dome, albeit reversed with the number following the destination. It held 50 passengers, not 53, with a fixed luggage pen but was the only example to have a fully automatic three speed gearbox, although this was replaced by a standard four speed semi-automatic box as seen on the other RELL buses. The standard semi-automatic gearshift included a position that opened and closed the passenger door. The driver was obliged to close the passenger door before selecting a gear, although there was a means of overriding this innovative safety feature.

The 564 shorts between Stroud and Nailsworth were the first routes

Jason Hire Tools operated branches at Gloucester, Cheltenham and Stroud. It was therefore fitting that their all-over advertisement bus 1278, usually based at Gloucester, should see service at Stroud. 1278 came on two occasions, once from December 1976 to March 1977 and again from January to April 1978, exchanged for Stroud buses 1038 and 1081 respectively. The vehicle was a dual door city fleet example but the central exit was blocked off when used at Stroud. *David Johnson*

to see RE operation in 1967, when 1017 arrived. This was followed by service 416 between Stroud, Eastington and Dursley. When able to do so following union agreement in 1969, Bristol Omnibus converted these buses for one-man operation. The first service converted in its entirety using REs was the 416.

In 1971, it was the entire 564 from Forest Green or Avening to Cheltenham via Nailsworth and Stroud that was to see the next trunk route conversion at Stroud to one-man operation. The withdrawal of the hourly 564 short workings between Stroud and Nailsworth enabled the resultant bus saved to be used on through journeys between the Nailsworth area and Cheltenham. Crew operated double deck shorts remained at peak times south of Stroud and this included a regular turn for an elderly Bristol LD double deck right up to the withdrawal of Stroud's last example, L8538, in March 1975.

Up to this point, through journeys had required two buses from Stroud and one from Cheltenham but now the situation was reversed, with just one Stroud bus being required. The reason for the switch was to transfer work to Cheltenham to compensate for a loss of work on the town's country routes. At the time, Bristol Omnibus was desperately trying to maintain some of its weaker country services in the expectation of grant aid from the county council (under Section 34 of the Transport Act 1968) and as a result was actually withdrawing more-or-less robust, commercial mileage to make its economies. Cheltenham suffered in this respect.

It was almost at the end of double deck operation on the 564 that, in December 1970, Stroud based double deck Bristol FLF no. 7275 overturned at Salmon Springs on the 1225 hrs Cheltenham to Forest Green. Having come off the road, the bus toppled over a 10-foot embankment before its fall was broken by two brewery tanks. The body was damaged along the entire nearside and the upper deck was pushed some six to eight inches out of line at the front end. Amazingly, none of the 11 passengers was seriously hurt and neither was Conductor John Muddle. Driver Ronald Short, who suffered nothing more than shock, is reported to have left his cab while the front off-side road wheel was still spinning. The bus took almost a year to be rebuilt, re-entered service in November 1971 and was one of the last crew operated double decks to work at Stroud over seven years later. During its absence, older Bristol LD double deck 8250 substituted.

50 seat RELLs 1293, 1294 and 1295 joined the fleet new in June and September 1972, replacing FLFs 7053, 7174 and 7203. 1293-5 enabled the conversion of a further trunk route to one-man operations – the busy

1967 Bristol RELH 2045 with attractive coach bodywork arrived at Stroud in 1972 and there it stayed for seven years, although it was renumbered and painted in bus livery from April to October 1979. Equally at home on stage carriage or tours duties, it was one of three such dual purpose vehicles featuring this coach shell and handsome front with dome housing a "T" style destination display. It is seen here in 1976 operating the 564 Cheltenham to Forest Green service. *Geoff Gould*

hourly 556 Nailsworth to Gloucester service, via Stroud.

Meanwhile, following the delivery in 1969 of 2050, June 1972 saw two more 47 seat coach shell high floor Bristol RELH semi-coaches, being 2045 and 2051 which replaced 1007 and 1081. For Stroud's management, these vehicles now totalling three represented the best of both worlds. To the casual eye, they looked very much like coaches. Indeed, they were marked out in half cream and half green. The chassis featured air suspension, a high floor and the bodywork was to coach trim specification, including sealed windows and forced air ventilation. Yet, the vehicles were equipped with Speed Setright ticket machine equipment for one-man operation bus work and featured automatic folding doors. These modern dual-purpose vehicles could perform equally well on stage carriage bus work up and down Stroud's hills or private hire, express coach or excursion duties. These vehicles were most at home on long distance work, however. It is said that one driver travelled as far from Stroud as Salisbury before realising that his RELH

Also transferring in to Stroud in 1972 was further RELH dual purpose vehicle 2051. Passengers enjoyed nine years of comfort on this well appointed vehicle. *Bristol Vintage Bus Group*

had five gears rather than the four on the RELL.

There arrived new in July, a matter of days before the change in registration suffix from K- to L-reg, a further dual-purpose RELH, numbered 2073. This was somewhat different to 2045, 2050 and 2051 as it looked like a standard bus similar to recently delivered low floor RELLs 1293-5. However, the vehicle came with a high floor, coach seats and a number of embellishments but, like buses, had ventilator and hopper windows rather than forced air ventilation. The reason why a bus rather than coach shell was used was to ensure that the vehicle, with its wide passenger entrance, qualified for the government's bus grant available at the time, which covered 50 per cent of each vehicles' costs. This was in an effort to modernise fleets and retire older vehicles that were not suitable for one-man operation. In spite of being slightly less well appointed than its coach shell predecessors, it still proved popular on tours work and with 49 rather than 47 seats, offered an almost like-for-like replacement for 50 and 53 seat RELL vehicles.

At the height of the summer, it was not uncommon to see three of the four RELH dual-purpose vehicles depart on excursion to Weston-

Retired staff line up at London Road before an outing on Bristol coach shell RELH 2050 in c.1971. Note the lowbridge double deck squeezing under the inside depot beam. From the left, George Guildford, Lawrence Cooke, ??, Rodney Stevens, ??, Driver Blick, George Gulliver, ??, ??, ??, Bill Mawler, Frank Washbourne, George Bray, Frank Cleaveley, George Churches, William Bourne, Ted Slad, Eddy Garnon, Walter Stevens, ??. *Chris Blick collection*

super-Mare. The revenue earned from tours work had always been a useful supplement to stage carriage revenue. Now, with the worsening financial position of the depot, such revenue was vital. Tours from Stroud were strong throughout the summer with many of the traditional destinations first started in the 1920s and 1930s continuing, albeit with the withdrawal of others. The range of destinations included the Elan Valley, Bath, Cheddar and Wells, Oxford, Stratford-upon-Avon, Birmingham and, of course, afternoon and evening mystery tours. Each was bookable through the Bus Station booking office at Stroud. Some trips going north would also call at Gloucester and likewise, some would start at Gloucester before picking up at Stroud on the way south.

The arrival of the four RELH dual-purpose vehicles added a further dimension to these tours. Because the season was busiest when schools were on holiday at Easter, Whitsun and during the summer, the vehicles would conveniently become available at the right time. Yet with 47 seats (or 49 in the case of 2073 and subsequent bus shell variants), there was sufficient capacity for these vehicles to be useful off-season, coping as they did with Stroud's peak travel patterns. By 1977, Stroud had seven such vehicles, or 14 per cent of the Bristol Omnibus total. In addition to those mentioned, these were of the bus shell variant, nos. 2077 and 2078 arriving in June 1975 and May 1977 respectively. Coach shell 2083 arrived in July 1975. Prior to reaching Stroud, 2083 had been down graded from a full 45 seat express coach but retained its red coach seats and trim associated with Bristol Greyhound. 2064 and 2062 were further RELHs to join Stroud in the 1980s. At least one full coach RELH with manual transmission and clutch arrived at Stroud for tours work in 1969 (no. 2117) but stayed only a short while.

Back to buses, Bristol RELL 50 seat single deck 1314 arrived new in March 1973 and this replaced single deck MW 2548. The next RE arrival was pretty much unique not just to Stroud and the Bristol Omnibus Company but in Britain. It was 1338, delivered new in February 1974, which was a test bed for future RE developments and featured among other things a power assisted spring-actuated hand brake (rather than the standard hefty ratchet parking brake). It was followed in 1977 by Bristol Omnibus' very last RELL numerically, no.1340 new in 1973, which replaced 43 seat Bristol RESL 524. Henceforward, National Bus Company subsidiaries were obliged to purchase the Leyland National, a vehicle jointly designed, built and promoted by British Leyland and the National Bus Company. However, for reasons peculiar to the town, Stroud was not yet ready for the National.

This meant that, over the remainder of the 1970s, Stroud collected an assortment of Bristol RELL single deck buses. Longer Bristol RELL no. 1067 replaced short RESL 501 in November 1976. This was replaced a month later by 1278, an all over advert for Jason Hire Tools, which in turn left upon the arrival of 1038 in March 1977 but reappeared again in January 1978. Nos. 1320 and 1337 arrived in September 1976 to replace crew operated double deck FLF Lodekkas 7063 and 7226. The other early short RESL 502 was replaced in July 1977 by RELL 1068. Similarly, 1034 replaced 7046.

By 1975, the number of departures from Stroud bus station had been cut by 19 per cent when compared to the level of service just 15 years beforehand and by 14 per cent when compared to the position in 1970.

Meanwhile, the funding crisis was reaching a head. During the mid-seventies, Gloucestershire County Council was facing the same financial pressures as any organisation and it could ill afford to fund more of the network. Yet, in following National Bus Company guidelines, Bristol Omnibus Company switched its method of calculating the subsidy it required, ratchetting it up in the process. Henceforward, full operational costing would reflect not only the costs of actual route mileage but contributions to fixed overheads whereas in the past, marginal costing made no allowance for such items.

The company had restructured its divisional management in parallel with the revisions to local government from 1974, when Gloucestershire lost its southern portion to Avon. The new divisional superintendent at Gloucester was entrusted with building relationships with the County Council which were successful, although centrally based Bristol management tended to be accountable for key financial negotiations. As the seventies progressed, tensions emerged between the County Council and company head office. On the one hand, Bristol Omnibus felt that council involvement was too restrictive, as the Council through its subsidy was able to dictate terms. On the other, the Council felt the company was too demanding. Up to and during 1975, this and other matters were discussed at length between Bristol Omnibus and Council staff. The economic climate of the time meant that the County Council was ill equipped to respond fully to Bristol Omnibus' subsidy requests. Council officers acknowledged that there was a basic "difference of approach" regarding negotiations. This translated into sometimes frank discussions. In the matter of servicing the National Bus Company's £93mil debt, following the holding company's set up, Council officers steadfastly refused the company's demands to pay increasing subsidy. In fact, the Council would always deduct the debt element before a subsidy payment was made. This left the company no alternative but to cut services or increase fares in order to balance its books. However, the Council agreed in future not to object before the Traffic Commissioners to fares increases.

By the financial year 1975/76, a number of other services were added to the loss-making list. These newly declared unremunerative routes were 401 to 404 (Nailsworth local services), 426 (France Lynch), 430/1 (Minchinhampton via Amberley), 436 (Ruscombe), 441 (Randwick), 443 (Westrip Turning), 453/4 (Kingscourt), 558 (Gloucester via Painswick) and 533 (Cheltenham to Standish Hospital via Gloucester), a route tailored to weekend and bank holiday visiting hours at Standish Hospital, introduced in the mid-fifties as 173, renumbered as 533 in September 1967 and eventually becoming 822). Losses on routes in the Stroud area now amounted to over £107,000 of an estimated £162,000

Later RELH dual purpose arrivals at Stroud came with a bus rather than coach shell. Seven such vehicles operated in the town, 2073 arriving new in 1972 followed by other long serving examples 2077 and 2078. Here, in a 1983 shot, 2062 descends towards Brimscombe from Minchinhampton. 2062 remains in local preservation. *Geoff Gould*

total but a year later were to grow to £232,000 in Stroud alone.

It was no surprise, then, that Bristol Omnibus agreed to make further economies in both 1975 and June 1976. In 1975, the company reduced the number of trips between both Stroud and Bristol (400) and Stroud and Framilode from six to five. One off peak bus in three on the 421 terminated at Stonehouse Doverow Avenue (now renamed Juniper Way) rather than Horsemarling Lane. Changes that were more significant took place in 1976, saving £20,000. The five Sunday return trips on each of 416 (Dursley via Eastington) and 433 (Leonard Stanley) were amalgamated into five departures on new service 437, to Dursley via Ebley, the Stanleys and Eastington. The 437, though taking longer in getting to Dursley, successfully combined the best of these former Sunday services. When renumbered 417 in 1979, this service was to operate during weekday evenings, as well.

Monday to Saturday journeys in 1976 to Bisley and Oakridge (425), Randwick (441) and Foxmoor Lane (442) saw a cut of about one third. Most 425 journeys were diverted along Bisley Old Road to the top of the town, thereby enabling Bristol Omnibus to withdraw the 439 to what had been Kilminster Road prefabs. At the same time, the Summer Crescent service 440, which partly paralleled the 439, was reduced from 13 to 11 departures. Buses to Minchinhampton via Amberley (430) and to Kingscourt (by now renumbered 446) were reduced by about a quarter. There were two Saturday departures fewer on the Minchinhampton via Brimscombe routes (447-9), one fewer on Mondays to Fridays and the service was dropped from five to two on Sundays. Ruscombe's service on 436, standing at six departures, went down to five per day and Cheltenham buses via Birdlip, from seven to six.

Things could not get any worse. Or could they? The position in September 1977 was still alarming. Only four services covered their costs in Stroud at this time: 421 (Chalford to Stonehouse via Stroud), 435 (Whiteshill), 442 (Foxmoor Lane) and 556 (Nailsworth to Gloucester via Stroud). Missing from this list of profitable routes was the trunk service between Forest Green, Nailsworth, Stroud, Painswick and Cheltenham (564). The £20,000 savings made on Stroud routes in June the year before had little effect as the net loss on routes in the Stroud area at September 1977 was now estimated at £146,400 for the financial year.

In parallel with the service changes of the early and mid seventies came the displacement of conductors. This process had restarted in

14 Bristol LH6Ls were operated at Stroud between 1975 and 1981. They found duties on almost every service whether rural, urban or inter-urban. 389, new to Stroud in February 1976, is seen in March 1976 at Bulls Cross, near Sheepscombe. *Geoff Gould*

1958 upon the one-man operation of Stroud's single deck Bristol LS and Bedford OBs and the delivery of Bristol MWs. In 1960, there were 10 one man duties and this had increased to some 22 in 1962. It continued throughout the sixties and particularly in 1968, when a number of further routes were converted and it was at this point that Stroud saw its first conductor redundancies, the first to leave the workforce compulsorily. Stroud had always hired up to nine students for conducting during the summer and this habit, too, dropped off.

Up to this point, a number of conductors had elected retraining as drivers rather than face redundancy. This process was not only a natural career progression, it coincided with a driver shortage at the time. From the company's perspective, it was the 1969 agreement that 36 feet Bristol RELL 53 seaters that allowed the progressive conversion of the remaining Stroud bus routes.

At the turn of the decade, the only services either completely crew operated or significantly so were 421 (Chalford-Stonehouse via Stroud), 425 (Oakridge), 429 (Rodborough-Minchinhampton via Stroud), 433 (Stonehouse Park Estate), 435 (Whiteshill), 470/558 (Gloucester-Malmesbury via Stroud), 556 (Nailsworth-Gloucester via Stroud) and 564 (Avening/Forest Green-Cheltenham via Stroud).

Of these, 433 and 564 were converted in 1970 and 1971. The arrival of more REs enabled the company next to convert the 556, in 1972.

One of the most unusual vehicles operated at Stroud was YHA 309J, Midland Red 6309 Ford R192 on loan during 1976 for evaluation. It was the only Ford PSV known to have operated at Stroud. *David Johnson*

Improvements to the Bus Station exit meant that Leyland Nationals, now common at most depots, could at last be introduced at Stroud. First to arrive in 1978 were 3052 and 3053, both almost new. 3052 sported an all-over yellow advertisement for the family of season and rovercards. *Mike Ede*

Because agreements with the unions now required extra time at termini for driver-only journeys to reverse the vehicle (if appropriate), complete the waybill and change route blinds, the conversion of 429 between Rodborough and Minchinhampton in 1972 forced the service to be split in two. This enabled a rationalisation at the Rodborough end and its amalgamation with the Kingscourt service. Also in 1972, the 421 (Chalford to Stonehouse) became one man operated each evening and on Sundays, beginning a process of gradual conversion throughout the decade. With the full conversion of 425 (Oakridge) to one-man operation in 1975, operation without conductors was almost complete, leaving only weekday daytime services on 421 and 435.

By the mid-seventies, the need to replace the aging Bristol MW 39, 43 and 45 seat single decks had became urgent. These vehicles, though many of them were underpowered for Stroud's steeper climbs, had proved themselves ideal for more lightly loaded rural routes. In search-ing for a successor, Bristol Omnibus alighted upon the 43 seat Bristol LH type (standing for "Lightweight, Horizontal") with ECW bodies similar in design to the last RELLs. The company had experience of operating six such LHs new in 1972 in Weston and Wells. However, by 1974, Bristol Omnibus had begun buying shorter 44 seat Leyland

Nationals for country services but there was a sudden change of policy in 1975, in favour of LHs. This was most likely because LHs were cheaper to buy and operate and at a meter shorter, were more manoeuvrable, but also because of the traditional links with the Bristol bus manufacturing arm. Bristol's bus works had become a separate company from 1955 and from the beginning of 1975, together with ECW bodybuilders and production of the Leyland National, was transferred again to a separate company, the joint responsibility of both National Bus Company and Leyland.

Between 1975 and 1980, Bristol Omnibus purchased 110 Bristol LHs. Stroud benefitted from a number of them. They proved to be more powerful on hills than the MWs. Being of a more modern design than their predecessors, the interior was bright and light. Each was fitted with a five-speed gearbox and steering was power assisted, still something of a rarity at this time. The seats were upholstered in light tan vinyl, rather than the moquette, as standard on MWs and patching was therefore less easy and sometimes messy.

The LHs did have more serious shortcomings, however. From a driver's perspective, the clutch was quite severe, in spite of power assistance. In an age when clutchless semi-automatic RELLs were still in use, drivers often stalled LHs in the early days at the traffic lights then yards from the bus station at the junction of Merrywalks, Gloucester Street and Beeches Green. This was in part owing to first gear being unpopular because of the gear arrangement, the LHs featuring a "Chinese box". In any case, selecting the appropriate gear was always difficult! Engineers complained of leaks, blown gaskets and break seizures. For the passenger, the ride was quite bouncy and noisy, owing to the thin plywood flooring. This earned the vehicles the nickname "Jacks in the Box" (whereas MWs and LSs were often referred to as "Spaceships").

The Northern Division of Bristol Omnibus tried to keep the LH at bay for as long as possible. Nevertheless, Stroud was the first depot to see them in 1975. Judiciously, on occasion it was possible to rearrange schedules to ensure that an RELL would replace the work of two LHs, something that was accepted at head office. That way, as few LHs as possible would be delivered to the area.

Stroud's complement of new, post 1975 LHs was 362 to 365, 384, 388, 389, 440, 441 and 448. 368, 419 and 421 were transferred in from Swindon in January 1979 although 368 had previously been used on service at Stroud for a week in September 1977 following repairs. It was the first of these LHs, no. 362, which crashed at speed into a 10-ton roadroller on Horsepools Hill near Gloucester in September 1976, with 53 pupils from the Stroud area destined for St. Peter's School. The passenger door, front of the vehicle and nearside wheel arch were severely damaged and the vehicle was out of service for a rebuild for 16 months. During its absence to January 1977, it was replaced by MW 2523, which was relicensed for the purpose.

There arrived in March 1977 a rather odd LH. This was numbered 347 in the Bristol fleet and was one of five bought at this time from Alder Valley, owing to a Bristol Omnibus-wide vehicle shortage. Unlike the new examples at Stroud, this LH was first registered in 1970 and therefore carried an older ECW body with a flat rather than bowed front and accommodated 41 rather than 43. It took two months for Stroud's fitters to refurbish 347 before being sent to Bristol for painting. It entered service in May. It was primarily used on the Nailsworth local services, replacing Bristol SUS no. 307, was temporarily replaced by similar vehicle 346 in August 1977 to evaluate the non-power assisted clutch, steering and handbrake characteristics following drivers' complaints and was withdrawn in September 1979 upon the arrival of new LH 448 and shortly after changes in Nailsworth.

Stroud hosted a trial of a vehicle not dissimilar to the LH during the autumn of 1976. This was a Midland Red Ford R192 of similar light-weight construction. Midland Red at the time were withdrawing such vehicles and Bristol wished to evaluate their suitability at Stroud. While the R192 had a certain novelty factor among the town's drivers, its front engine design meant that it was noisy from both a driver and passenger perspective. The high revving engine did not help in this regard. The trial was just that – a short-lived experiment.

It is worthy of note that in spite of the three-pronged attack of fares increases, labour cost savings owing to one man conversions and reduced mileage following journey withdrawals, the position still remained stark for Stroud's bus services. This was duplicated elsewhere on Bristol Omnibus. At the close of the 1970s, it became clear both to the National Bus Company and to Gloucestershire Council that something more radical was required. This far-reaching solution is something for the next chapter in Stroud's bus history but in the meantime, further revisions to services continued, in 1977, 1978, 1979 and 1980.

The 1977 changes continued the downward spiral of cutbacks. Three journeys on Saturdays to Bristol (400) were withdrawn and this balanced the number operated on Mondays to Fridays. Changes to services via Cashes Green meant slightly more buses to Westrip Turning, where there had been considerable building, and Ruscombe,

The arrival of five more new Nationals in March 1979 meant the final with-drawal of Stroud's last five half-cab, conductor-operated Bristol FLF double decks. 7206 operated a tour of duty along former FLF routes that month and is seen at Stancombe on the 426A (425 from 1967). *Bristol Vintage Bus Group*

and slightly fewer to Foxmoor Lane. The Ruscombe service was renumbered 443 in the block of routes operating via the expanding Cashes Green estate (441-444, the 444 operating to Randwick via Paganhill). Journeys between Stroud and Gloucester via Painswick (558) saw a marginal increase as did direct buses from Stroud to Cheltenham (564). However, those on the opposite leg to Nailsworth and Forest Green lost four journeys, at peak times. Buses on 564 no longer bifur-cated at Nailsworth to either Avening or Forest Green and hencefor-ward, all 564s would terminate hourly at Forest Green, another area of considerable 1970s building. Changes to 423/4 (Stroud to Malmesbury) to compensate meant that there were 12 buses between Stroud and Avening (nine from Nailsworth), compared to 14 beforehand (also nine from Nailsworth).

With the exception of the 421 (Chalford – Stonehouse), changes in 1978 were more modest with buses to Oakridge (425), Whiteshill (435) and Foxmoor Lane (442) seeing minor changes. Those affecting Stroud's principal local service, the 421 (otherwise known as "The

Track") were more significant. July 1978 was the date chosen to introduce one man operation at off-peak times on this route. At the same time, the frequency outside the peaks dropped to a bus every half-hour. The peak service continued at twenty minute intervals utilising Bristol FLF double decks requiring conductors. There was a rather awkward break in the through service at between 0917 and 0930 and again between 1500 and 1520 on Mondays to Fridays as the service changed between conductor-operated double decks to one man operated Bristol REs and vice versa. Saturdays operated at 30-minute intervals throughout, using one man operated vehicles. This was a sad state of affairs indeed. Not since 1944 had the frequency dropped below every 20 minutes and the reduction was a true litmus test of the lack of profitability at Stroud.

It is interesting that Stroud hung on to its double decks as long as possible. Stroud did not wish to see the introduction of single decks on The Track at this stage and even considered converting the FLFs to one-man operation. Eastern Counties had been successful in converting semi-automatic gearbox examples. It is probably as well that such a conversion was ruled out at Stroud, as there was still plenty of short hop passengers on the service, even at this stage.

Journeys between Stroud and Minchinhampton via Brimscombe on 447-9 were withdrawn in their entirety in 1978. The replacement offered was the diversion of Malmesbury journeys previously travelling via both Nailsworth and Minchinhampton away from Nailsworth in favour of Brimscombe and Burleigh Hill. The net affect for Minchinhampton via Brimscombe was a reduction from 16 to nine departures on Mondays to Fridays and from 16 to eight on Saturdays. A Nailsworth – Minchinhampton local service at four per day was introduced following the rerouting of the 429. Journeys to Highfields on 448 transferred to 430, although journeys offering this particular diversion were numbered 432 from 1979.

February 1979 saw yet further changes. There were minor retimings on journeys to Cirencester, Uplands, Summer Crescent, Kingscourt, Nailsworth to Gloucester and Forest Green to Cheltenham. Service 426 (France Lynch) saw a slight cutback, the 427 (Framilode) was renumbered 414, 433 renumbered 413 and the 415 to Dursley via Uley was revised to absorb local Dursley service 413. Wednesdays only 417 from Quedgeley to Stroud, introduced in 1976 with joint Gloucestershire County and Stroud District funding to form a link from the fast expanding Quedgeley to the town responsible since 1974 for its local affairs, was withdrawn. A solution similar to that made to

Sunday services in 1975 was imposed on 416 (Dursley via Eastington) and the 433 (the Stanleys), although these were now numbered 417 and 418 rather than 437. The long-standing works service to Oldends Lane (434) was withdrawn but partly replaced by an early morning 417, which also operated via the Stanleys. In 1980, there was even a proposed 419 Sunday service which combined journeys to the Stanleys, Stonehouse and Whiteshill in something of a marathon!

It was also on 11 February 1979 that Stroud gained its first two minibuses, for Nailsworth and between Stroud and Cheltenham via Birdlip. These, like the preceding SUSs, had more-or-less been tailor made for Stroud's particular circumstances.

The vehicles chosen were two Reeve Burgess bodied Ford Transit 17 seat dual-purpose vehicles. Some five years ahead of the arrival of commercial minibuses used on high profile, frequent urban services at Cheltenham and Gloucester and later at Stroud, the "Reeburs" were for rural routes where demand was lowest. The vehicles themselves, numbered 302 and 303 in the Bristol Omnibus fleet, were actually owned by Gloucestershire County Council in an experiment that, if successful, could be mirrored elsewhere in the county. They certainly stimulated requests from others. They were liveried in green and yellow, in one of five livery styles considered. These were joined between September 1980 and June 1982 by a third vehicle, no. 301, a Leyland 440EA minibus with a strange Ascough 17 seat body, which previously had spent much of its life rather unsuccessfully on Gloucester's City Centre service, then in Weston and after that on the Windmill Hill Community Bus, where it proved to be too small.

In Nailsworth, with the active support of the town council which since 1976 had been frustrated in buying a community minibus through lack of funds, the company and Gloucestershire County Council took the opportunity to recast local services 401 to 405 plus shorts on 400 between Nailsworth and Horsley. The services became more customer-focused with the introduction of an element of hail-and-ride plus dedi-cated drivers. In fact, Tony and Paul Deakins, a father and son team, were to win an award for their customer service. With the withdrawal of the 30 seat Bristol SUSs in November 1977 and March 1978, the time was right for the smaller minibuses to use new roads previously unserved. This included buses to Bunting Hill and a new circular serv-ice twice a week to North Woodchester via Watledge and Theescombe. Fares were even cheaper downhill than up!

Between Stroud and Cheltenham via Birdlip, the council and company took a similar approach, even though there was less scope for innovation. Part of the 565 (Cranham) was incorporated into the 563 minibus operation and the minibus was able to serve Sheepscombe village for the first time, rather than the road across the top at Jack's Green.

Launched as "The Bus for all Reasons", both vehicles were available for hire complete with Bristol Omnibus Stroud drivers during evenings and weekends, in an effort to defray costs. It was for this reason that vehicles were fitted with dual purpose seats. This worked best in the Nailsworth area where the local community really felt that the vehicles were their own and as a result, private hires were relatively busy. This arrangement was not the original intention, however. The County Council wanted the minibuses to be turned over to the community for use by trained volunteer drivers during evenings and weekends. The Transport & General Workers Union were concerned at the effect unpaid labour would have on drivers of both the Bristol Omnibus Company and smaller coach firms. The company's view was that the

New in 1979 were two Ford Transits with angular Reeve Burgess 17 seat dual purpose bodies for Nailsworth local services and the 563 Stroud to Cheltenham via Slad and Birdlip. Both vehicles were bought by Gloucestershire County Council as an experiment to provide improved yet cost effective services and predated the use of minibuses on a commercial basis at Stroud by 12 years. *Geoff Gould*

community bus revenue generated might actually contribute towards safeguarding employees but nevertheless was concerned about the insurance surrounding the project. To be fair to the union, it did agree significant changes to wage rates for driving the minibuses after hours, which ensured that they were available for hire at reasonable rates. Nevertheless, this debate was partly responsible for holding the project up for the best part of a year, as the initial press release giving details of the scheme in Nailsworth to come went out in March 1978.

In fact, in March 1978 the press was immensely interested in what the Western Daily Press called "The Bus of the Future". In the excitement, the Western Daily Press stated "Mayor of Nailsworth, near Stroud, yesterday waved a glad farewell to lumbering single-deck buses and the problems they have brought his town" while the photographer focused not on local services 400 to 405 but on standard Bristol RELL 1105 in Nailsworth Bus Station clearly showing "Gloucester 556". Not only was this 11 months premature, it was rather unfortunate in the choice of a trunk service but the event did little real damage. The Nailsworth and 563 minibuses carried on until replaced from October 1984 by three further vehicles owned by Gloucestershire, Mercedes 608Ds, numbered 600 to 602.

By 1978, other Bristol Omnibus country garages had received considerable numbers of single door, 52 seat Leyland Nationals. As successors to the Bristol RELL 50 seat bus, they represented the most modern single deck vehicles then available. The 11.3m single door country models first arrived on Bristol Omnibus in 1975, although dual-door "city" examples of the same length but with 44 seats were in service on town routes in Bristol, Bath, Gloucester and Cheltenham from 1972. Manufactured jointly by Leyland and the National Bus Company, its subsidiaries were "encouraged" to buy the product, even though many bus company engineers regarded it as expensive to buy and run. In its favour was a warmer winter passenger interior, a quieter engine than the RE, free of the infamous gearbox whine, and bodywork that suffered less from the early rattles associated with the ECW body on the Bristol RE chassis. The more utilitarian interior comprised of darker creams and beiges, with brown plastic seats, was somewhat sombre when compared to the RE. For the driver, they came with modern switchgear, power steering, a small steering wheel of almost car-like proportions and what at the time was a curious semi-automatic gear shift to the right of the driver.

Apart from Wells, Stroud was the last garage to receive the National when in November 1978 3052 and 3053 came. The decision to

A down graded motorway RELH coach arrived in 1979. Delivered in 1972, numbered at the time 2161 but renumbered 2089 as a dual purpose vehicle, it was surprising for the fact that it was powered by a Gardner rather than Leyland engine. It also had bodywork by Plaxtons whereas all RELHs to date had more familiar ECW bodies. *Geoff Gould*

exclude Stroud in no way reflected Bristol Omnibus' desire to run the town's fleet down. In fact, Stroud of the sixties and seventies could boast a line up of modern and appropriate vehicles. No, the delay was simply because the bus station exit, constructed in 1968 as a means of relieving the congestion caused by buses entering and leaving at a single point, caused Nationals to ground. On the rare occasion that Cheltenham sent a National rather than RE on the 564, the driver had to leave via the Stroud bus station entrance, under the supervision of an inspector.

The road surface at the bus station exit was built up on 30 November 1978 and 3052 and 3053 arrived on that very day! They had been used in Gloucester since April, swapped with the garage's RELLs 1333 and 1334 until the situation could be resolved. 3052 wore an all-over advertisement for the Rovercard family of season and other discount tickets. 3053, although painted in leaf green with "Bristol" fleetnames, was actually owned by Hants & Dorset, showing a Bournemouth address on its legal lettering. 3053 together with five other Nationals leased by Bristol Omnibus from new in August 1978 were all "swapped" on paper in October 1979 with six which had been bought outright by Hants & Dorset, thereby improving Hants & Dorset's cash flow without the need to swap vehicles physically. 3053 and sister vehicle at Gloucester 3064 received Hampshire Bus legal lettering upon the split up of Hants & Dorset.

The improvement in ground clearance paved the way for more Nationals. No. 1456, a dual door example from Cheltenham painted silver for the Queen's Silver Jubilee but by this time advertising Rovercards etc, saw service on loan to Stroud between the last days of December 1978 and the end of February 1979. The next to arrive, 3073 to 3077, were significant. New in February (with 3076 being slightly delayed) and into service in March 1979, these five vehicles directly replaced the last five Bristol FLF Lodekkas and, in theory, meant that conductors were no longer required at Stroud. The Lodekkas had been sent to Cheltenham for the Gold Cup, Stroud sending four or five such vehicles throughout the fifties, sixties and seventies. When they returned, the Lodekkas were used for a couple of days and finally departed, with 7206 being the one chosen to come back on 11 March 1979 for a parting tour of routes. Stroud was the first main Bristol Omnibus garage to bid farewell to its FLFs, even ahead of the small country depot at Wells.

The FLF Lodekkas were the last "half-cab" vehicles at Stroud. Though their departure caused considerable regret, the drivers' operating environment, sitting immediately next to the heat and noise of an engine for potentially a whole eight hour shift, was particularly harsh when compared to modern vehicles, although drivers accepted this situation.

It is a curious fact that the Nationals perpetuated the 20-minute peak service on the 421, with conductors. Nothing changed except new Nationals replaced older double decks. The off peak and Saturday workings stepped back to half-hourly as they had since 1978. The reason for the conductors' continued use was simply a matter of route running time: the 20-minute service would not work with the additional layover required for one-man operation. However, the amount of changing required by passengers was reduced as, when the conductors came off, the vehicle could be used on 421 with a driver only.

The 435 to Whiteshill, which had progressively become one man operated from 1977, was similarly affected. In 1978, all 435 peak work was converted to one man operation, creating a rather haphazard frequency. Conductors were still required to maintain the off-peak service at half-hourly intervals. The round trip time with conductors was 27 minutes and without, 29 minutes, because of the five minute wait. In fact, conductors remained on both the 435 off-peak and 421 at peak times Mondays to Fridays until July 1981. The Nationals were used consistently on both the 421 and 435 but would see evening duties on the 556 (Nailsworth-Gloucester).

During the early 1970s, Bristol Omnibus had announced that it saw the long single deck as the preferred model in country districts and, indeed, the only vehicles purchased for any stage carriage operation, rural or urban, between 1967 and 1972 were single deck Bristol RELLs. It would only be purchasing modern, front entrance double decks suitable for one man operation for city type services, and this it did in large numbers, for Bristol but also for Gloucester city, Cheltenham town and

Stroud's environment can be a difficult one in which to operate buses, as this picture of RELH 2045 demonstrates. The dual purpose vehicle is passing through Nympsfield on the Dursley to Stroud service 415 in January 1979. Nympsfield itself is about 800 feet above sea level and, in common with other settlements atop the Cotswold scarp, experiences snow when Stroud sees rain. Most rural routes suffer annually at the hands of snow and for many years, for example, snow fences were erected across Minchinhampton Common. In extreme weather, Bristol Omnibus would send two buses to Bisley, one via Bisley Road and the other via Bisley Old Road, in the hope of at least one getting through. Inspectors would never be sure whether a bus made it until a driver telephoned through to report conditions. *Geoff Gould*

eventually Swindon town services. In the public's eyes, this announcement caused some consternation as Stroud's passenger had failed to see what Bristol Omnibus already knew: that loadings were generally insufficient to warrant double decks.

Nevertheless, between 1975 and 1977, Bristol purchased 27 of these modern double decks similar to those in use on intensive city type services, but with single doors. These were classed as VRTs ("Vertical Rear Transverse") and were deployed on busier city and town routes in Bath, Weston, Gloucester and Cheltenham. A couple found their way to smaller depots, one of which was 5512 which, fresh from being repainted from silver jubilee to leaf green livery, joined Stroud from Bristol's Marlborough Street garage in March 1978. This vehicle replaced 5518, on loan from Bath between 30 September 1977 and 4 March 1978, which in turn had replaced Cheltenham's 5511, at Stroud for five days before that.

The transverse engine at the rear offside corner enabled a passenger entrance opposite the driver which, for the first time at Stroud, meant that a double deck could be used without a conductor. However, the low rear overhang created by the engine also meant that the bus would ground at the bus station exit, as had the National single decks! The vehicle could only leave via the bus station entrance. Yet, 5512 and its predecessors on loan had been on regular service a full year before the road camber was sorted out. This was an apparently crazy situation but the pressing need for economies on the 423 (Stroud to Malmesbury via Nailsworth and Tetbury), owing to a heavy school movement to Malmesbury, ensured the introduction of a one manned double deck. 5512 also worked the 443 to Westrip Turning and the 1735 journey from Stroud to Oakridge which, even in 1979, often carried more than an RELL load, but only for the first mile out of town to Mason Road. Thereafter, between zero and five continued for the remainder of the journey via Bisley.

Meanwhile, trouble brewed as road staff took strike action in 1979 following what they claimed was the unjust dismissal of a colleague. The action lasted four days but was particularly harsh as pupils were left stranded, causing some ill feeling among the public. Strikes were rare as relationships between unions and management at Stroud were generally good. An example of this was the reaction to a Leyland Leopard coach which, when down-graded to a dual purpose vehicle, was deemed to be unacceptable to union stewards at Bristol's Marlborough Street but entered service at Stroud without problems.

The seventies had been a decisive one for Stroud's buses. It finished with a considerable reduction in departures from Stroud bus station (down by one third in a decade) at the same time as the County Council had been pumping in considerable and increasing amounts of money. Crew operated double decks, standing at 24 in 1969, had been eliminated and two minibuses introduced. The total vehicles based at Stroud had gone down from 59 in 1969 to 47 in 1979. It became clear to both the company and County Council that the continued "cut and cut again" approach could not continue. There needed to be a radical reappraisal of services. This was to follow in 1980 and the resultant changes in 1981 were to be of the utmost significance. Yet even as the 1980 review was taking place, there were further cuts in April, which resulted in the saving of two single decks, four drivers' and two conductors' duties, bringing an end, for example, to the 20 minute Monday to Friday peak service on the Chalford to Stonehouse route and Sunday buses to Bristol.

CHAPTER 8

1980–1989
DEMAND,
DEREGULATION AND
DENATIONALISATION

During the eighties, Stroud's bus services were dominated by three major events – deregulation, denationalisation and demand & supply.

Faced with the gloomy prospect of continued cuts in service in the early eighties, Bristol Omnibus applied a radical solution. During the previous decade, the reaction to declining passenger numbers saw fares rise ahead of inflation and year-on-year service cuts, resulting in about one third of Stroud's departures being wiped out by the end of the decade. Rather than stemming the decline, this approach tended to perpetuate it. Bristol Omnibus' approach was nothing short of fire fighting and, if the future was to be more secure, a more measured and forward-looking response would be required. It was this environment that the Market Analysis Project of the early eighties was designed to provide.

The Market Analysis Project, or MAP as it was known, had its origins in 1977 with the Viable Network Project of National Bus Company subsidiary Midland Red which, at the time, faced mounting financial problems associated as much as anything with the passing of a number of its core, profitable services to West Midlands Passenger Transport Executive. Following its success at Midland Red, MAP became corporate National Bus Company policy, with a team of specialists centrally and within each National Bus Company region to oversee it. It later spread throughout the Scottish Bus Group and even to a number of municipal undertakings.

MAP's main objective was to balance supply with demand to

produce a viable network. This was to be achieved by adjusting services (and fares) to match passenger demand, without undue cross-subsidy between areas, routes or groups of passengers. The tools open to operators in assessing demand were on-bus passenger demand surveys, which included speed and punctuality checks, and off-bus passenger attitude surveys. Each operator would then assemble new timetables, consider the vehicle types required for services and how best these could be scheduled. The resultant viable network would clearly expose to local authorities those areas or routes which were weakest and the cost of subsidy required for them. In fact, Gloucestershire County Council fully supported the MAP ethos as it was concerned at increasing subsidy levels. In the year to March 1980, Gloucestershire contributed £300,000 in revenue support towards Bristol Omnibus' £413,000 Gloucestershire deficit. This had risen from nothing at all ten years before. To put this into context, Avon County Council contributed over £1mil and Wiltshire £372,000, towards a total Bristol Omnibus deficit of more than £2mil.

The Bristol Omnibus MAP-inspired changes were first seen in October 1980 in Bath, with Gloucestershire country services and those in north Avon together being the third of the Company's projects, introduced in July 1981. The planning process itself was started in April 1980, with passenger and attitude surveys completed in Stroud by the autumn. Employees, their spouses and college students were used to time services and distribute and collect simple one-page on-bus passenger questionnaires in which the passengers were asked to state their origin, destination, journey purpose, etc. It was thought at the time that some students invented their own answers! As electronic ticket machines were at least six years away, surveys of this type were the only means by which managers could fully understand their businesses.

Meanwhile, during the MAP planning process, there remained the need to make further economies to bus services. There were changes to services in January, July, September and October 1980, most of which were minor in nature. The most notable January 1980 change was to the 558 (Stroud – Gloucester via Painswick) which was diverted through Upton St. Leonards. Those in July were more severe, saving two single decks, both Leyland Leopard former coaches, four drivers and two conductors duties. The changes included the withdrawal of Sunday services between Stroud and Bristol (service 400) and to Whiteshill (435); the final adoption of a 30 minute frequency throughout the day on Mondays to Saturdays on the Chalford-Stroud service (421) plus the reduction in the number of buses terminating at Standish

The late summer and early autumn of 1981 saw the reintroduction of a batch of double decks at Stroud. These were to fulfill duties following the major Market Analysis Project. Stroud's solitary double deck between the withdrawal of Bristol FLFs in March 1979 and the new arrivals had been Bristol VR 5512, principally to accommodate school traffic on the Stroud to Malmesbury via Tetbury route and it is on this route that new VR 5535 is seen six months after arrival and still in as-new condition. *Geoff Gould*

Lodge to three per day; the retiming and rerouting of buses after 1700 between Stroud and Dursley via the Stanleys (416/7/8), the consequent withdrawal of peak afternoon mileage on the 413 (Stroud to Leonard Stanley) and the curtailment of Sunday services at Claypits; the renumbering of the Aston Down service from 420 to 422 and the co-ordination of service 422 (Cirencester) with Chalford-bound 421 buses; the withdrawal of four trips to Uplands (438); and the withdrawal of late evening buses which had by this time operated only on certain days of the week, to Dursley via the Stanleys (418), Eastcombe (426), Minchinhampton (428), Whiteshill (435) and to Oakridge (425), although a once-a-week late departure for Bisley Road/Mason Road was maintained. The 2230 service to Minchinhampton via Amberley swapped from a Friday to a rather unusable and unsatisfactory Monday. The September 1980 changes were again of a minor nature, although the 563 timetable was rewritten. Those in October 1980 were confined

1977 Bristol VR 5527 on the other hand, came a year after MAP to facilitate paint trials in exchange for 5528, new in 1981. It is seen entering Nailsworth from Spring Hill on revised service 555 which, with 553, 554 and 556 from April 1983 saw hourly through services to Gloucester and opposite hourly shorts between Forest Green, Nailsworth, Stroud and Whiteshill. *Geoff Gould*

to changes to the Nailsworth minibus services, including the withdrawal of some Shortwood journeys (402) and a new Tuesday only 406 between Nailsworth and Nympsfield via Spring Hill, Tinkley Lane, Nortonwood, Windsoredge and Bunting Way.

In parallel with this good housekeeping, the results of the MAP demand surveys were being compiled and analysed by the National Bus Company and there followed the design of a viable network. The process, though relatively quick, was not a smooth one. When information became publicly available, it provoked more criticism from passengers, parishes, district councils and MPs than at any other time, with what can only be described as a mountain of letters to both the company and county council. Among the correspondence were suggestions, good and bad, and not a little anger. The initial services were modified and, in considering the matter, Gloucestershire decided to buy back £164,000 worth of services throughout the county. This equated to about half that previously spent on revenue support.

The consequent timetable revisions were at a sufficiently firm stage in March 1981 for the proposed amendments to be submitted before the Traffic Commissioners. There followed a two-day hearing during which time Stroud's services were dealt with on the second morning. Somewhat prophetically, the Chairman of the Traffic Commissioners for the Western Region, Major-General Sir John Potter, concluded that "Whether or not we like it, the public are now simply not going to get the bus services which they have been used to in the past, and the days when people could always count on a bus, even for just the odd person, are dead and gone" and "unless there is a determined effort by the public to help themselves, I do not think they are likely to get all that good a service in the future."

MAP services in Stroud were launched on 26 July 1981. To encourage their use, Bristol Omnibus offered a 10p voucher towards bus fares in the local newspaper. The theory was that a MAP-inspired network would be free of the historical development in bus services over years gone by. It would better reflect current passenger demand – and at Stroud there was evidence to support both of these claims. Some

September 1983 saw the Bristol Omnibus Company's Northern Division split off to form the Cheltenham & Gloucester Omnibus Company. Two months afterwards, the local identity "Stroud Valleys" was introduced which Bristol RELL 1337 amply demonstrates. Bus services were also progressively renumbered in two phases the following year, starting in May, the 440 to Wotton-under-Edge becoming 40. *Mike Ede*

commented instead that MAP was no more than a tactical withdrawal.

For example, the new network reflected the painful truth that buses beyond Cashes Green estate were not viable. Up to this point, Cashes Green had been served by a combination of services to Randwick, Ruscombe and Foxmoor Lane. Few travelled beyond Cashes Green. The result of MAP was a new, half-hourly circle of Cashes Green as service 436/7. Peak services to Randwick and all services to Ruscombe did not form part of the viable network but the Council bought back just three off peak services to Ruscombe (433) and a peak service from Randwick via Ruscombe using one of the rural minibuses. Randwick saw five departures on Mondays to Fridays, six on Saturdays and a "late" service each Thursday at 2120, compared to 12 on Mondays to Saturdays.

Three daytime, two evening and all Sunday journeys between Stroud and Gloucester also operated via Whiteshill as 555, although the service was only open to local passengers between Stroud, Paganhill and Whiteshill after 1900 on weekdays and all day Sunday. This meant that MAP actually reintroduced Sunday services to Whiteshill. The weekday diversion followed a two round trip Saturday working of the 556 Stroud-Gloucester service via Whiteshill from December 1980, something for which Whiteshill Parish Council had been pressing since 1977. There were proposals at one stage to link Cashes Green services across Stroud to Whiteshill. This was not pursued and, under MAP, Whiteshill continued with a half-hourly standalone daytime service, albeit with fewer early morning, school and evening journeys. However, the cross-town link was actually made in March 1982, when 436s and 437s worked through to Whiteshill and the 435 number was discontinued.

The seasonal Saturday limited stop services between Stroud, Bristol and Weston-super-Mare (830) saw only a slight retiming. However, the weekday Stroud-Bristol service 400, introduced in 1950, was curtailed at Yate as 440, of rather limited use to Yate passengers and only marginally better from Wotton-under-Edge and Horsley to Nailsworth and Stroud. There was substantial opposition to this cutback from communities along the 400's route. However, over the years, the Stroud area had naturally grown away from Bristol as a regional shopping centre and the fact that most passengers on the 400 wishing to get to Bristol were not prepared to tolerate the slow, rural ramble was now sadly reflected in the revenue figures. The Nailsworth minibus services, including journeys to Horsley, remained untouched, as this was the subject of a special funding arrangement between company and

Council since 1979.

Services via Amberley to Minchinhampton (430-2) were linked across Stroud to those via Kings Stanley to Leonard Stanley (413) and renumbered 412 via London Road, 413 via Park Road and 414 via Highfields. The company maintained an hourly daytime service on each leg, though evening services to Minchinhampton and Sunday services to Claypits via the Stanleys were withdrawn. The 421 to Stonehouse was diverted to serve Park Estate, previously covered by the 413 on certain extensions beyond Leonard Stanley. Services to Dursley via Eastington (416) remained almost intact, although passengers found that the last direct 416 via Ebley at 1745 became a 418 via the Stanleys at 1740, with a resultant additional 12 minutes journey time.

Gloucestershire stepped in to protect the Nympsfield to Dursley via Uley section of the 415 service, though not the extension beyond Dursley to Berkeley. Even so, seven Dursley journeys were reduced to five. It was at this time that a works journey from Tetbury via Nailsworth, Nympsfield and Uley to Lister's at Dursley was included.

Under MAP, it was proposed that the four journeys per day between Stroud and Cirencester (422) would be withdrawn. In the event, Gloucestershire subsidised three return trips on Mondays to Fridays only. Similarly, MAP saw no future in delivering services on the Malmesbury corridors beyond Tetbury. The Council again bought back two trips per day on Mondays to Fridays between Tetbury and Malmesbury, where previously there had been seven on Mondays to Saturdays, while the level of service on 429 to Minchinhampton via Brimscombe Hill was reduced from nine to seven per day Mondays to Fridays with one fewer on Saturdays; and that via Nailsworth, renumbered under MAP as 448/9, was cut from seven to five journeys.

The eight buses daily to Bisley or Oakridge (425) were reduced to six, with only limited intervention from Gloucestershire and the 11 each day to Summer Crescent (440) became just four under the revised number 427. However, MAP originally proposed just a single return shopping journey to Summer Crescent, the remainder being bought back by revenue support. There was an element of co-ordination between the 425 and 427 over the common section of route to Summer Street, although this was but a shadow of the half-hourly combined service enjoyed previously to this point.

Services to France Lynch (426), which had been diverted along part of the spine road constructed in 1978 at the start of the major Manor Farm housing development rather than via the Ram Inn at Bussage,

Numerically Bristol Omnibus' last Bristol RELL single deck bus, no. 1340, arrived at Stroud in 1977, transferred to the new company and is seen here in its Stroud Valleys identity at the Chalford terminus of what was the 421. *Mike Ede*

saw a reduction of 13 to nine buses per day, with Gloucestershire buying back a "late" service at 2120 on Tuesdays and Fridays only (replacing the Mondays to Saturdays departure at 2140).

The service to Uplands was due to be withdrawn in its entirety but Gloucestershire safeguarded just three of the pre-MAP ten return trips on Mondays to Fridays but did nothing on Saturdays. Services to Kingscourt, 446, were about halved to eight on Mondays to Fridays and nine of Saturdays. The 563 to Cheltenham via Birdlip, always a weak service and one the subject of a special arrangement with a minibus, was due to be withdrawn entirely save for school journeys but Gloucestershire's funding enabled its continuation, albeit at a much reduced level. Weekday services to Cheltenham reduced to a Thursday only operation.

Both the Nailsworth-Stroud-Gloucester (556) and Forest Green-Nailsworth-Stroud-Cheltenham (564) trunk services were largely untouched by MAP during the daytime. However, the half-hourly Saturday 556 from Stroud to Gloucester was reduced to the Monday to Friday hourly frequency. Certain weekday and all Sunday journeys operated via Whiteshill and the evening service, particularly from Stroud to

181

The launch by Cheltenham & Gloucester of the "Cotswold" coaching brand in 1983 was a bold and significant step. The flagship coach was Leyland Tiger 2211 and it was allocated to Stroud. It initially received green and red stripes but was later repainted in this post-1986 livery of white with green and red flow lines. *Mike Ede*

Nailsworth, was thinned. The 564 saw some morning and evening withdrawals.

Gloucestershire County Council recognised that the traditional form of area timetable book produced by Bristol Omnibus had become somewhat obsolete and in any case was not easily accessible. It wished to see the best use of its investment in local services and it recognised that it had a vital interest in keeping the viable network as sound as possible. The Council decided, therefore, to invest in smaller, localised timetable booklets. That for Stroud included the rail timetable and the few services operated by the council itself. 64,000 copies were printed and it was delivered free from door to door. This format became the norm in the early eighties but for a short period after MAP, Bristol Omnibus did revert back to its larger, comprehensive Gloucestershire timetable book.

The net result of MAP changes was a level of service less than half that operated thirty years before, at the height of passenger numbers. Had the Council not intervened, this would have been at about 40 per cent. It is hardly surprising that such a reduction required fewer staff and fewer buses. On the rural Gloucestershire network, 38 jobs in total, including five clerical staff, were shed and this included the last two conductresses at Stroud, one of whom, Audrey Gay, had previously been employed at Western National as a secretary and the other, Evelyn Gardiner, by Red & White as a conductress. Perhaps more than any other of the road staff, these two were very well known to generations of the Stroud travelling public, visibly working up and down the bus gangway rather than being stuck behind the wheel. Both had been on notice since January 1981 and while Evelyn retired, younger Audrey left to begin a successful private hire taxi business, something she has maintained well past state retirement age! There is no doubt that had she wished to be, Audrey would have been Stroud's first woman bus driver. Those remaining crew drivers, such that there were, retired at this time.

Audrey recalls walking between her native Whiteshill and Stroud to the first and from the last buses. There simply was no other way of getting to and from work. The four mile walk was downhill to Stroud but steeply uphill, of course, in the opposite direction. She recalls collecting enough grit on a bus' rear platform at Farmhill to help in the steep ascent to Whiteshill and passengers in the late forties on the last journeys home silently climbing the rear ladder of single deck buses fitted with roof luggage racks. Audrey also recalls an incident just after the war and not long before she started conducting when a driver forgot to chock his front wheel at the Whiteshill terminus, there being a large wooden block for this purpose attached by a chain to the large Western National timetable board. On this occasion, the company had to pay for a new kitchen as the runaway bus demolished part of a nearby house! Later, one hot summer afternoon, Audrey and her driver fell asleep in the sun during a 30 minute layover at Framilode. Upon waking, this resulted in their being an hour late but because they rarely saw any passengers between Frampton-on-Severn at Leonard Stanley, they were able to make up time and, in fact, arrived promptly at Stroud!

Aside from the conductors being forced to leave in 1968, there had previously been no compulsory redundancies at Stroud. Even in the difficult years of the seventies, natural wastage had applied. Now, the MAP revisions marked the end of what was once viewed as a job for life on the buses. Matters could have been worse. Gloucestershire's buy-backs ensured a greater retention of staff than a purely viable network would have allowed. As part of the MAP process, there was also talk among the MAP team of closing Stroud depot, running services in the area either from Gloucester or Cheltenham garages with nothing larger than a small Stroud-based outstation. This had been the first time that such a thought had been mentioned.

Vehicles required for the new network were just 39, as opposed to 47 beforehand. Flexibility was the word in vehicle allocation on the MAP network. Services had been recast to create as many well-loaded peak journeys as possible. The weaker services had been withdrawn or drastically thinned. With fewer vehicles actually needed but a similar number of passengers to be carried, there was no longer the requirement for the smaller, 43 seat Bristol LHs. All 11LHs were withdrawn from Stroud, even though the oldest was just seven years old and the youngest had been allocated to Stroud in 1979. Interestingly, two lower capacity 44 seat Leyland Nationals did arrive at this time. Had the LHs been such a disaster? They certainly were not liked by fitters or drivers but in replacing MWs on rural services, they had plugged a gap at the time. Their estimated nine year life was never achieved at Bristol Omnibus and, indeed, MAP was to see the back of virtually all such vehicles throughout the company, the exceptions being in the south of Bristol's territory where 12 were in use in 1984. Some surplus newer Bristol Omnibus LHs did see further service with other National Bus subsidiaries, particularly Hants & Dorset.

It was a case of the higher the capacity of the remaining post-MAP vehicle stock, the better. In the early seventies, Bristol Omnibus had announced to a somewhat sceptical public that henceforward single decks would replace double decks altogether on country services. Now, to cope with the new network's demands, double decks made a welcome return to Stroud. Thanks to a parallel MAP exercise at Hants & Dorset which rendered its new double deck order unnecessary, six single door "country" Bristol VRT double decks with 74 seat ECW bodies were diverted to Stroud. These joined Stroud's solitary double deck, also a VR, 5512. However, none was ready for the launch of the new network and on temporary loan came six Bristol City fleet examples, nos. 5107, 5108, 5110, 5112, 5117 and 5118. These replaced five Bristol RELL single deck buses and one RELH dual-purpose vehicle.

The dual-door city fleet VRs came with the customary centre exit, used to speed unloading in busy city environments. During the first few days of the new network, this seemed odd to passengers. They were often hesitant as to exactly where they should stand in order to leave the vehicle. The use of the central door was quickly banned in Stroud Bus Station on safety grounds. Longer term dual-door vehicle loans, such as the Bristol RELL single deck all-over advertisement for

Former National Travel Leyland Leopard 2088 operated at Stroud for two periods. On its second visit, between January 1985 and March 1986, it received the early version of the "Cotswold" Livery in the revised National Bus Company local coach style. This consisted of a broad band of leaf green used at Stroud at the rear blending with the red used at Cheltenham and Swindon at the front merging into stripes which extended diagonally forward to the front wheel. The vehicle is seen leaving Bristol for Stroud. *Daniels collection*

Jason Hire Tools (no. 1278), would have the centre exit blocked off by two pieces of wood. The vehicles themselves were almost grounded by the union because of concerns over visibility leaving Stroud bus station, owing to a different lower deck passenger seating configuration compared to Stroud's single door example. However, most of Stroud's brand new single-door double decks had arrived by the end of August. Looking back at this period, the use of city fleet dual door vehicles seemed rather pointless as they started during the summer school holidays and most were out of service by the end of August, before the return to school and work peak loadings in September.

Stroud's new single door VRs settled down to regular duties on revised services 421, 436/7 and 555/6. However, there were changes during the 1980s. At the time Swindon's depot adopted a poppy red livery in 1983, some Stroud VRs were swapped with Swindon's. This was because a couple of Swindon's vehicles had been painted in an

Still within state hands as part of the National Bus Company and with deregulation of bus services looming, the loss of network subsidy and the threat of competition, Stroud Valleys introduced its commercial network in May 1986, five months ahead of the statutory date. This brought about a number of changes, the most significant of which was the announcement of the complete withdrawal of service 46 between Stroud, Painswick & Cheltenham. In the event, Gloucestershire County Council secured a rescue package, although the level of service dropped from hourly to some five per day. One of Stroud's first two Leyland Nationals, 3052, previously an all-over advert but now in standard National Bus Company leaf green livery, has recently arrived on the 46 from Cheltenham. *Brian Ward-Ellison collection*

experimental long-life green paint finish. As Stroud's buses were to remain in leaf green at that time, it seemed sensible to transfer across Swindon's green VRs to Stroud so that the tests could be completed. Transferred out to Swindon were 5512, 5527, 5530 and 5532 while in their place Swindon's 5611, 5612, 5613 and 5616 arrived in October 1983. All were 1974/75 vehicles acquired by Bristol Omnibus earlier in 1983 from West Riding.

It was at this time that the Bristol Commercial Vehicles factory at Brislington in Bristol, closed. It had supplied Bristol Omnibus, its predecessor and the nationalised transport sector with vehicles for 75 years.

The vehicle changes at the end of 1981 and during 1982 were mainly swaps. National 3073 went to the Central Repair Works in 1982 for six months and an eighth, no. 3024, arrived during this time. 47 seat

RELH dual purpose 2051 was withdrawn in November 1981 and replaced 49 seat 2064 which in turn left the following January. Five months later 2089, an unusual Plaxton Panorama Elite-bodied downgraded RELH coach, which itself had arrived in May 1979, transferred out. Unlike other RELHs, 2089 had a Gardner rather than Leyland engine as it was originally ordered by, but never delivered to, Western National. From 1982, the bus shell RELH vehicles acquired an all-white livery with a single green waistband, a reversal of the standard bus livery.

It might have been assumed that the MAP revisions of July 1981 marked the low point in Stroud's bus services. Sadly, this was not so. While there were some minor changes between September and March 1982, mostly to put right some of the MAP's mistakes but also including a new works service in November 1981 between Hattersley Newman Hender at Woodchester and Stonehouse and the extension of

Changes in April 1983 had seen the withdrawal of five Bristol RELL service buses at Stroud, thereby halving the number at the depot. The May 1986 revisions saw Stroud's remaining five RELLs as surplus to requirements. Also no longer required was dual purpose RELH 2073 which had left Stroud in 1983 but returned in 1985. In all, some 50 REs in various guises had served the town since the type was first introduced in 1967. The last REs lined up for the camera were from left 1340, 1338, 1337, 1320 and 1305. 1338 had been new to Stroud and had featured experimental modifications. *Mike Ede*

certain journeys beyond Leonard Stanley for Stonehouse on 413 and 414 in March 1982, the downward spiral had began again in April 1983, the cumulative effect had been the withdrawal of another two per cent of mileage.

It had taken a little over two years for the company's position, stabilised first in Bath under MAP, to worsen again. Virtually all services were again affected in some way, including running time adjustments, in a review that encompassed much of the company's area, including town, city and country services in Weston, Bath and Gloucester. It was at this time that economies forced the closure of Trowbridge depot altogether, although the threatened Bristol city Winterstoke Road depot was saved. So far as Stroud was concerned, on the positive side, all journeys not terminating on the 413 and 414 at Stonehouse now did so. On the other hand, the Tetbury to Dursley works service on 415 was withdrawn but replaced with one operating from Stroud via Nympsfield and Uley. Although there was an additional departure for Dursley on 416 at 2120 on Mondays, the overall level of service was reduced. The 440 was curtailed at Wotton-under-Edge and the 448/9 at Tetbury (although the standalone but still limited services continued beyond, for Malmesbury). The level of service via Brewery Lane in Thrupp was again reduced. The 1750 workers journey on Mondays to Fridays to Whiteway was withdrawn on 563 as were the limited "late" evening departures to Oakridge (425) on Mondays, France Lynch (426) on Tuesdays and Fridays and Randwick (434) on Thursdays and Saturdays. The 418 evening variant to Dursley via the Stanleys was withdrawn entirely, albeit with a part replacement on 421.

Two other changes were of the highest significance. The first was alterations to the Chalford-Stonehouse trunk service (421). This was to see the Stonehouse leg largely intact at its pre-MAP half-hourly level of service but the transfer of certain journeys at the Chalford end to either 422 to Cirencester via Chalford or 426 to France Lynch, thinning the Chalford service. The half-hourly service was maintained as far as Brimscombe Corner and Bourne Bridge before the 426s, every two hours, left the main road for France Lynch. The welcome reintroduction of Saturday services to Cirencester was the result of this change.

The other significant change was a range of measures affecting Gloucester, Cheltenham and Whiteshill services. Both the Cashes Green to Whiteshill services (436/7) and the Cheltenham-Forest Green (564) services were curtailed at Stroud and as a consequence, most Nailsworth-Gloucester journeys diverted via Whiteshill. Shorts from

By this time, it was the Leyland National that had become the mainstay of Stroud's single deck fleet. This London Road line up of Nationals in National Bus livery, each with the "Stroud Valleys" name and NBC "Double N" logo is headed by 10.3m short 44 seat National 576, transferred to Stroud in December 1985. *Mike Ede*

Whiteshill to Forest Green operated opposite these journeys. With the extension of the hourly Gloucester-Nailsworth through services also to Forest Green, the pattern of services that emerged was not dissimilar to that beforehand in terms of local movements, just a redistribution of the way they operated. It produced an horrendous list of service number variations for Gloucester services depending upon whether buses travelled via Dudbridge (553, 554), Whiteshill (553, 555), Pitchcombe (554, 556) or Golden Cross (555, 556).

April 1983 also saw interesting and welcome developments so far as evening buses were concerned. Yes, there had been withdrawals at this time but also some remarkable reintroductions. These revolved around the ever-popular Mecca Bingo Hall, near Sims Clock. The building had reinvented itself as a bingo hall in 1973 following the closure of the Apollo (formerly Odeon and Gaumont before that) cinema, seeing an immediate bingo membership of 1,200. It was a popular source of entertainment especially amongst those less likely to have their own transport and the bus company capitalised on this, in conjunction with

funding from the bingo hall operators, with the introduction of services which terminated at Mecca, even offering a special return fare,
initially of just 50 pence.

On Tuesdays to Saturdays, a 2125 service 449 from Stroud bus
station operated via Mecca before continuing to Nailsworth,
Minchinhampton, Avening and Tetbury. The Mondays to Saturdays
2120 Chalford to Stonehouse passed Mecca before Stroud bus station.
This particular service diverted via Cashes Green and the Stanleys but
also served Ebley, as had the 417. On Tuesdays and Fridays, there was a
departure for Uley, Wotton and Dursley and on Wednesdays,
Thursdays and Saturdays for Frampton, Cambridge, Sharpness and
Berkeley (now the only link between Berkeley and Stroud!). There was
an amendment to Mecca services in November 1984, with revisions to
the Gloucester service to include a Mecca journey in each direction on
Tuesdays to Saturdays. Such Mecca services lasted until the early 1990s
when the bingo hall finally closed.

Consequent upon the April 1983 reductions, five Bristol RELL
single decks, being the last of the "flat-front" type at Stroud, were
withdrawn, although one of these (1070) plus former Stroud vehicle
1038, were to see further service with Potteries Motor Traction in
and around Stoke-on-Trent. RELH dual purpose 2062 and short
Leyland National 559 were both drafted in to replace two of the
RELL buses.

1983 was a decisive year for Stroud's transport in another way. In a
final outworking of the MAP process, which sought to ensure that bus
companies might better reflect the areas they served, including the
local political geography, the National Bus Company announced in
June 1983 that it was to split Bristol Omnibus into three. Stroud's operations, together with those at the Gloucester, Cheltenham and
Swindon depots, including Cirencester outstation, were to be transferred to a new concern called the Cheltenham & Gloucester Omnibus
Company Ltd, with its head quarters at the northern divisional offices
at 47 London Road, Gloucester. The rump of the company, which upon
the 1983 split formed Citybus and Country Bus (later Badgerline) divi-
sions, was to remain under the name Bristol Omnibus. The third
organisation was the old central works at Lawrence Hill, to be called
Bristol Engineering, which was designed to provide engineering
support to both companies. The move would cost the jobs of 48 head
office staff at a saving of £250,000 but Bristol Omnibus promised no
bus service cuts as a result. Bristol Omnibus' General Manager at the
time, Michael Wadsworth clearly stated that "I sincerely believe these

The summer of 1983 saw the extension of the popular X30 beyond Weston-super-Mare to Burnham-on-Sea. The X30 was often Bristol VR operated by this time and here a well loaded journey to Burnham is no exception, photographed when passing through Bristol. The X30's history can be traced back to the 702 which started in December 1971, was renumbered 830 in 1976 and again in 1982 as X30. Note the advert for Billy Graham. The X30 operated specials for Graham's Mission England event in Bristol. *Daniels collection*

changes can only lead to better services in due course. Very soon all three companies will be talking of growth in their business which must mean greater stability for the future and a better chance of breaking even financially."

National Bus appointed two able, young stewards to take the new concern forward, Mark Thomas as General Manager and Norrie Thomas, Commercial Manager. Both formally took up their positions ten days ahead of the 11 September 1983 official company launch. Before that, there had been interviews in July for other managers at which time Harold Smith, Stroud's District Traffic Superintendent under Bristol Omnibus, had been appointed Manager at Stroud. Smith had risen through the ranks, from a Red & White's fitter's mate in 1947 to driver, to inspector in 1956, senior inspector, and superintendent in

1980 and was well respected in the town.

Whereas the Bristol Omnibus rump of Bath, Weston, Wells and Bristol itself could be said to have a strong sense of cohesion, the same was definitely not true at Cheltenham & Gloucester, a company which was perceived to have scooped up the odds and ends. The choice of the name "Cheltenham & Gloucester" had not been a good one and the decision had been taken by National Bus and Bristol Omnibus. It immediately caused bitterness among Gloucester's politicians who felt aggrieved that they were not consulted over the move – in spite of the special relationship between city and company with its joint advisory committee – and who believed that one town was placed ahead of the other.

In fact, the company name did not matter at all, as the Thomases set about creating strong local brands. The public would see them as four separate companies, a low profile head office and the promotion of the local manager as the front man, with much autonomy. This was an absolute necessity given the lack of territorial cohesion and the huge differences between local markets. National Bus gave grudging agreement to the request to paint Gloucester's buses aircraft blue, an unusual colour which had seen little expression in the National Bus world of either leaf green or poppy red. In a popular move, Cheltenham's buses went red again and Swindon's followed suit. Green was fast disappearing but the decision was taken to retain it in Stroud as it better reflected the rural nature of the area.

Thus the seeds where sown for central and local managers to turn around a company that was perceived, certainly in Bristol, as being of little worth. Cheltenham & Gloucester management, in turn, felt that Bristol Omnibus had been inflexible. While this might have been the case centrally, it was not necessarily true of the Northern Divisional office. However, the new company was also no longer associated with the stronger Bristol union powerbase.

In Smith, Cheltenham & Gloucester had a strong local motivator who knew his area and market well and who enjoyed good relations with the local press. It was Smith who, without hesitation, suggested the name "Stroud Valleys" at his interview back in July, though this was a result of kicking around alternatives with his then Assistant, Christopher Blick. One such idea had been "Five Valleys Buses" and while geographically correct, it was rejected by Smith and Blick as giving insufficient identity to the network. The chosen identity struck the right tone in creating the image that the Thomases were after. Two months after the September 1983 split, the Stroud Valleys fleet name replaced Bristol, still in National Bus block style but unusually not side-by-side but with a larger "Stroud" above a smaller "Valleys", the first vehicle treated being double deck VR 5613 for the Cheltenham & Gloucester press launch in November 1983. It was as well, immediately upon the completion of MAP two years earlier, that Bristol Omnibus, unlike virtually all of its contemporaries, had decided against applying a gimmicky or idiosyncratic brand name to its local buses. The strong Stroud Valleys brand was to prevail at Stroud, in one form or another, for a further 18 years.

The 1983 reorganisation had other effects. The reduced number of vehicles at Stroud plus the need to operate on as firm a footing as possible meant that only one of the three senior inspectors was required. Two, Vic Watkins and Harry Wand, were almost at retirement and agreed to take redundancy if the younger, John Holmes, was appointed. All three were well respected and had been involved with buses and coaches almost man and boy. Holmes was indeed appointed and worked from 0530 to 1330. Thereafter, the Stroud cashier, Stan Roberts, would take over duties to 1800 under the revised job title of Cashier/Supervisor, wearing the black uniform of inspector. Such shifts as there were after 1800 became self-supervised. This arrangement might have been unusual but it proved a practical solution to supervision at Stroud. Following Holmes' own retirement in 1995, he returned to Stroud in October 2001 as a part-time monitor while in his early 70s in response to the concerns of the Traffic Commissioner over punctuality and reliability, not looking a day older than when he retired and still commanding the respect of drivers. Holmes also filled a role not seen at Stroud for many years: a visible presence on the bus station platform for passengers. With the barring of the public from entering the upper storey at the bus station buildings, hitherto all complaints and concerns became unjustly focused upon staff in the travel office who had difficulty directly resolving them.

Stroud's fleet upon transfer totalled 34 and comprised two Reebur bodied Ford Transits, three short 44 seat Leyland Nationals (two of which were to the more utilitarian "B" type specification), eight longer 52 seat Leyland Nationals, 10 Bristol RELL buses, three RELH dual purpose vehicles, a Leyland Leopard coach now downgraded to dual purpose work, and seven Bristol VRT double decks. Of the 11 now almost life expired RELL buses transferred to the new Cheltenham & Gloucester company, 10 were at Stroud.

There is no doubt that Wadsworth was right when he predicted that there would be company growth. There was a renewed confidence in the local industry at this time, much needed after 13 years of severe cutbacks. There were two main examples of company growth and both were linked. One was the "Cotswold" coaching arm and the other, particularly at Stroud, of "Pursesaver" limited stop "X" routes aimed at the leisure market. The Pursesaver network, to become branded under the Cotswold name, was a way of encouraging extra revenue from traditional and not-so-traditional bus users alike. Interest in new limited stop routes had actually started under the older regime with the introduction in July 1982 of the weekly X24 and X28 from Cheltenham to Stratford-upon-Avon and Worcester, respectively. That very month also saw the X26 service each Wednesday from Cheltenham to Bath via Gloucester, Stroud and Nailsworth. A second

Following the commercial network, it was only a matter of months until Cheltenham & Gloucester Omnibus passed from the state control of the National Bus Company to be purchased by its management. The new company did away with the National Bus Company "Double N" logo while leaving intact "Stroud Valleys" in NBC block. Bristol VR 5532, new to Stroud in 1981, is seen in Nailsworth Bus Station. Note the destination display for the post-May 1986 service from Nailsworth to Cheltenham via Stroud and Gloucester which replaced direct buses on 46. *Mike Ede*

departure on Saturdays was added in September and the route, invariably double deck operated, continued with modifications, including the introduction and withdrawal on Tuesdays and Thursdays of shorts from Stroud between March and December 1997, which fitted around school commitments, and the withdrawal of the Wednesday journeys on school days in 2000, right up to July 2001 when a severe driver shortage at Cheltenham forced its withdrawal.

In August 1982, the 830 limited stop service to Bristol and Weston-super-Mare was renumbered X30. This continued on Saturdays only over the winter period, starting from Nailsworth and operating as usual via Stonehouse but was curtailed for the winter at Bristol. An X35 between Stroud and Oxford via Cirencester was introduced experimentally over the 1982 summer and continued afterwards.

April 1983 saw further changes. When the summer season began for the X30 in April 1983, the service was extended beyond Weston, to Burnham-on-Sea via Brean. This was to be extended further, to Bridgwater, in 1985. A new X31 between Stroud, Nailsworth, Wotton

The next stage in the post-privatisation process was to apply a new Stroud Valleys logo to vehicles that had yet to receive a new livery. The NBC block remains but, as shown on 3073, one of the 1979 batch of Leyland Nationals, the new logo was applied to the vehicle's front. *Mike Ede*

To emphasise the change of control, buses began to appear in a new livery of mint green with a mid-chrome yellow flash. Leyland National 3048, wearing the single deck version of this livery, is seen on Cheltenham Promenade on the 92 service linking Cheltenham, Gloucester, Stroud and Nailsworth. The first single deck to appear in this livery was sister vehicle 3046. *Mike Ede*

and Bristol was introduced that April, with two departures Mondays to Saturdays to Bristol, thereby restoring something of the 400 service severed two summers before. For the Gatcombe Park Horse Trials near Minchinhampton over an August 1983 weekend, special X services operated from Swindon and from Gloucester via Stroud bus station, non-stop from Bath to Stroud as X26 and from Bristol as X30 before ascending towards Gatcombe.

The most ambitious service was the X68 between Stroud and Stratford-upon-Avon which from the end of May replaced the X28. It acted as a local express service Sundays to Fridays from Stroud and Gloucester via Cheltenham, Winchcombe, Broadway, Chipping Camden jointly with Midland Red South. There were two trips from Stroud and a further two from Gloucester. The service was short-lived, however, and withdrawn within a year.

It was the new Cheltenham & Gloucester company that was to market and mould these services into the undoubted commercial successes they became. Building upon the strengths of the X26, in October 1983 the new company launched a Mondays only X28 from

Stroud to Bath via Stonehouse, Dursley and Wotton which continued beyond its experimental period of January 1984. Then came the Saturdays only X33 from Stroud to Pontypridd (for the market) via Stonehouse, Dursley, Thornbury, Newport and Cardiff, the first stage carriage service from Stroud to Wales since the withdrawal in 1972 of the 415 Chepstow extension. Also in October was a Tuesday only X37 to Moreton-in-Marsh (for the market) via Stonehouse, Gloucester, Brockworth and Stow-on-the-Wold. This service was deliberately designed to have a short life, up to Christmas that year.

From March 1984, there were further X route developments. The X28 Bath run offered additional dropping off points at Yate and Chipping Sodbury. The X30 to Burnham was extended to start at Mason Road. Special X30s were laid on for Mission England with the great evangelist Billy Graham, between 12 and 19 May. The X31 became Wednesdays only and, in May 1984, the Wednesday only X38 was

The double deck version of the new livery had the yellow flash positioned differently as displayed on Bristol VR 5613, a relatively elderly ex-West Riding example which reached Stroud in 1983. It is seen at Maidenhill School on service 14 (formerly 414), operating via the Stanleys. This vehicle was one of the examples painted blue in the nineties principally for use on school contracts. *Mike Ede*

launched, again to Stratford but via Stonehouse, as well as Gloucester, Cheltenham and towns otherwise served by the X68. Then in September, Stroud Valleys launched an X32 on Fridays to Bristol via Stonehouse. A number of these services were suspended for the winter but it is of note that the X26 boasted connections and through fares from as far as Tewkesbury from November 1984.

Why were these services so well supported? First, they offered something different to the average bus service destination. Secondly, care was taken to ensure local pick-up points, where possible. Thirdly, fares were nothing if not reasonable. Fourthly and most importantly, while traditional excursions were declining in both importance and passenger numbers, the regular timetabled X service offered the leisure traveller something that they had not experienced to date: a regular, walk-on service without the need to book a seat, although the downside of this last point was that the service had to go regardless of numbers. There was no such constraint applied to the traditional tour.

Double decks were used on the X routes at appropriate times. Mostly, the vehicles were dual-purpose vehicles, coaches downgraded to be used on bus duties as required. This was where the "Cotswold" brand came in. At the company split, Cheltenham & Gloucester had inherited its share of the old Bristol Omnibus' final order of full coaches. Four Leyland Tigers with Plaxton Paramount bodies, were duly allocated to Cheltenham & Gloucester, plus two ordered by the company in its own right, five of which received National Express livery of base white with red and blue stripes, two for Gloucester for Edinburgh expresses and three to Swindon for London services. This left one spare, which was allocated to Stroud in a bold new livery of green and red on white. The vehicle, 2211, delivered in December 1983, became the flagship of the entire Cheltenham & Gloucester fleet. 2211 had replaced aging bus shell Bristol RELH dual-purpose vehicle 2062 which itself had only arrived at Stroud in April and which is currently preserved by the Stroud RE Group.

The open day venue for the launch of the Cotswold livery and concept was the Ryeford Hotel, between Stonehouse and Stroud. Taking addresses from the yellow pages for a mailshot, there was an opportunity to see a brand new coach.

It was shortly after this launch that the National Bus Company coaching subsidiary Black & White based at St Margarets Road, Cheltenham was effectively put under the control of Cheltenham & Gloucester, although the coach operator itself actually ceased trading a year later, in April 1985. An established and once large coaching name could so easily have ended up killing the Cotswold brand and, had events happened the other way around, Cotswold would undoubtedly have been stillborn. In the event, Cheltenham & Gloucester effectively bought some of Black & White's vehicles for £1, some being repainted into a new Black & White style, others appearing in Cotswold livery.

One of the first big Cotswold successes was in October 1984 when McEvoy of Woodchester (formerly Hattersley Newman Hender) hired 15 coaches to transport its entire workforce to London following a Queen's Award for Industry. Along with Stroud's vehicles, coaches were brought in from Cheltenham, Gloucester and Swindon for the purpose. This meant an 0500 start for some drivers and a return the following day at 0330. Only two of some 700 passengers taken to London the day before failed to make it back with Cotswold!

Coaching was one obvious direction in which a newly formed bus operator could develop its business, especially with the constraints on the local bus network placed on it by the county council. Cotswold coaches were available for private hire from Stroud, Swindon or Gloucester, with Black & White being the logical coach brand from Cheltenham. In addition to working certain limited stop journeys, they were available on traditional tours work to a variety of destinations and at a variety of fares. Yet even in Stroud, where the brand was most meaningful, the project was of a relatively small nature and created no more than a ripple among the established private hire coach operators of Rover (Hand's), Davis and Beavis.

Meanwhile, the Cheltenham & Gloucester company was now on its feet. Within a few months, the senior engineer at the time, Chris Sheppard, adapted the company's systems and procedures to dispense with the services of Bristol Engineering. Fewer vehicles needed to undergo the traditional seven-year rebuild and the depots themselves developed under Sheppard, allowed the company to take total control of its fleet. Meanwhile, because there were no joint services south of Stroud into Bristol Omnibus territory, relations between the two managements were not necessary and the one never met with the other.

The last service changes made at Stroud under the former Bristol Omnibus Company, in early September 1983, were minor alterations to buses to Randwick (434), Uplands (438), Kingscourt (446), Gloucester (555 only) and Cheltenham (564). The first under the new administration was a minor schooldays only change to the 564. There were further minor changes in November, including a one way loop for Uplands buses via Folly Lane and Peghouse Rise, an additional peak

Two Leyland Olympian double decks arrived at Stroud in May 1986 for use on the Cheltenham via Gloucester services 92 and 93. New four years previously, they represented a considerable improvement in vehicle quality over the Bristol VRs. 9521 swings into Gloucester Bus Station on a 92 journey heading from Cheltenham to Nailsworth. *Daniels collection*

Delivered new to Devon General in 1978, Bristol VR 5619 arrived at Stroud in 1987. It is seen at Whiteshill on service 37, a number introduced in May 1986 for the half-hourly service to Cashes Green via Stroud. *Mike Ede*

departure from Kingscourt to Stroud (446) at 0838 and the operation of the Saturday only "Bingo Bus" to Tetbury (449) additionally via Forest Green. Changes of this nature continued in January, March, April and May 1984.

It was in May 1984 that the company began to flex its muscles by renumbering some, though curiously not all, of its Stroud services. Gloucester services 553 to 556 became 55A, 56A, 55 and 56 respectively while the Stonehouse-Cirencester service 422 dropped the first digit while working alongside the three digit 421! Nailsworth locals became 1 to 6 and the 429 Stroud to Tetbury, the 29. The 447/8 between Tetbury and Malmesbury was renumbered 63 and 63A while services between Stroud and Tetbury via Nailsworth (449) and Tetbury and Cirencester (452) were combined as new through service 32. At the same time, a new minibus service operated with two return journeys Mondays to Fridays between Minchinhampton and Cirencester as service 64 and from July 1984 a further new service operated as 15A at the same level and on the same days between Stroud and Bisley Road via Bowbridge Lane and Park Road.

With the exception of X services which were unaltered, September 1984 saw the remainder of services renumbered, by dropping the initial digit "4". Exceptions were the 420 (Minchinhampton to Downfield Schools, renumbered 29A) and 564 (Cheltenham, 46, it's "traditional" number). In addition, the 15A introduced four months previously was renumbered logically as 27A. This renumbering in two chunks was actually more logical than it sounded. By not renumbering in May those services the company knew would see timetable changes in September, passenger confusion was minimised.

The cycle of minor changes continued throughout 1985, the most visible being the introduction in May of service 24 between Stroud and Thrupp Brewery Lane (with an extension in November to Lewiston Road, The Bourne), replacing a diversion on the 29 on Mondays to Fridays and the extension of 64 journeys from Minchinhampton to Chesterton Estate in Cirencester. The X services continued with their seasonal variations but with a five minute extension beyond Moreton-in-Marsh to Batsford Park. New in November 1985 was the Saturdays X57 from Gloucester to Swindon via Stroud and Cirencester. Also in November, services were reintroduced to Ebley Foxmoor Lane as service 20, following a 40-month absence, with two return journeys on Mondays and Wednesdays only. A further new service that month was a Thursdays only Stroud to North Woodchester service, numbered 57. The 33/33A Ruscombe and Randwick services were revised to connect at Whiteshill with the 55/55A, with through tickets being available.

By this time, deregulation was looming. Throughout 1984, Cheltenham & Gloucester management had towed the National Bus Company line in opposing the transport white paper by sounding the appropriate alarm bells, up to the assent of the Transport Act 1985. The Act was designed to deregulate bus services and return the bus industry to the free market. This was to be achieved by the removal of the stage carriage licensing system introduced in 1931 to check the worst excesses of competition at that time. As a result of the 1931 Act, fierce competition in Stroud between Red Bus and Western National evolved into peaceful co-existence and later, with successor company Red & White, into more-or-less full co-operation. Unlike that for express services, deregulated in 1981, there had been no changes to the legislative framework surrounding stage carriage services since the adoption of the licensing system.

Route licensing had done much to protect the position of existing operators in exchange for the maintenance of near comprehensive networks. Stronger services cross subsidised the marginal routes. The Conservative government of the mid-eighties felt that this was too protectionist, that increasing network subsidies stifled innovation and that competition might reinvigorate the industry. Smaller operators, with fresh ideas and lower overheads, should be allowed the opportunity of competing for passengers and be able to grow the market in the process. The then Transport Secretary Nicholas Ridley looked no further than an operator in his own Gloucestershire constituency – Pulham's of Stow-on-the-Wold – as an example of a small family run business successfully operating stage carriage services.

Whatever the rights and wrongs of deregulation, it certainly had a profound effect throughout Cheltenham & Gloucester Omnibus and its Stroud Valleys operation. Henceforward, operators simply needed to register those services it could run commercially and in this respect, the Traffic Commissioners would act merely as librarians for fuel duty rebate. Their power to grant or refuse new and varied services was taken away. The cushion of network subsidy was removed entirely. In most cases, transport authorities such as Gloucestershire County Council were required to tender any replacements for services not provided commercially which the authority considered as socially necessary.

The appointed day for deregulation was 26 October 1986 but Cheltenham & Gloucester had chosen to bring forward its commercial network to the preceding May. The changes were profound and the reasons for doing so were twofold. First, management wished to take control of its business. Since 1971, council involvement and funding had increased to the extent that by the time Cheltenham & Gloucester was formed, any sensible economy put forward by the company would result in an attempt by Gloucestershire to claw back network subsidy. This had the tendency to result in the status quo. Cheltenham & Gloucester's young management had not been party to the ever more complex deals struck with the former Bristol Omnibus and was therefore at something of a disadvantage. Secondly, a projected £349,000 shortfall in revenue support meant that action would have to be taken in any case.

The launch of the commercial network in May 1986 meant that services needed to stand on their own two feet. Although there were redundancies at Cirencester, which had come under the management of Stroud Valleys from September 1983, there were none at Stroud itself at this time. This was a remarkable achievement given the amount of revenue support required to keep the company afloat beforehand. Of course, the County Council did buy back certain services and a number of them have been tendered ever since. The mere fact that from now on the business would never have the prop of network subsidy ensured that great care would be taken in the running of the company. It was also surprising what the threat of competition could achieve in terms on the one hand of cutting overheads and on the other running services at break even that once fell into the loss-making category. Freed to control its own destiny, Stroud Valleys and its parent were able to identify and develop specific markets. This had been the basic flaw with MAP's more universal approach. Even so, in the early years, there is no doubt that there was an optimistic approach to what was and what was not commercial and, of course, the desire to win back tendered work meant that the Cheltenham & Gloucester pencil was sharpened considerably in a bid to retain work.

The introduction of the commercial network affected Stroud, Cirencester and Dursley rather more than in other parts of the county. Its proposals withdrew all remaining Sunday services, although here Gloucestershire stepped in, and reduced virtually all rural bus services. In this area, before any Council intervention, the network proposed the loss of bus services to 33 villages, 15 outlying urban areas, one hospital and six OAP communities. However, the result was that the viable network was able to support a number of enhancements on the more urban parts of the network. The greatest shock was undoubtedly the complete withdrawal of what had been the first ever motor omnibus route in Stroud, that between Stroud, Painswick and Cheltenham (46), previously operating at hourly intervals. Gloucestershire County Council came forward with a £100,000 rescue package for the entire county for the 22 weeks to deregulation and this included a fragmented service on the 46 with a four return journey service with a somewhat untidy timetable designed to provide, in as few journeys as possible, for the needs of as many shoppers and commuters as possible.

This rather negative aspect of the commercial network needs to be balanced against developments on the Gloucester corridor. Stroud Valleys introduced new service X4 from Forest Green and Nailsworth to Cheltenham via Stroud, Pitchcombe and Gloucester, with certain journeys, especially at peak periods, via Whiteshill as X3. Not only did this perpetuate an hourly service from Stroud to Cheltenham (albeit via Gloucester), it re-established a link from Nailsworth to Cheltenham, previously cut in April 1983.

Between Gloucester and Cheltenham, the service was designed to run as an extension of the "CG Flyer" via the Golden Valley by-pass, opposite the X1/X2 from Dursley, introduced in September 1984. The Cheltenham to Gloucester market was clearly one that the company wished to exploit in the brave new world and, in fact, is one that currently contributes much to its strong financial position. It was at this time that Stroud gained its relatively new Roe bodied Leyland Olympians, new in 1982, in order to upgrade the quality of vehicles operating the X3/4. Although not brand new like the VRs in 1981, the vehicles represented a significant improvement in passenger comfort. This "direct" service from Stroud to Cheltenham via Gloucester ceased in 1990 except at peak times and service 46 via Painswick to Cheltenham was strengthened to every two hours to compensate.

The changes to the Gloucester routes and diversion of most services via Pitchcombe affected Whiteshill buses. Where previously these had gone through to Nailsworth, in future they again extended across Stroud to Cashes Green at half-hourly intervals as service 37, replacing in part 55/55A. The circuit of Cashes Green was revised to operate in the same direction on each journey. To complement the hourly X3/X4 to Forest Green, Stroud Valleys introduced hourly service 34 from Stroud, giving Nailsworth the same level of services as before but improving that to Forest Green to half-hourly. Gloucestershire funded a limited evening and Sunday service which extended to Gloucester via Whiteshill.

With the reduction in Whiteshill to Gloucester services on what was the 55/55A, Stroud Valleys introduced a new shoppers' service 30 between Tetbury, Minchinhampton and Gloucester operating on Tuesdays, Wednesdays and Fridays via Whiteshill and on Mondays, Thursdays and Saturdays via Stonehouse, the latter diversion in part replacing service 51 between Stonehouse and Gloucester. The Gloucester extension lasted until May 1993.

There was some rationalisation and withdrawal from the Dursley direction on the evening "Bingo Bus" network. Meanwhile, weekday daytime service 16 journeys operated via Park Estate and were extended beyond Stroud to Uley, service 15 (Dursley to Uley) becoming much reduced. Also significantly reduced were buses to Bisley and Oakridge (25/25A), including some journeys now operating on various days of the week only, although shorts on this service to Mason Road were improved, with a broadly hourly service.

The viable network saw the uncoupling of direct services between Chalford and Stonehouse, a feature since 1919. Standalone services to Stonehouse (21) once again offered a 20-minute service. Gloucestershire funded a limited Sunday operation. Between them, buses to Chalford (22, now broadly hourly), France Lynch (26) and Minchinhampton (broadly two hourly on each route) offered a half-hourly combined service as far as Brimscombe Corner. In all, five journeys extended beyond Minchinhampton to Tetbury (service 30).

Minchinhampton buses via Amberley (renumbered 28, formerly 14) were henceforward to operate at two-hourly intervals, rather than hourly. Through services between Minchinhampton and Leonard Stanley were withdrawn. Leonard Stanley retained hourly services but, other than at certain peak periods, the extension to Stonehouse was withdrawn. Kingscourt saw an improved service with hourly buses.

Buses were rationalised between Stroud and Tetbury with the 29s running between Minchinhampton and Stroud, while Tetbury and Cirencester journeys on 32 curtailed to operate east of Stroud only with the new albeit limited service to Gloucester on service 30, as stated above, as a partial replacement. This also partly replaced the withdrawal of service 51 between Eastington, Stonehouse and Gloucester. The Randwick and Ruscombe services became 33 only and saw some rationalisation. Certain journeys on the 58 (Painswick to Gloucester) were again extended to start in Stroud, in part to compensate for the loss of hourly 46s along this road. The usual seasonal X services restarted either at or near this time, together with a new weekly X27 Cheltenham to Bath service via Brockworth and Stroud.

To fill other gaps, Gloucestershire County Council tendered some services for the 22 weeks to deregulation, the total cost for Stroud services being £43,000. A number of these passed to smaller firms, under contract. This was the first time that there had been independent operators running services in Stroud since Red & White. With the support of Stroud Rural District Council, Dursley Rural District Council had asked the Traffic Commissioners to consider smaller firms on unremunerative routes as far back as July 1968, as a response to continued fares increases. In 1986, these smaller concerns were now given a chance on uneconomic routes. Calypso Travel and KB Coaches operated the Gloucester – Stonehouse or Eastington services (14/51), supplementing Stonehouse service 30 journeys, KB's providing fare paying school services between Eastington and Maidenhill School plus a morning shopper. Abutting the Stroud Valleys network, Davis' of Minchinhampton provided services between that town and Tetbury and Rover Coaches (Hand's) of Nailsworth operated between Chalford

Throughout the 1980s, limited stop "X" services filled the gap in terms of leisure travel left by the reduction in the number of tours operated, although a parallel but less extensive excursion programme was operated throughout the decade. Important in attracting additional revenue for the company, they appealed to regular bus users and non-regulars alike. Cotswold liveried vehicles were invariably used such as 2113, a Leyland Leopard based at Stroud for two years from May 1987, seen here on one such limited stop route, the X35 between Stroud, Cirencester and Oxford. *Mike Ede*

and Cirencester and from Nailsworth to Malmesbury at school and other times, including some Saturday journeys. Large Gloucestershire independent Swanbrook Coaches operated under contract between Arlingham, Framilode and Stroud on Tuesdays and Fridays, replacing service 11, withdrawn under the viable network. Gloucestershire County Council itself took on a number of journeys but in Stroud perpetuated the weekly Salt Box to Cheltenham service, something it had operated since MAP, and between Stroud and Cirencester. Withdrawn service 20 between Stroud and Foxmoor Lane was not replaced.

Gloucestershire County Council's revenue support budget for the entire county, now targetted on tendered service replacements and de minimis payments, rather than pure network support, rose from £430,250 in 1985/86 (before deregulation) to £489,500 in 1988/89. These figures included the operation of Stroud Bus Station. Council officers calculated that the projected level of expenditure under previous network support legislation would have been £19,000 extra in 1986/87, £8,000 extra in 1987/88 but less in 1988/89.

The May 1986 revisions saw a fond farewell to the remaining Stroud Valleys Bristol REs, the last at Cheltenham & Gloucester. REs had played more than a significant part in Stroud's bus history. At 36ft, operated by the driver only, capable of carrying passengers not far short of the double decks at use only one year before their introduction, with wide, open entrances and pleasant interiors, these were the first "modern" buses at Stroud. Their use at Stroud spanned almost twenty years. Adding the RELL buses to the RELH dual-purposes, Stroud saw over 40 examples in use during these years. The last REs were bus numbers 1305, 1314, 1320, 1337, 1338 and 1340 (with 1287 having been withdrawn the previous February) and dual purpose 2073. At was fitting that 1340 should be used on a farewell tour of routes. Four Nationals were drafted in as replacements, although Stroud also lost three other Nationals at this time, which included no. 3500, Stroud's first Series 2 Leyland National, new in 1980 but entering Stroud service in 1984, although 3514 appeared that August. National 2s, similar to the Mark 1 but with a protruding front and without the roof pod so associated with the earlier National, were to become more common at Stroud after a number of second hand units arrived from Ribble and Cumberland from 1993.

Because of the premature introduction of a commercial network, deregulation D-day on 26 October 1986 brought with it few surprises so far as Stroud was concerned, unlike in many parts of Britain. The threat of competition from other operators did not materialise, although Circle Line, operating in Gloucestershire on local services for the first time in May 1986 upon the withdrawal of City of Gloucester's Slimbridge to Gloucester service, stepped in with additional contracted services between Stroud and Tetbury on the 30. Later, Circle Line was to operate between Stroud and Standish Hospital, again under contract. In October, many Stroud Valleys services changed but only in minor ways. There were, for example, the reintroduction of through journeys between Dursley, Uley and Stroud (15), the consequent deletion of the Dursley-Uley extension on 16, a marginal improvement in the number of journeys to Oakridge (25/25A), Summer Crescent (27A), the reintroduction of a Saturday service for Uplands (38) not seen since July 1981 and the withdrawal of the 45, a 46 variant from Cheltenham to Stroud via Painswick, Cranham and Birdlip.

Within days of deregulation came the announcement, on 1 November 1986, that the Cheltenham & Gloucester Omnibus Company Ltd had been sold to its management for some £980,000. Privatisation was the second strand of the Transport Act 1985 and the state owned National Bus Company had begun the task of selling itself off. Cheltenham & Gloucester's was the fourth completion. Being at the head of the queue had great advantages. First, the likelihood of a sale to a hostile bidder was small as interest in the process beyond in-house management bids developed only with later sales. Secondly, the price was favourable, the management team bought a bargain and was able to bid for other National Bus companies, a holding company by the name of Western Travel being formed to do so. Illustrating this point, Western Travel became the owners of far-less profitable Midland Red South in December 1987 but had to pay £3 million for it, the stakes having been raised by the likes of Brian Souter's Stagecoach.

The management buy-out began a period of considerable optimism for the company. The company had built a successful business having detached itself from Bristol's remote management, created a branded coaching unit, restructured prior to deregulation, promoted strong, local brands with competent local managers, found itself in an environment free of local authority control and, finally, had gained control over its own destiny. Little wonder that there was a renewed willingness to succeed, probably more so than at any other time in Stroud's bus history.

To emphasise the transformation from state to private ownership, Cheltenham & Gloucester adopted new liveries, dispensing the National Bus drab styles. Based on the initial colours adopted at the launch of the company in 1983, they were to a completely new design.

From June 1987 for two summers, the X35 was extended beyond Oxford to Woodstock. Leyland National 2 no. 3514, dating from 1980 but at Stroud from August 1986, was one of four such vehicles based in the town. It is seen at Woodstock. *Mike Ede*

Launched in November, Stroud's was a darker "mint green" with a "mid-chrome yellow" stripe. Although it might be argued that an individual brand and livery for each of its main operations – Stroud, Swindon, Cheltenham and Gloucester – would cause engineers headaches as vehicles moved from depot to depot, the need once again to reinforce strong local branding in distinct markets was of paramount importance. Even the drivers' uniforms and tickets were colour coded to match the vehicles at each depot.

The green and yellow at Stroud had been inspired by Badgerline's livery. However, it was sufficiently different. The mustard yellow flash extended on double decks from the middle third of the roofline first to the rear lower deck and then extended forward in an L shape to a point towards the front wheel. A similar design adopted for single decks starting at a point over the passenger entrance/driver's cab and extended and broadened along the roofline to the rear before it dropped to the rear wheel arch in a broad and acute L shape.

Its application may have been conservative by today's standards and it even might have been described as somewhat crude but at the time it was original, fresh and it certainly set the vehicles apart, exactly what management wanted. Although a family resemblance was adopted throughout the company, it was Stroud's livery that was the most

No. 600, a PMT bodied Mercedes-Benz 608D, arrived in 1984 as the first ever new vehicle in the fleet. Together with sister vehicles 601 and 602, which directly replaced the 1979 Reebur Transits, they were ordered initially by Gloucestershire County Council for use in Nailsworth, Stroud and Cirencester. Painted in Cotswold livery of the time but with the Stroud Valleys rather than Cotswold name, the vehicles also operated with the Gloucestershire County Council crest. No. 600 was unusual in having no built-in destination display. By the time this photograph had been taken, the National Bus Company logos by the side of the Stroud Valleys name and on the upper red stripe at the front had been removed. *Mike Ede*

successful with its strong contrast in colours. It was also in keeping with the rural parts of the area, cheap to apply and left sufficient space for commercial advertising.

Another added advantage was that the company now in private hands had already been through the process of cutting costs and restructuring for the viable network. Nevertheless, the negotiations leading up to the sale were quite harrowing. Here was a mostly young management team prepared to put their continued faith in a company about to face an entirely new operating environment. No one could be sure what competition might be around the corner, or the extent of any such competition.

Service changes in the first years of deregulation happened often although, with some obvious exception, they tended to be relatively minor in nature each time. By this time, Stroud Valleys had begun to issue individual timetable leaflets rather than a network booklet as had previously been the case. They were cheaply produced in house and offered great flexibility. These were supplemented by Gloucestershire's own leaflet publicity, principally along corridors in which the county had a tendered interest. The early years of deregulation saw a considerable number of minor changes to both commercial and contract networks and it became increasingly difficult for passengers to keep up to date with the number of changes and build up a picture of exactly what was operating. Added to this difficulty was the need to request leaflets at Stroud bus station – there was no self-service at this time – which did little to promote the entire network to passengers.

The overall number of these minor changes was actually quite immense. This reflected the ease with which managers could make decisions and the amount of information now available via the electronic, computerised Timtronic ticket machines now being used (even though these were somewhat unreliable and sometimes disrupted services), which for the first time gave accurate passenger boarding and alighting data. This was perpetuated by Almex Magnet machines in April 1989. It is worth noting that prior to the Timtronics, Setright manual ticket machines had been used since the merger of the fifties. It became easy for managers to adjust specific journeys and if this caused confusion with the travelling public, at least it meant that experiments could be put in place or taken out quickly and effectively. Management was able to react quickly to customer demands and suggestions. One example of the scale of changes was service 30: there were no less than ten leaflet issues within the first two years of deregulation! In the period from 10 October 1986 to the end of the decade, there were no fewer than 180 separate changes to services.

Some of the most significant changes between D-day and the end of the eighties included on-street running at both Bristol and Bath, from January 1987. This reflected the conditions and charges imposed on "foreign" operators using other operators' bus stations. Other X services were also revised. New among them was a seasonal service from Stroud to Wotton-under-Edge, Bath, Wells and Wookey Hole (X32). For a limited time, Stroud joined the "South Coast Express" in summer 1988 with the operation of the Gloucester to Weymouth service via Stonehouse, Stroud and Nailsworth, picking up at 0830 at Stroud and arriving at Bournemouth at 1122, Wareham 1155 and Weymouth 1230. The departure from Weymouth was 1630. Stroud Valleys lost the

Swindon council-owned operator Thamesdown Transport operated infrequently between Cirencester and Stroud in the late eighties. New to London Transport in 1977, 39 seat Bristol LH no. 43 loads at Cirencester Market Place. Such a vehicle type had not been seen at Stroud for some eight years. Note the vehicle's condition which reflected the narrow roads along which it travelled. *N P Daniels*

contract for Cirencester journeys via the intermediate villages (64) to Thamesdown Transport in January 1989 plus Sunday work and some journeys to Tetbury. Thamesdown operated LHs on the 64 and even resulted in that type's reappearance at Stroud after eight years, on the Saturday variant of this service.

It was in February 1989 that no smoking was introduced on all Stroud Valleys buses.

The ICI Fibres contract was lost after 31 May 1989. Known by the pun "The Nylon Run", it operated up to three times a day from Stonehouse, Ebley and Stroud to Brockworth via Painswick and Cranham and had been a feature of the town's bus operation since the British Nylon Spinners (and before that the Gloster Aircraft Company). For many years, it had been the first bus off Stroud Bus Station at 0445 out to Stonehouse and, should a driver not turn up, the duty inspector who booked on at 0430 had to take the bus out.

In spite of the continual though minor adaptations, the years between 1986 and 1990 were good ones at Stroud as the company had increased control of its own destiny. This new-found confidence would stray a little into the next decade.

CHAPTER 9

1990–2003
FROM MOTORBUS
TO STAGECOACH

The overwhelming optimism felt among management and staff at Stroud Valleys over the previous half-decade was to continue into the early nineties. Stroud's buses maintained its very own green and yellow identity and livery and its able local manager, Harold Smith, had for the previous four years played a commercial as well as operational role.

Smith who in 44 years at Stroud had taken only three days' sick leave, retired in June 1991. The stability that had been Smith's, and had seen a small band of managers since 1950 as district traffic superintendents in Herbert Sollars, Roy Burnett and from the mid 1970s, Peter Collins, was to end. Collins' post reflected the emerging importance of the county council as he was area traffic superintendent for Cheltenham and Gloucester but based in Stroud. From the nineties onwards, there was a period where managers seemed to come and go as regularly as the buses themselves. Henceforward, managers would on occasion be anything but local, controlling either Swindon or Cheltenham as well as Stroud. The reduced fleet in the town, by now no more than around 35 vehicles, did not always require a local manager in an age when overheads needed to be cut.

Yet, there were plenty of management decisions and innovations to be made. One in the early nineties was the introduction of minibuses in large numbers, for both urban and rural use. Unlike the experiment of 1979 with minibuses on the lightest routes, a new breed were progressively to find themselves the backbone of rural routes, regardless of vehicle types previously in use. A number of them came into play in the late eighties with the conversion, for example, of certain journeys on services 15 (Dursley via Uley) and 30/1 (Tetbury area and to

Gloucester) in September 1988 and January 1989 respectively. This brought in two additional minibuses to Stroud in January 1989, which were Alexander converted 16 seat Ford Transits, new to Cheltenham & Gloucester Omnibus in 1985.

The minibus was set to hit Stroud big-time on 9 December 1991, however, with the delivery of 607, 608 and 609 from East Kent and 611 and 612 from Go Ahead Northern, plus at around this time, native registered 616. All were 16 seat Ford Transits converted by either Dormobile or Alexander, initially one in Stroud Valleys' green and destined for rural services such as to Oakridge (25) as straight replacements for larger vehicles. The others were designed for an improved service to Cashes Green. There was scorn from some of the drivers collecting the Transits when it was discovered that one of their number took a tow-rope with him, yet this was actually required on the homeward trip! In addition, one of the vehicles boiled on the M25 motorway.

The Cashes Green route was numbered "C" and, like a number of urban services in Gloucester, Cheltenham and Swindon, were branded as "Metro", a bus service which offered something different. Metro had been phenomenally successful for Cheltenham & Gloucester Omnibus. Introduced in Cheltenham as routes A, B and C in October 1985 to Charlton Kings and Springbank, the concept was swiftly followed two months later in Gloucester to Matson, Coney Hill, Wheatway and Abbeydale. Other routes followed as Cheltenham & Gloucester saw their potential. This was a remarkable turnaround for the two managers whose views on the minibus operation had earned them the nickname within National Bus circles as "the Doubting Thomases" just two years earlier. Yet, the success of Metro was such that some routes saw a 40 per cent growth in business.

Metro offered something of an alternative to the traditional bus service. First, being minibused, it stood out as obviously different and ideal for urban environments with congested highways and estate roads. Secondly, frequencies were set at 10 minute intervals at the very least, which meant that passengers no longer needed to refer to a timetable. Thirdly, Cheltenham & Gloucester took great care to ensure that the livery did not resemble the traditional service bus. It was devised by the company's managing director, by then Norrie Thomas, who happened to be driving a metallic silver car at the time (during a period when such a colour was less common as nowadays) and, to him, there seemed no reason why buses should not also be metallic. To this silver-grey base were applied red and blue stripes used on the vehicle representing the two base operating colours at Cheltenham, Swindon and Gloucester in a similar fashion to Caryle demonstrators. The effect was finished off by the addition of "Metro" in large white letters on the side.

Stroud Valleys therefore applied the Metro thinking on the Cashes Green route. Before C took over from conventional buses, it operated a parallel service for a week beforehand in shadow. From its inception to October 1994, it operated as a "hail and ride" service around Cashes Green. There is no doubt that C was a successful move but the passenger growth was never as strong as elsewhere, at about 25 per cent. The urban minibus had by this stage began to play itself out as a force for change. Nevertheless, some Metro C 16 seat Ford journeys did find it hard to cope with loadings. Prior to route C, buses to Cashes Green had operated at half-hourly intervals beyond Stroud to Whiteshill with double decks but this route was now operated to Whiteshill only.

Generation was also partly to do with the service terminating not at the bus station but on-street. C was the first route to find itself back in the town centre itself since 1960. This, again, followed the situation in Cheltenham. At the earliest opportunity, Cheltenham District country services had abandoned the somewhat down-trodden and tucked away Royal Well bus station for on-street running adjacent to the town centre shops, a situation which better fitted the company's image. More buses became visible to more people and passengers welcomed the change as proved by the positive, even buoyant, effect on revenue generation.

Would such a system work wholesale in Stroud? Up to his retirement, Smith had been open-minded about the approach. However, something had to be done about Stroud bus station no matter what. The bus station had passed from Bristol Omnibus to Cheltenham & Gloucester at the new company's formation. By 1984, Cirencester's bus station had closed. It was before privatisation that talks began in September 1985 between company and county council over the disposal of Stroud's site for commercial redevelopment but local authorities considered that its closure would increase town centre traffic congestion, this being before the construction of the east-west by-pass. To overcome this situation, the local authorities agreed to take on a lease for the site so that it might be retained as a public amenity for the time being, held by Gloucestershire County Council. The lease was due for renewal in 1991. At this time, Stroud Valleys offered the two covered bays at the multi-storey end for hire and they housed some industrial relics which were awaiting a more permanent site (eventually at Stratford Park museum). The bays had previously been used for lubri-

Long serving employee Harold Smith, left, retired in 1991, after 44 years. As District Traffic Superintendent since the seventies and later manager, Smith had considerable ability. In fact, the depot had been labelled "Harold's Buses". In this retirement shot, Smith is joined by traffic assistant Christopher Blick who during the nineties was himself to take over as manager. In the background is 498 FYB, former Black & White Leyland Tiger CDG 207Y, which passed to Cheltenham & Gloucester in 1985. *Chris Blick collection*

cation, washing and fueling and were demolished four years later.

By 1991, planning permission had been granted for the Stroud Valley's London Road garage site as part of a deal which included the adjacent Stroud District Council land, used for maintenance vehicles. However, the economic climate was not right at this time. Nevertheless, with the completion of the by-pass and a perception that the bus station's location was not convenient, Cheltenham & Gloucester was keen to look at on-street running, the company believing that at Rowcroft, George Street and Russell Street, there was sufficient space for buses.

In November 1990, there were warnings of considerable expenditure needed on the bus station's fabric. The concrete apron had in 1960

The age of the minibus began at Stroud in earnest in December 1991 with the arrival of six second-hand 16 seat Ford Transits. One was painted in the green and yellow Stroud Valleys livery of the time but with the yellow flash arranged not as standard single decks but in a similar fashion to those on double decks. The others operated in "Metro" livery of base metallic silver grey with blue and red stripes and were used on new route C to Cashes Green. *Mike Ede*

been constructed on bad ground and it needed replacement at a cost of £100,000 or the annual lease costs, payable by the County and District Councils jointly on a 70:30 basis, would need to rise from £32,000 to £70,000, it was estimated. It was felt that now was the ideal time to abandon the bus station in favour of on-street running.

The town council objected, stating that the bus station should be retained as ideally situated. Nevertheless, the majority of passengers arriving in Stroud from Minchinhampton, Chalford, Oakridge and France Lynch, who had a choice, already opted to alight at a set-down-only stop at the junction of London Road and Russell Street at Sims Clock rather than continue to the bus station. The police also objected, on road safety grounds, especially concerning the large numbers of school children changing buses. The issue of children was to be overcome by using the larger reservoir space in the bus station at school times only.

The reaction from passengers on Metro C to town centre running had proved positive. With the minimum of fuss, Stroud Valleys hurriedly arranged site meetings for town centre locations and agreed a date for change in February 1992. Buses would henceforward use stops at Rowcroft, the Subscription Rooms and Russell Street. Stroud Valleys' publicity at the time trumpeted on-street running, branding the bus station as "edge of town". Certainly, by this time Merrywalks Shopping Centre above the bus station could be viewed as increasingly marginal to the economy of the town centre. Stroud Valleys opened travel shop premises at No. 3 John Street at the same time as the move from the bus station.

What was the town's response to this potentially radical change? Although there was modest growth in passenger revenue following the decision, indicating a certain popularity with passengers, it was criticised from nearly all quarters. A protest march was called but in the event saw only some 30 marchers. While some drivers were open minded about the switch, others felt the loss of their own bus station amenities. Drivers were expected to carry a day's takings across town to pay in. With the town's street pattern making it impossible for an

The idea was that the Metro branded Transits would appear solely on Route "C" but from time to time, traffic requirements dictated otherwise. Here 612, an ex-Northern vehicle, is seen at Nailsworth Bus Station preparing to depart for Minchinhampton, a service usually reserved for green examples of this vehicle type. *Geoff Gould*

observer to see all departures at once, inspectors found it difficult to control drivers and vehicles and, should a driver not turn up to relieve a through bus, passengers both on board and at the stop would be left stranded, wondering what was going on, until someone noticed.

Traders complained that doorways were used as shelters and that there was insufficient pavement space for queuing passengers, let alone those wishing to walk around the town. There were complaints of litter on the streets at bus stops. The buses were also causing congestion, in spite of fewer cars now needing to enter the town centre, following the construction of Dr. Newton's Way. A number of cartoons hung in the company's office drawn by employees illustrating the chaos and these found their way to the press.

Taxi drivers also opposed on-street running. They were unhappy that their rank outside King Street Parade was moved and as Rowcroft was also used as a reservoir for buses, taxis were banished to Rowcroft Retreat. In retaliation, taxi drivers offered to pick up passengers waiting at bus stops free-of-charge upon return to the town, having previously dropped off a fare. Drivers would display a blue "T" on a white background to alert passengers to this free service and, although it soon fizzled out, it had the greatest impact on town routes. It also generated more negative publicity and was, in fact, filmed. In spite of all this, buses remained steadfastly on street for much of the nineties.

The early 1990s saw their share of service changes. In March 1990, buses between Forest Green, Stroud and Gloucester were extended to Cheltenham at peak times only rather than hourly throughout the day, and this followed the improvement of service 46 to Cheltenham to two hourly. February 1992 was also the date of some major service changes which included two services per hour to Stonehouse (20,21) and one per hour to Dursley (16) diverting via Stonehouse to give a combined 20 minute service over the common section. By 1994, the 16 had extended to Uley, providing an hourly link to Stroud, importantly via Dursley. Stroud Valleys also provided an hourly link to Chalford (22), the extension (again!) beyond Leonard Stanley for Stonehouse (14), co-ordinated hourly departures between Stroud and Minchinhampton, either via Amberley (28, now extended to Tetbury in place of 29) or Brimscombe (29), more direct buses for Cheltenham (46), though still broadly every two hours, and a new circular service for Mason Road, operating hourly as 35.

Adjustments to this network were made in 1993, 1994 and 1995 but the initial excitement of deregulation and privatisation, which fostered rafts of minor changes at short notice following the scrutiny of each

February 1992 saw the closure of Stroud Bus Station to passengers, except at school times. Buses moved on street at that time. There were many within the town who felt that the streets were unsuitable for buses. The point was illustrated by this shot of Russell Street where Leyland National 3050 with a Leyland Olympian pause at a stop while the driver of Bristol VR 5540 waits to find a space, the vehicle's near side indicator flashing. In the midst is Inspector Ian Taylor. *Mike Ede*

individual journey on a route, gave way to a more stable, network approach. The "Bingo Buses" were gradually withdrawn: the 2130 Stroud-Gloucester (93) at the end of October 1994, and the 2133 Stroud-Dursley via Cashes Green, the Stanleys and Stonehouse in October 1995. The 2130 Stroud-Tetbury ran on Tuesdays to Saturdays only until October 1994 then continued on Thursdays to Saturdays for a further year. All remaining evening journeys, including services to Painswick and Chalford fitted in before the Bingo Buses, were withdrawn in October 1995. For those without a car, this meant that the clock had been turned back one hundred years. Between May and October 1992, there was a Saturday only late night service 92 from Gloucester at 2345 to Stroud via the Peel Centre, which included a cinema.

Those concerned at the appearance of the town held sway over those who wished to see buses on the streets and following its purchase by Stroud District Council, buses returned to the bus station in April 1997, save initially for those to Cashes Green ("C", five per hour, from Rowcroft), Kingscourt (36, hourly, from Russell Street) and Summer

Internal company humour at the so-called chaos sparked a number of cartoons, some of which found their way to the local press. One such cartoon was by local employee *Alan Davies*

Crescent and Mason Road (34/35, hourly, from the Subscription Rooms). These three services eventually migrated to the rest in the following November. This left just one service on the streets of the town, which was the infrequent Wednesdays only 67 from Stroud to North Woodchester which moved from Russell Street and George Street to London Road that very November.

The sale of the bus station was somewhat coincidental as Cheltenham & Gloucester had always wished to see it sold and any future development would be easier if the site was in council, rather than company, hands. The deeds ensured that the council, along with the Merrywalks developer, should be given first refusal if the site was to go. Meanwhile, a 33 seat PSV traffic ban was put in place in 1997 along London Road preventing buses negotiating the town centre, a move that operationally seemed odd as services from Minchinhampton, Chalford, Oakridge and France Lynch had to turn left just prior to a potential major passenger destination, avoiding the new Waitrose store!

It was the sale of the London Road garage site in 1992, reported to be for over £1mil, in use since the 1920s and extended in both 1936 and 1963 with the parking area paved in 1967, that enabled Waitrose to construct its new premises in the town. The supermarket itself was actually on the former District Council yard with the bus garage site being used for car parking. There was nothing particularly life-expired about the London Road premises, save perhaps for a spot of minor subsidence and the deal was similar to those being taken throughout the industry at the time, to improve the company's financial bottom line. It had taken several years to reach a situation where an unnamed concern was interested in the site and the deal was closed as swiftly as possible. Buses continued to be stabled at the London Road site even during the supermarket's construction. Nevertheless, the company identified premises at a former hauliers at Bowbridge and this became fully operational by the summer of 1993. It was not ideal but better suited the commercial realities of Stroud's buses. Some work, including maintenance on Stroud Valley's double decks, passed to Gloucester

London Road garage had been in use since the close of the 1920s and seen several improvements over the years but apart from that, it was very much as it was when new, as this internal shot shows. It was sold in 1992 as part of a deal which would eventually see a Waitrose supermarket in the town. In the depot building are Leyland Nationals 3048 and 3050, Olympian 9517, VR 5535 plus an unidentified VR and two Transits. 3050 shows Cirencester local service 9 on its blind. Traffic and engineering responsibility passed between Stroud and Swindon depots over the years and on this occasion, Cirencester's route network was Stroud's responsibility. *Mike Ede*

depot. At the same time, Stroud District Council invested in the bus station, buying it outright for what was reported as £250,000. The original Cheltenham & Gloucester plan had been to use the bus station for maintenance.

Many services, in fact virtually all of them, were extended from their street side terminus to Waitrose in November 1993. This logical step, being easy to serve as it was relatively close to the town centre, proved disappointing in traffic terms and was soon dropped, from February the following year on "C" and all other services from that October with the rather peculiar exception of the limited service between Stroud, Nympsfield, Uley and Dursley which served Waitrose to July 1995.

November 1993 saw the off-peak frequency on "C" reduced from every 10 to every 12 minutes. "C" became 37 in October 1994, was further reduced in frequency to every 15 minutes and has remained at this level, save for a short period from March 1997 to April 1998, when it became six per hour again.

October 1994 saw a fairly widespread reduction in levels of service on Saturdays, though most of this has subsequently been reversed. For example, the direct buses to Stonehouse via Ebley were stepped down from every 20 to every 40 minutes after 1500 on Saturdays. At this time, there were no departures at all on Saturdays on the 29 to Minchinhampton, including onwards to Tetbury (restored December 1998) and the 38 Uplands service was withdrawn on Saturday afternoons. Even the Forest Green-Nailsworth-Stroud-Gloucester trunk service saw reductions on Saturday early mornings and afternoons.

Industrial relations during this period were not always at their best. During the negotiations surrounding both the bus station and garage site, drivers saw the potential for large profits yet in Stroud at any rate, there was only a small possibility of a pay rise owing to the poor trading position of the company. This prompted Stroud Valleys' Driver Brian Dutton to pen the following poem, which appeared in the February 1992 issue of the company's house newsletter. It makes mention of the intense competition between Cheltenham & Gloucester and Circle Line, something that did not affect Stroud, of course.

Lets feel sad for the poor bus driver,
Of the Cheltenham and Gloucester fleet,
All we want is a simple fiver,
Which our bosses just won't meet.
So we keep the pressure on them,

Tell them 'On their bike',
That we don't believe the bulls***
But we can't afford to strike.

For bulls*** to me it appears to be
As the money still seems to flow,
They can revamp the station, sell London Road
Where's my share, that's what I want to know?
The money still finds its way to the top
And there it seems destined to stay
Yet us mortals below have to take a chop
And we'll stay there if they have their way.

So Norrie get your skates on
As our claim is surely just
All we ask for is a slice of the bun (A cake is too big)
Before the lot goes bust.
Lets have no more hard luck story
But one day all things will be fine,
If we can't get a piece of the glory
We may all go to Circle Line.

Brian Dutton

Thomas, Managing Director, entered the spirit of the occasion by
replying to Dutton, also in verse:

Let's not feel too sad for the driver
Who, at least, can have that fiver.
The company has offered to increase the rate
And let those who need it, work extra late.

Bulls*** in Stroud it may appear to be
But there the competition we don't see
London Road is an extra liability
Relocated we improve our profitability

Bust is not a state we can allow
We must protect our position for now
Or surely we'll end up in Hempsted one day
All of us at Circle Line's rates of pay.

Norrie Thomas

During the building of the Waitrose supermarket, buses still used the area for parking, as shown by Leyland National 3011 which, at the time of the photograph, was shortly to be withdrawn. *Mike Ede*

Meanwhile, in a surprise decision taken in the Spring of 1993, Cheltenham & Gloucester decided to abandon its coaching activities in order to concentrate on its commercial core bus services. Coaches attached to bus operations had played more of a significant part at Stroud than any other local depot, for more than 70 years, apart from during the Second World War. Often, they had been dual purpose so that they could be used on local bus services when not required for tours, private hires or express reliefs. Since the 1950s, there had been a fine heritage of Bristol LS, MW and RE type dual purpose vehicles. The 1993 Cotswold vehicles at Stroud certainly fell within the dual purpose category, even though the larger vehicles were actually by now full coaches capable of bus work which, over the past couple of years, had acted as Stroud's spare vehicles, as the number of buses was progressively reduced. This reduction meant that coaches could only be used as such during school holidays and this meant that coaching made less business sense.

Between 1989 and 1993, coaches would be used on school specials, private hires, limited stop X services and Cirencester school services 82

The depot moved to a site at Bowbridge in 1993. It offered plenty of secure parking and provided facilities more in tune with the realities of bus operation at Stroud in the nineties. Officially opened on 12 October 1993, it afforded the Chair of Stroud District Council, Cllr Sybil Bruce, the opportunity to realise the ambition of a lifetime by sitting at the wheel of a Mercedes-Benz. *Chris Blick collection*

to 85, won and operated from 1990 now that Cirencester had been under the control of Stroud since the late eighties. The garage was still undertaking coach tours in the late 1980s but these were constrained by the need for spare vehicles, as previously mentioned. Coaches were also used for rail replacements as Stroud was ideally placed in the middle of the line from Swindon to Gloucester. They were perfect in terms of comfort and by this time had replaced double decks on rail replacement duties. Staff had proven that they could react quickly with vehicles and a coach could be at almost any point on the line within half an hour.

Stroud was more affected by the coaching decision than any other Cheltenham & Gloucester depot. It had a separate 10 driver EU coach roster. However, the vehicles were now aging and elsewhere on the company, vehicles had already been sold. Stroud Valleys had made it known that given an investment, management would make coaching work but this was not to be and there was some bitterness at the corporate decision to withdraw. Among Stroud's vehicles receiving Cotswold livery since the brand was introduced were minibuses 600,

After the initial six Ford Transits, minibus arrivals at Stroud improved in size and quality with the arrival of the first of a number of Mercedes-Benz. Among them was 677, a 25 seat Mercedes 709D which was painted with a blunt yellow stripe. *Mike Ede*

601, 602, 678 and 679 and full sized vehicles 2111, 2112, 2113, 2211, 2213 and 2124. 2111, AFH 198T, withdrawn in 1987, was an elderly Leyland Leopard with Duple bodywork new to Cheltenham in the fleet of National Travel (South West), as Black & White had become at that time.

Between 1990 and 1991, three of Stroud's Mark 1 Leyland Nationals entered the Cheltenham & Gloucester "National 3" refurbishment programme. The project was to upgrade a number of former Bristol Omnibus vehicles but was confined to 13 examples only, refurbished when there had been a major engineering failure. The project suited Cheltenham & Gloucester well at the time as it was not keen to rush into any new conventional bus purchases during competition at depots other than at Stroud but needed to upgrade its stock. Re-engined with a DAF unit and with a totally upgraded interior including extra stanchions, non-slip flooring and improved heating, the budget for each vehicle was between £20,000 and £25,000. Each vehicle was marked out with a "National 3" badge and operated in a revised livery dependent on the depot's base colour, in Stroud's case with an angular yellow L shaped stripe and grey window surrounds edged with white. Only one

National 3 operated at Stroud, this being former native 3046 (renumbered 306 after refurbishment), having been withdrawn for upgrade in March 1991, entering service afresh a month later but leaving Stroud for Cheltenham that December.

Further minibuses were introduced in August 1993 for bus service work, this time new to Stroud and registered in the previous month. The 1993 four Mercedes 811Ds with Marshall 33 seat bodywork (803 to 806), joined later by a fifth of the same batch, directly replaced 52 seat Mark 1 Leyland Nationals, by now showing their age. At this time, Stroud had gathered an eclectic mix of such vehicles, operating as many as 15 in 1986 and 16 by 1990. 3012 and 3037 were both former Midland Red vehicles and another, 3011, was ex-Badgerline.

There were protracted negotiations at the introduction of 803 to 806 and 12 drivers were downgraded to a lower minibus rate of pay. The arrivals plus a similarly L-registered Mercedes 709 with PMT body were the first brand new purchases in any quantity for Stroud since the 1981 Bristol VRT double decks and the three minibus replacements, actually funded in 1984 by Gloucestershire County Council. In the

Mercedes 709D nos. 678 and 679 were curiously used in "Cotswold" white, green and red livery even though they were built with 25 bus rather than dual purpose seats. *Mike Ede*

years to 1981, Stroud had seen its share of new vehicles as investment at the depot had remained high. The fact that there had been few brand new arrivals since – with second hand Nationals predominating – indicated the need for peak time school capacity rather than a requirement for large numbers of minibuses. In any case, Cheltenham & Gloucester saw few conventional vehicles from new.

Stroud Valleys was to see major alterations as 1993 closed, one that would signify lasting change for the town and its buses. Western Travel, the holding company, sold its bus interests to acquisitive Perth-based Stagecoach Holdings in November 1993. This had followed some considerable time when Stagecoach had pressed the Western Travel board to sell, by now comprising five directors compared to the original 10. Aside from the fact that the earlier prices were below expectations, Western had made it clear that it did not wish to sell. However, Stagecoach had contacted the company again six weeks beforehand with an improved offer of cash and shares. The amended offer came at a time when Western was seeing increasingly bitter competition on its acquired South Wales subsidiary Red & White's routes and had only recently acquired a costly 49 per cent interest in Circle Line, an independent on its home turf whose competitive activity ceased the previous May.

The offer was made and accepted within 24 hours. In order that Stagecoach, newly floated since April on the stock exchange, could demonstrate that its momentum was continuing, the giant insisted that the offer be accepted quickly, the day before Badgerline was due to float, in fact. The imperative was therefore on Stagecoach to offer a good deal, which brought wealth to a small number of men. Mark Thomas, by then Western Travel's chairman and Norrie Thomas, its development director, left the company as Cheltenham & Gloucester came first under Stagecoach Midlands and later Midlands & North. Stagecoach had not wished to buy Western Travel's Chipping Campden hotel interest, which had been purchased upon the advice of investment bankers who recommended that the board needed to diversify, and this was subsequently sold later. On the sale of Western Travel, Mark Thomas commented that it was in the best long-term interests of staff, customers and shareholders. The Cheltenham & Gloucester era at Stroud had been a good one and 1994 saw a new company at the helm of Stroud's buses.

At the time, Stroud Valleys staff were somewhat despondent at the sale. Rightly or wrongly, Stagecoach had developed a negative reputation in their eyes. There were parallels with the situation 43 years

In spite of Stroud Bus Station being used for passengers only at school and college times, the site remained open for supervisory staff, drivers and the parking of buses. Leyland National 2 no. 3502, by this time renumbered as 362, is seen leaving the Bus Station to take on service at a town centre bus stop. The vehicle has by this time received Stroud Valleys "refurbished" livery which included grey window surrounds, a white roof, a white waistband and a sharp yellow flash. Although in Stroud Valleys livery, the operator had passed to Stagecoach by this time and there is a Stagecoach liveried minibus following 362. *Brian Ward-Ellison collection*

before at the takeover of both Red & White and Western National by Bristol Omnibus. In the 1990s, times were changing, however. Even in the late eighties and early nineties, there had been staff who had worked for many years throughout the Bristol Omnibus period and been molded by it. Stroud had a reputation for families working together on the buses. On the other hand, Stagecoach was perceived as remote and uninterested in Stroud's future. Stagecoach would, however, enable the fleet to be updated with relatively modern, though often second hand vehicles, which would have been difficult to achieve had it remained in the hands of Western Travel.

Coincidentally, Christmas 1993 saw the 25th and final Stroud Carol Bus season. Sponsored by a Woodchester rail tour broker, Stroud Valleys also donated diesel and maintenance free-of-charge. During a quarter of a century, this Stroud tradition had raised over £140,000 for local charities. It was also as good an example as any of the "family atmosphere" on Stroud's buses. Nevertheless, with the reduction in the number of staff at Stroud and increasing fears over the vehicle's relia-

Stagecoach, as new owners from November 1993, set about repainting the entire fleet, a process that was to take two and a half years. Freshly painted in Stagecoach corporate white with orange, red and blue stripes but as yet without the "Stagecoach Stroud Valleys" logo above the driver's cab window, is Bristol VR 5528 undertaking a swimming bath run for Bisley's Bluecoat School. New to Stroud, it had arrived back following a stay at Swindon. *Mike Ede*

bility, since 1984 former city fleet Bristol FLF Lodekka double deck 7246 dating from 1966, the committee decided that the idea had played itself out. Added to this was the fact that the vehicle was now stored at Gloucester which meant that preparation was more time consuming both in terms of travel and the need to move several other buses before work could start. A further key consideration was that, year-on-year, the amount collected had increased and there was a real concern that, at some stage, the previous year's record would not be broken. Cheltenham & Gloucester did, in fact, offer a Ford Transit 16 seat minibus as a replacement for the double deck to the Stroud Valleys volunteers but, understandably, the gesture was turned down! It was ironic that as service buses were being replaced by minibuses, so potentially was the Carol Bus.

Following the takeover in November 1993, Stagecoach Holdings set about stamping its mark on buses and operations. Announced in February and implemented in March, a company-wide reorganisation saw two jobs redundant at Stroud, one administrative and one managerial. The manager was local man and magistrate Christopher Blick who, following a career in the armed forces, had settled into 27 years' service at Stroud first as conductor, then driver, then inspector and, as Smith's right-hand man, as traffic assistant. Upon Smith's retirement, Blick had become traffic manager under Bill Bishop. Blick had been honoured in 1985 with the British Empire Medal for his work for charity, which had included many years' commitment to both the Carol Bus and Bristol Omnibus Welfare Committees. The Transport & General Workers' Union did not blame Stagecoach for its streamlining but deregulation itself. In an interesting comment, which forgot that few wheels turned after darkness at Stroud, the local representative commented that the redundancies had been necessary to ensure that Stroud remained as competitive as possible against potential challengers creaming off daytime buses. Blick's replacement was to be Bob Sewell but this never actually happened. In a remarkable turn of events, Blick found himself reappointed in August 1994 as manager until his early retirement in 1996.

Stagecoach also applied its corporate thinking to the buses themselves, adopting the name of "Stagecoach Stroud Valleys" for its Stroud and Cirencester operations, although Cirencester became "Stagecoach Cirencester" from 1995. It began repainting buses immediately in the livery adopted by Stagecoach some 12 years earlier, in base white with three stripes in orange, red and blue which ran along each vehicle's entire length below window level before sweeping up at the rear in a chevron, first towards the front and then towards the rear. The repainting process was a long one and it was not until July 1996 that the last green bus, EWS 743W, a Bristol VRT double deck, formerly no. 5535 but by then renumbered 228, received the white treatment. Not surprisingly, the passing of green buses, which had been a feature of the town since the Western National days and the unstoppable tide of white, drew criticism from drivers and passengers alike. Steve Evans, acting manager at Stroud Valleys, observed that there had been a lot of comments about the change.

On and off throughout the nineties, particularly between 1990 and 1995, there were driver shortages, more acute at some times than others. On one occasion, Circle Line stepped in. This followed Stagecoach's acquisition of the remainder of the Hempsted firm, although it remained as a separately liveried low cost unit of Stagecoach till it closed in 2000. The situation at Stroud had become reliant on drivers' willingness to undertake overtime to keep services going and this went on so long that eventually such work was banned

A Nottingham preservationist is restoring Bristol FLF 7246, which retired as Stroud's last Christmas Carol Bus in 1993. Dating from 1966, the vehicle was the first ever purchase by the Cheltenham & Gloucester Omnibus Company, on behalf of the Stroud Carol Bus Committee, in November 1983. Significant progress is being made in its restoration to full Bristol Omnibus condition but at the time of this shot in April 2003, one panel is left as a reminder of its former duties. *N P Daniels*

because drivers became jaded as a result. The temporary solution was for the entire 93 service between Forest Green, Nailsworth, Stroud and Gloucester to pass to Circle Line in 1995 in an effort to overcome the paucity of drivers. On another occasion, in 1997, drivers banned overtime again, this time because of management imposed revisions to terms and conditions. Circle Line again found itself on the Stroud trunk route but Stroud Valleys' drivers would not permit those from Circle Line to use canteen facilities and this resulted in Circle Line breaks being taken upstairs in the bus station building.

Minibus deliveries continued throughout the nineties and they dominated the town insofar as rural and non-trunk urban routes have been concerned, especially since the withdrawal from the Bulk Scholars Agreements. In 1998, half the fleet was made up of such vehicles, whereas between 1990 and 1993, the percentage varied from 10 to 18. Over the years, the quality of these minis has improved from the 16 seat Transits from 1991 and early Mercedes 608s with 18 seats to the current 709s and 811s with between 25 and 33 seats. Six Mercedes-Benz 709Ds arrived new in 1995 and 1996 with Alexander Sprint 25 seat bodies to be followed by five Mellor bodied 17 seat Iveco Daily minibuses arrived new at Stroud in 1997. By this time, Stagecoach locally was beginning to move away from vehicles with such a limited seating capacity, with the earliest Ford Transits being withdrawn by 1994 and later Transit imports by 1997. With such a limited seating capacity, it was not surprising that the Ivecos lasted in some cases just over a year. The 12 subsequent minibus purchases, by now all second hand, were with 25 or 33 seat bodies.

It is pleasing to record that towards the end of the nineties and into the 21st century, the decline in bus service has to some extent been reversed, even if in 2003 the situation again looks bleaker. True, evening services are non-existent and those on Sunday extremely thin but Stagecoach Stroud Valleys, from October 1996, began to make some significant and major improvements.

Funding from the Rural Development Commission from October 1996 saw the introduction of a Monday to Friday peak return service from France Lynch, Brownshill and the burgeoning Manor Farm estate

The white and stripes of Stagecoach had now become familiar in the town during the mid and late 1990s. This shot, outside the Subscription Rooms, was taken during the month before most services returned to the Bus Station in 1997. *Geoff Gould*

at Bussage via Bisley to Cheltenham on Mondays to Fridays. Branded "The Bisley Flyer", the 47 started from France Lynch at 0750 and operated to Cheltenham rail station, returning at 1730 and tended to have regular driver Alan White behind the wheel. It was specifically designed to encourage modal shift from car to bus. Improvements to the road infrastructure had not kept pace with the huge Manor Farm housing development since 1978, with the minor roads toward the Air Balloon via Througham and Foston's Ash seeing considerable increases in Gloucester and Cheltenham commuter traffic. Those few passengers using the 47 commented that the fares were reasonable when compared to car parking but the loss of flexibility, especially regarding the return time from Cheltenham, meant that passenger support for the service was disappointing and it lasted to August 1997.

Using the Flyer's down time in Cheltenham to greatest effect, in an unusual development, Stroud depot operated hourly Cheltenham Town Service "S" between the general hospital, railway station and Springbank between October 1996 and February 1997. Because it was the Bisley Flyer bus, the vehicle was branded not for Cheltenham but Stroud itself, although it would have to take an observant member of the public to have noticed anything different or unusual about the vehicles used. Cheltenham drivers covered meal breaks. Prior to "S", the Stroud bus found itself temporarily on the "M" and "P" routes to Swindon Village and Ewens Farm, both currently operated by Beaumont Travel.

1996 saw a brief resurgence in works service activity. During the forties, fifties and sixties, and to a lesser extent in the early seventies, the bus had been the backbone of Stroud's valley bottom industry, to factories such as Sperries Gyroscope, Hoffman's, Newman Henders, RHP, ICI Fibres and Lister's. Lister's at Dursley had subsidised Rovercards but this arrangement had ceased. With the relocation of Cirencester firm of Mycolex from a site adjacent to the former Bristol Omnibus depot at Love Lane to Bourne Bridge, came a works service which commenced in July 1996 from Cirencester at 0622 to the site and on to Stroud. The dead journey out of Stroud became a service bus which met an earlier coach to London at Cirencester. The journeys were withdrawn in June 1999.

The April 1997 changes included most services returning to the bus station, more regular services and simplified routes. Key among the changes was the introduction of a half-hourly service between Stroud and France Lynch on Mondays to Fridays (26), where previously it had been hourly. It recognised the potential growth of housing from 1978 at

Leyland National 2 no. 3514 as renumbered 368 pulls away from Gloucester Bus Station in1996. Services between the Stanleys, Stonehouse and Gloucester have seen various levels of service throughout the years and are now largely supported by Gloucestershire County Council following agreement with Stagecoach. The vehicle itself was modified to carry wheelchairs. *Dave Farrier*

Manor Farm between Eastcombe and Bussage on the hill to the north of the Golden Valley and has paid off with services being sustained at this level up to April 2003 and the inclusion of Saturdays at half-hourly intervals in 2002. Other April 1997 developments included hourly buses between Stroud, the Stanleys, Stonehouse and Gloucester (service 90) initially between 0900 and 1415 but later throughout the day (as service 14). Also, Cashes Green benefitted from the reintroduction of a 10 minute frequency, now numbered 37/37A/37B rather than "C", with certain journeys via Sainsbury's, opened on the Red & White depot site at Dudbridge from March 1997. Nailsworth minibus routes were curiously renumbered 61, 61A, 61B, 61C, 62, 62A, 62B and 62C by Gloucestershire County Council. June 1997 had seen the diversion of Forest Green to Gloucester buses via Dudbridge, Dudbridge Hill and Bath Road.

Stroud's buses were to get as far as Swindon for a short time from November 1997 as the 77 service from Cirencester to Swindon via

The growing proportion of minibuses has continued under Stagecoach's ownership. Flanked by 805 and 804, two of four 33 seat examples purchased new for Stroud by Cheltenham & Gloucester in 1993, are two ex-Red & White vehicles, nos. 1403 and 808. All are Mercedes-Benz 811D chassis and all are currently in service at Stroud as at the time of writing. *N P Daniels*

Lechlade was extended to start from Stroud. Stroud's buses reached Lechlade last from 1920. The new activity resulted from the award of the 77, previously operated by Thamesdown two months earlier, which became Stroud's responsibility owing to a paucity of staff at Cirencester. The timetable was somewhat distorted with morning journeys towards Swindon and afternoon returns. Of the three vehicles used on this service, one operated an 0730 Swindon start.

Also, from October 1997, the direct Cheltenham service (46) saw a major boost with the welcome reintroduction again of hourly services plus quicker journey times. However, services 18 and 19 which acted as works journeys for Lister's were withdrawn in December; they had previously been under contract to Gloucestershire County Council since January 1996.

Building on the 1997 changes came more good news for Stroud's passengers in July 1998 with the increase in service from 60 to every 30 minutes between Stroud and Gloucester, alternately via Whiteshill (92) or Pitchcombe (93), a level of service not seen at Stroud except on Saturdays to 1981. Both the 92 and 93 continued to start at Forest Green. However, buses to Cashes Green (37/37A/37B) now operated at 15 minute intervals via alternate journeys via either Paganhill or Sainsbury's. The Tetbury service 29 saw more departures while there were hourly services to Uplands.

From 1997, Stroud depot operated five Iveco minibuses with unusual Mellor bodies. 606 was one of them but they lasted no longer than two years, owing to their restricted seating capacity. *Dave Farrier*

July 1998 was the time when Stagecoach Stroud Valleys severed its links with the Bulk Scholars Agreement, something that had been a feature of Stroud's operation for many years. Under the agreement with the local education authority, Stroud's service buses carried pupils entitled to free school transport on the local service network. Over the years, this was true of services to Maidenhill, Manor and Highwood Schools but especially to schools with large catchment areas, namely St. Peters, Tuffley and the Downfield schools of Marling and Stroud High School for Girls, off Cainscross Road.

The Bulk Scholars Agreement was unique in the former Bristol Omnibus' Northern Division and reflected Stroud's geography. In order to ensure free transport for those qualifying for it under the terms of the Education Act 1944, Gloucestershire County Council had entered into a symbiotic agreement with Bristol Omnibus which saw the greater part of the area's pupils travelling by ordinary service bus. Not only did this have a considerable affect on the company's bottom line, it governed the size of buses required. Because the agreement was simply for transport from A to B without time constraints, it allowed Bristol Omnibus the flexibility in some circumstances to operate two schools each morning and afternoon with one vehicle. The Downfield schools, both grammars, had significant catchments but the agreement meant that some pupils would be able to board buses soon after the close of school at 1550 hrs while others had to wait to 1605, 1620 and, for those travelling to Bisley, Oakridge and France Lynch during the seventies, 1630 or even 1640.

During the sixties and seventies, Cainscross Road would be a sea of green as buses queued for Downfield pupils with the exception of a contract run to Frampton-on-Severn by Locke and later, upon take over, by Ladvale.

In spite of this, the agreement did pose its problems and proved to be something of a constraint. In the mid-seventies, it accounted for 13 vehicles used solely at school times out of a Stroud allocation of some 50 at that time. It also stifled the growth of commuter traffic, which was obviously put off by hordes of pupils. After protracted and careful consideration, during which time Stagecoach concluded that the economics of the agreement were not as sound as they looked, notice was given in an attempt to grow the commuter market and to rectify the hiatus suffered by fare paying passengers where everything either stopped or altered at 1430 for scholars. It meant fewer large, conventional buses, an increase in cheaper minibus provision and was moderately successful in achieving its objective.

It also meant that with a few early exceptions (two double decks to Minchinhampton and a bus to Painswick, both now lost), most scholars travelled on vehicles provided by smaller operators, with Ebley Coaches being a particular winner at Downfield. However, because Stagecoach Stroud Valleys was the only local operator to offer double decks, contracts operated by Stroud depot included the retention of buses to St. Peters and from Stonehouse, Stroud and Chalford to Cirencester at school times plus the movement of some college students. Stagecoach Stroud Valleys did accommodate pupils upon its network where space permitted, provided that there were no specific alterations to times and routes for them, as there had been in the past. Drivers viewed the end of the agreement with some concern as it appeared to them that the company was throwing away solid revenue.

One other problem associated with the Bulk Scholars Agreement was the minor trouble caused by pupils at the end of the school year. It was not unknown for a school to pay for a conductress to have her hair permed or dressed following a "flour and eggs" episode. However, discipline at schools was strict and this only presented itself as a problem on occasions. It was rare for a pupil to be ejected from the bus, though this did happen. One driver recalls that a pupil was thrown off the bus a short while from Stroud at Lightpill one afternoon, only to be picked up by the driver's own son who was working the following bus to

Stagecoach adopted a revised image in 2001, dropping the name "Stroud Valleys", in use since 1983, in favour of "Stagecoach in the Cotswolds". At the same time, the company modernised its corporate livery. First to be repainted at Stroud were the four Dennis Dart super low floor vehicles with Alexander ALX200 bodywork, nos. 932 to 934 plus one of the Olympian double decks, 105. *N P Daniels*

Nailsworth and who knew nothing of the incident that had occurred minutes before. Son overtook father along the route and the boy arrived at the bus station ahead of his original bus.

Other changes from May 2001 included the reintroduced of hourly through running between Forest Green, Stroud and Cheltenham; improvements to Mason Road, Uplands and Kingscourt which all enjoyed at least hourly and at times half-hourly frequencies on new circular town services 8/8A, with daytime levels of service similar to or better than their 1970s level; extension of all weekday, daytime services between Stroud, the Stanleys and Stonehouse to and from Gloucester; and the extension to Nailsworth of the Stroud-Amberley-Minchinhampton service. From this date, Stroud local small operator Cotswold Experience, previously specialising in bespoke tours centred on Bath plus school contracts, was successful with County Council local services to Standish Hospital, to Cheltenham via Slad and Sheepscombe, to Oakridge via Bisley, to The Bourne, North Woodchester and on Nailsworth local services. The firm's proprietor,

Andrew Lawton, won a Eurosolar UK environmental award in 2002 for his innovative use and promotion of vegetable oil sourced biodiesel which he used across his fleet. The fact that Lawton had been able to retain the same drivers during a period of driver recruitment problems at Stagecoach would seem to indicate that he was a fair employer. Three of them were formerly Stagecoach employees.

April 2002 saw additional changes including the withdrawal of the town service 8/8A journeys via Sainsbury's, further funding from the County Council to secure service 28 (Stroud - Minchinhampton) but with the withdrawal of the Minchinhampton - Nailsworth section and further thinning of the Stroud - Dursley via Uley service. The linking across Stroud of the 26 and 92 resulted in hourly through running between France Lynch and Gloucester and the reintroduction of conventional vehicles to France Lynch. The April changes in all saved two minibus workings with only minimal changes to the number of departures from Stroud.

At this time, other Stroud firms began to see increases in work. Smaller companies had started on local bus services at the introduction

Bus no. 104 was one of five high capacity Leyland Olympians with Alexander 87 seat bodies new to Cheltenham & Gloucester for Swindon in 1990. Four of the five have been based at Stroud, reflecting the need for moving large numbers of school pupils. Here, 104 sports the new livery. *Daniels collection*

by Stroud Valleys of its commercial network in 1986. Ebley Coach ran occasional Saturday services from Minchinhampton. They had began by operating services from Stroud and Painswick to Gloucester via Cranham or Birdlip as well as to Standish Hospital in the early nineties. Ebley also took over the Tuesdays only 32 service from Camp to Cheltenham which had been Stagecoach Stroud Valleys on an emergency tender for three months. Swanbrook Coaches provided the Sunday service to and from Cheltenham (46) and the Mondays to Saturdays Stonehouse-area Village Link Red Route, one of three bookable, demand responsive services. From April 2002, Beaumont Travel were successful with most 40 journeys between Stroud and Wotton-under-Edge. The era when first Cheltenham & Gloucester and then Stagecoach sought to defend its territory at any price was now over. If commercial or tendered work could not pay its way, it was sacrificed and if this meant a smaller operator winning it, so be it.

Nationwide, from January 2001 Stagecoach reorganised its bus division. Cheltenham & Gloucester, together with services in South Wales and those remaining in the Forest of Dean after many purges, merged under an operation called Stagecoach West & Wales. The name was deliberately chosen to avoid confusion with the train operating company Wales & West Trains though almost nine months after the Stagecoach reorganisation, the rail operator split and the Wales & West name disappeared. The regional head office for buses operating as far afield as Cardiff remained at Cheltenham but, unlike the days of the mid-eighties when Stroud was largely responsible for its own development, there was to be much less local control, as the Stagecoach bus division in Stockport henceforward began to have a greater influence. Matters had gone full circle. Yet in May 2003, coinciding with structural changes at Stagecoach's bus division, it became apparent to Stagecoach that the growth associated with free concessionary travel in Cardiff from 2001 and elsewhere in Wales from 2002 should reverse the West & Wales merger. Stroud's operations again found themselves within a subsidiary akin to that operating before 2001, albeit with Ross-on-Wye added to the Cheltenham & Gloucester Omnibus depots.

Of particular interest was the introduction in 1998 of initially two and then a further two nearly new former Stagecoach Oxford super low floor "easy access" Dennis Dart/Alexander ALX200 single decks, initially labelled "LoLiner", for evening and Sunday contracts between Stroud, Stonehouse and Gloucester, which demanded vehicles of this type. During the day, they were used on the Stroud-Stonehouse (21) and Stroud-Dursley via Stonehouse (16) routes, which in combination

Mirroring trends elsewhere, smaller operators are currently winning tenders for socially necessary bus services. Since 2001, Cotswold Experience has been operating to Standish Hospital (service 19), Slad, Miserden, Cranham & Cheltenham (23), Oakridge (25), The Bourne (27), Randwick & Ruscombe (30) and the Nailsworth local services. In April 2002, the firm moved from the Bus Station to Cornhill, were two Mercedes-Benz minibuses are seen seven months afterwards. *N P Daniels*

under Stagecoach had returned to daytime 20 minute frequency between Stroud and Stonehouse. The vehicles were successful in generating business. From May 2001 all renumbered as service 20, the four vehicles with one other (double deck 105) were the first to carry Stagecoach's new livery and "Stagecoach in the Cotswolds" branding in 2001. This new branding, which had a softer, swirling look and feel and was introduced as part of Stagecoach's 2001 reorganisation, recognised that the public throughout Britain could identify with the Stagecoach image and colours but disliked the aggressive stripes associated with it. "Cotswolds" branding was seen not just in Stroud and Cirencester. Two vehicles outstationed in Pulham's yard at Bourton-on-the-Water for a contract that lasted from December 1998 to September 2001 were also given this treatment and one duty even involved one of these vehicles running dead each day from Cirencester to Stroud for refueling and cleaning.

Also acquired in 1999 from Stagecoach Manchester via Cheltenham were two Marshall 40 seat single deck Dennis Darts (these had been acquired when Glossopdale was taken over) which were supplemented by three similar Darts and three Volvo B6s all with Alexander Dash bodies which were transferred from Swindon and Gloucester a year later. Also from Manchester in 1999 were six Volvo B10M-55 buses with 49 seat Alexander PS bodywork. New three years previously, they were intended for trunk routes 92, 93 (to Gloucester) and 46 (to Cheltenham) and were seen as ideal for this purpose but in February 2003 were replaced by five high capacity Leyland Olympian double decks, all ex-Stagecoach London and all one year younger. These joined the three stretched Leyland Olympians with Alexander 87 seat double deck bodies bought brand new for Swindon in 1989 but transferred to Stroud principally for school work, one in 1995 and two others in 2001.

The last bus of Bristol Commercial Vehicles manufacture was withdrawn at Stroud in 2000, being a Bristol VRT double deck, no. 223, formerly a Gloucester vehicle converted from a dual-door to a single-door layout. Thus ended a long association of Bristol manufactured vehicles with the town going back to the Western National days. The Bristol bus manufacturer had closed in 1983. It is worth noting that the Bristol VRs new to Stroud in 1981 were the last brand new conventional buses for the town and the subsequent large bus fleet has been second hand. This contrasts sharply with the days under Bristol Omnibus when Stroud had as high a proportion of brand new vehicles as any country depot. The change had resulted from Stroud's lack of commercial robustness and was inevitable, especially when compared to the commercial success that was in nearby Gloucester and Cheltenham.

Severe driver shortages again surfaced in the years from 2000, although some believed that this was more about driver retention. During the summer of 2002, there was reported to be insufficient staff to cover as many as 17 duties and, as a result, drivers were drafted in from as far afield as South Wales, Scotland and the north of England, all staying at the Imperial Hotel in Stroud. Road and supervisory staff from both Swindon and Cheltenham were also used at Stroud.

9 July 2001 was the last Saturday operation at Stroud bus station's booking office. A six days-a-week facility had been available in Stroud in both the Western National and Red & White days. There was also a reduction in Monday to Friday booking office operation from this date. The Saturday closure in particular was much criticised. Indeed, it was a popular day for the sale of National Express tickets, business that has now transferred to the Tourist Information Centre at the Subscription Rooms.

The trend towards more healthy and positive developments continued in April 2002 when services between France Lynch to Stroud were extended as 92 to Gloucester, providing a new and important through link from the growing areas of France Lynch, Chalford Hill and Manor Farm to Gloucester. This necessitated the improvement of Saturday services to half-hourly, previously hourly even after the 1997 improvements. Not only this, it introduced conventional vehicles once again on the France Lynch route, though the corresponding short working to and from Stroud on the opposite half-hour remained a minibus. This development was to be short-lived, however.

The Town Service 8/8A, though continuing to serve Uplands, Summer Crescent and Mason Road at existing levels of service, saw changes with the withdrawal of the Kingscourt and Dudbridge/Sainsbury's sections. Dudbridge and Sainsbury's continued to be serviced on the Nailsworth and Cashes Green routes while Kingscourt saw the reintroduction of a dedicated, hourly service 36.

The section of route between Minchinhampton and Nailsworth on service 28 was withdrawn as Gloucestershire County Council stepped in to secure what is now the Stroud - Minchinhampton service via Amberley. The withdrawn section saw two buses a day in each direction only, as service 62. Service 28, now largely a secured service, was to have been withdrawn in its entirety. It is hard to believe that up to the 1970s the route saw half-hourly operation as either 428 or 430/1 to Minchinhampton via Amberley.

Most other services saw minor timetable changes. The 35 (former 15, Stroud - Selsley - Uley - Dursley) was further cut backs to one return trip on Mondays to Fridays. May 2002 brought fares increases of between 10 and 15 per cent to reflect the need to address the scarcity of drivers and increased insurance costs. In otherwise low inflationary times, an increase of this magnitude brought with it renewed public criticism over fares hikes. Passengers felt that the service should improve in proportion to the increase but had failed to do so.

However, Stagecoach continued to feel the pressure of falling demand and increasing wage bills and, following some considerably negative press coverage and complaints from passengers who, after 17 years of deregulation, still misunderstood the commercial nature of the bus industry, put in place revised services throughout Gloucestershire from 27 March 2003. These were mitigated following some £100,000 worth of additional subsidy from Gloucester County Council throughout the county.

In actual fact, withdrawals were relatively minor in nature at Stroud. This included an hourly rather than half-hourly service between Stroud and France Lynch (26). However, because the half-hourly service introduced in March 1997 had actually served Eastcombe, Brownshill and Tanglewood Way (Manor Farm) on an hourly basis in any case, Stagecoach planners' replacement loop meant that as few people as possible suffered loss of frequency, although arrivals in Stroud at 0712, 0812 and 0932 were somewhat difficult to bear for workers and scholars when compared to the previous 0715, 0740, 0805, 0840 and 0915.

Last minute negotiations with the County Council ensured that the planned withdrawal of half the weekday hourly service between Stroud, The Stanleys, Stonehouse and Gloucester (14) did not take affect. The 14 through The Stanleys had seen quite a chequered history in recent years: it was first extended to Gloucester via Stonehouse hourly in May 1993 and renumbered 90 but 17 months later operated hourly between Stroud and Leonard Stanley and every two hours beyond to Stonehouse and Gloucester. In March 1997, along came an hourly service to Gloucester but only in the off-peak. In April 1998, it was diverted from Bristol Road in Gloucester to serve Cole Avenue while in July 1998, the whole service was curtailed at Stonehouse and renumbered 14 again before going through once again to Gloucester hourly that December!

From 27 April 2003, the Sunday service 14B saw a reduction from five to four journeys and its complete withdrawal over the Sunday only Stroud to Forest Green section. However, services 14B and 46 along this road had ran on top of each other in any case. Service 46 between Nailsworth, Stroud and Cheltenham passed from Swanbrook to Ebley Coaches and although extended to start at Forest Green, it, too, was reduced, from four to three journeys. Through ticketing became available between Ebley Coaches and Stagecoach to maintain a Forest Green to Gloucester link.

What remained of the Stroud to Dursley via Nympsfield and Uley service passed from Stagecoach to Ebley Coaches who since May 2002 had been operating a school journey. That between Nailsworth and Minchinhampton (62) also passed to Ebley and the operator combined the two to provide a Minchinhampton to Dursley service via Nympsfield, albeit of a limited nature.

Direct services between Stroud and Cirencester as service 54 improved to hourly intervals in September 2002 to enable Stroud drivers once again to operate Cirencester local services, enhancing and replacing the 22 to Chalford. However, the little used Fridays and Saturdays journeys operating between the two towns via Minchinhampton and Daglingworth and the Mondays only service from France Lynch to Cirencester were withdrawn without replace-

Other smaller operators picking up work in the Stroud area have included Beaumont Travel (service 40 to Wotton-under-Edge, from April 2002), Swanbrook and Ebley Coaches. Swanbrook has been operating between Nailsworth, Stroud and Cheltenham on Sundays since 2000 on which route SB51 SBK, a Marshall bodied super low floor Dennis Dart, is seen in August 2002. However, the route passed to Ebley Coaches in April 2003. *N P Daniels*

ment. These services had been reduced to very infrequent levels in 1993.

Stagecoach chose to uncouple its hourly services between France Lynch and Gloucester which was only introduced a year before. France Lynch could not justify the level of service provided to Gloucester plus the opposite shorts to Stroud which combined to give a half-hourly service. The replacement hourly service to France Lynch served as many points as possible and its journey time prevented its marriage to the Gloucester service.

Instead, Stagecoach in the Cotswolds provided an hourly Tetbury to Gloucester service via Minchinhampton with alternate journeys via Brimscombe (92) and Amberley (92A), replacing and indeed enhancing local movements between Stroud and Minchinhampton. Notwithstanding the somewhat limited facilities associated with the 30 between Tetbury and Gloucester from 1986 to 1993, there had been no through services of any significance between Tetbury, Minchinhampton and Gloucester since the withdrawal of the 558 in 1971. The April 2003 changes actually enabled passengers from the

Gloucester bus to go through to Bath on the 620 at Tetbury. The 620 from Tetbury operated via Chipping Sodbury and Yate, was subsidised by South Gloucestershire Council and operated since its start by Stroud depot in January 1999.

April 2003 also saw the reintroduction of a direct link from Stroud and Nailsworth on Mondays to Saturdays to Bath following the demise in 2001 of the popular Wednesdays and Saturdays only X26.

Finally in April 2003, in an interesting development described in Stagecoach in the Cotswolds publicity of the time as introducing "a more convenient town centre pick up", service 36 to Kingscourt again reverted to an off-peak town centre terminus in Russell Street, as well as the bus station. The Kingscourt service was among the last substantial services to remain on street after 1997.

The prospect of Stroud Bus Station's closure and temporary accommodation has found resistance from some quarters. A public exhibition in November 2001 outlined plans for a new interchange at the rail station, something likely to be delayed or downgraded or both. Temporary measures were proposed while the existing Bus Station site is redeveloped as a cinema. Meanwhile, in September 2001, passengers raised a 400 signature petition against the Bus Station's closure and even used an empty unit in Merrywalks Shopping Centre to help with their cause. *N P Daniels*

Meanwhile, the District Council continued to market the Stroud bus station site. In moves that would see a cinema more-or-less on the site occupied by the 1939 Ritz, Stroud District Council wished to see leisure facilities on the bus station site as part of a refurbished and expanded Merrywalks shopping development. Negotiations had been on-going for several years and received a considerable boost following controversial planning permission and opening in April 2003 of a nearby McDonald's fast food cafeteria on the former Merchant & Lusty site on Merrywalks. Plans for the cinema on the bus station site were submitted for formal consideration in January 2003, 30 years after the closure of the Odeon/Gaumont at London Road.

Stroud District Council officials were present at 1700 hrs on 8 May 2003 to receive the keys to the bus station buildings from Stagecoach at the expiry of the lease. Stagecoach transferred its accommodation to a unit within the Merrywalks Shopping Centre from the following day, while the bus station itself remained open for passengers, for the time being. Ebley Coaches' offices in the former waiting room also closed that day. Ebley had erected a somewhat confusing notice inferring that the bus station was about to close when, in fact, they meant the offices only. All this activity indicated that the bus station was nearer to total closure than at any time in recent years.

Gloucestershire County Council planned to integrate buses with trains at the rail station site in the town but this is likely to be two years away. This was subject to external funding by the Strategic Rail Authority through its Rail Passenger Partnership (RPP) process and during the gap between the bus station redevelopment and new interchange, a much criticised temporary terminus was to be in place from April 2003, split partly on the old bus station and partly on the car park at the bottom on Rowcroft Retreat. Owing to the shortage of RPP funding, the interchange may be implemented initially on a smaller scale until contributions from the Cheapside development become available. While Stagecoach welcomed the rail station interchange, it was less than happy with the temporary situation which, at the time of writing, has yet to be finalised.

Public opinion in Stroud was split between retaining the existing bus station terminus site and moving to the new one. The idea of a transport interchange was actually mooted as far back as 1968 during the Merrywalks planning process and first seriously discussed between Bristol Omnibus and Gloucestershire County Council as far back as 1975. Other than being able to move between bus and train, it had level access to the town centre in its favour. The closure of the bus station had been something of an on-off process throughout the years from 2000 but in readiness, Cotswold Experience took out its bus services in April 2002, perhaps to stake a claim on a stop at Cornhill (space at the temporary bus station was to be limited) and perhaps in part because of health and safety fears in the current bus station itself. The services affected were council contracts to Oakridge, Standish Hospital, Randwick/Ruscombe, The Bourne, Woodchester and Birdlip, though in reality this represented an average of only 12 Monday to Friday departures per day. This does, however, present any traveller wishing to transfer to these services with a problem, although some Cotswold Experience services still drop off in the bus station, without picking up.

At the turn of the 21st century, there were again rumours that Stroud might close as a depot at the time of the loss of the bus station. However, in spite of cuts over the years and its operation more or less as a large, engineering outstation, Stroud's operation was still felt to be too large for such a move. Such a decision would give other operators more of a foothold in the town.

With out of town supermarkets built from the late 1980s onwards, major medical facilities transferred from the seventies to the main Gloucester hospital, on a site outside the city centre, the relocation of the District Council offices from the town centre first to Tricorn House, Cainscross in the seventies and then to Ebley Mill at the end of the nineties, with expansion in the eighties of warehouse style shopping at Cheltenham, Gloucester and Swindon, the popularity of Cribbs Causeway plus the unremitting rise in house prices which attract affluent and longer distance commuters, it is easy to sink into despair as far as Stroud's buses are concerned. The transport interchange and indeed a Transport Strategy for Stroud which encompasses improvements for pedestrians and cyclists does offer some renewed hope.

In spite of the most recent cut backs, the future of bus services at Stroud remains rosy, especially for trunk bus services. The ex-Stagecoach Manchester Volvo B10M single decks delivered to Stroud in 1999 and used on the 46 (Cheltenham) and 93s (Gloucester), though solid performers, have since 2003 been replaced by 83 seat Alexander bodied Volvo Olympians, cascaded from London. Slightly newer than the Volvos and once smartened up following their hard London life, the vehicles were designed to offer a renewed level of passenger comfort. Stagecoach in the Cotswolds found that the B10Ms were too small to cater for Saturday and school holiday loads, especially to Cheltenham, and this resulted in Stroud's older double decks being used on service just at a time when the most impressionable passengers

Where it all began. In use by Stagecoach in 2003 is 424, one of six Volvo B10Ms with Alexander PS bodywork which arrived second hand in the late nineties. Designed for the trunk services 46 (Cheltenham) and 92/93 (Gloucester), 424 is seen on the 46 heading towards Stroud with the Falcon Inn Painswick behind. The Falcon held local offices for the GWR, who operated Stroud's first motor buses. *Geoff Gould*

were travelling. Far better, then, to offer a good level of service to everyone, all the time. This is a remarkable turn of events given that the 46 route itself was deemed to be unprofitable in 1986 and was all but withdrawn. The 46's renaissance owes much to the ascendancy of Cheltenham as the sub-regional shopping centre of choice. The five Olympians inter-worked both the Cheltenham and Gloucester services, swapping from one to the other at Forest Green.

Even traditionally more rural services have seen some benefits. Stagecoach has wherever possible aimed to ensure that each service operates at a clockface frequency, at the same times past each hour. Gloucestershire's contract service to Wotton-under-Edge, now with Beaumont Travel, is clockface two-hourly. The town services (8/8A), services via Leonard Stanley (14), Dursley and Uley (20), France Lynch (26), Minchinhampton (92/92A), Kingscourt (36) and Cirencester (54) operate at regular intervals where not so long ago, the schedules were anything but even.

With new partnerships emerging between company and council and the blurring of commercial and subsidised journeys, the more rural services are still holding their own, in spite of reductions designed to ensure stability. If the decrease from half-hourly to hourly between Stroud and France Lynch is a backward step, it needs to be remembered this level of service is still better than at the height of the bus service in the early fifties, in spite of mass car ownership in the 21st century.

As at January 2003, 39 buses, now all renumbered in a Stagecoach national system, were stabled at Stroud. Stroud has been allocated depot code "SZ" in the Stagecoach scheme of things. Staff totaled 60 in number. Nearly two million passengers are carried per annum. Cotswold Experience, Ebley Coaches and Beaumont Travel also operate services and employ, pro rata on local bus services, some seven drivers.

APPENDIX 1

CHRONOLOGY

1903	GWR steam railmotors start following actual and threatened road competition
1905	GWR begins motor bus operations at Stroud with service to Painswick
c.1907	Arnold's motor buses serve Avening, Nailsworth and Stroud. The business is sold to National in 1920
1908	Combe operates motor bus services between Stroud, Eastington and Stonehouse
1919	Established Painswick horse bus operator Ireland buys motor buses and is acquired by National a year later
1919	Pegler operates motor bus services between Stroud and Framilode
1919	National Steam Car Company Ltd establishes its first presence in the south and west of England
1920	Bristol Tramways & Carriage Co begin operations in the Stroud area
1920	National opens branch at Wotton-under-Edge, which it closes three years later
c.1920	Grey Motors begins operations between Minchinhampton and Stroud
1923	The Bear bus service extends beyond Rodborough Common to Minchinhampton, to be acquired by National three years later
c.1923	Reyne's Red Bus Service commences
1926	GWR expands to Rodborough and Kingscourt
1927	National moves into London Road premises which served the town to 1993 and offices at 8A George Street
1928	Two London express services start, operated by Red Bus and Blue Star
1929	National becomes Western National and GWR services in Stroud merge with that company
1931	Route licensing system introduced
1931	Western National becomes part of the Tilling Group, to be joined by Bristol Tramways a year later
1932	Red Bus becomes incorporated a year ahead of its sale to independent Red & White

1933	Thorp's services taken over
1934	Following agreement between Tilling and Red & White, Stroud area services are rationalised and reorganised among the three main operators
1935	First brand new Red & White vehicle arrives, being a Bristol G type double deck
1939	Wartime rationalisation of services begin in September
1944	Twenty minute weekday frequency begins on Stroud's most important local service, that from Chalford to Stonehouse, to continue at this level for approximately 35 years
1948	Western National and Bristol pass to the nationalised British Transport Commission and Red & White sells to the State within two years
1950	Western National and Red & White add their land-locked Stroud routes to Bristol Tramways' own in a post-BTC rationalisation which sees the Bristol company in ascendancy. This facilitates a new Stroud–Bristol service. Western National continues on the now joint service to Trowbridge until its division at Malmesbury in 1957. Tetbury - Malmesbury section divided as late as 1983
1951	The transfer of Red & White's Coleford operation to Bristol facilitates a vehicle exchange which sees most of Stroud's Albions pass back to Red & White
1954	The Bristol LS arrives, the first underfloor engined single deck bus, thereby increasing seating capacity, to be followed by Bristol MWs of similar design in 1959
1955	Revolutionary "Lodekka" double decks arrive, with one-step entrance, two rows of double seats upstairs and no sunken upper deck gangway
1957	Stroud's first Bristol Tramways vehicles operate without a conductor, although there had been one-man routes before the merger. More services are converted progressively to one man operation
1957	The Suez Crisis forces the withdrawal of some mileage
1957	Two damaging bus strikes at Stroud
1960	Stroud Bus Station opens – ending on-street running in the town
1961	Universal Bristol coat-of-arms replaced by "BRISTOL" fleetname in block to be replaced from 1965 with the famous Bristol scroll common at that time on Bristol-manufactured buses
1962	Bristol SUS4As arrive, replacing Bedford OBs as the last non-Bristol manufactured buses not only at Stroud but with the entire company
1964	Railmotor service closes
1966	With the opening of the Severn Bridge, operations between Stroud and Chepstow commence with connections for Newport and Cardiff. Withdrawn six years later
1966	Last Bristol K double deck withdrawn from company service, this

being a Stroud example previously transferred from Western National in 1950

1966   Nailsworth Bus Station opens

1967   First 36ft single deck arrives in the shape of Bristol RELL6L 1017 and with its conversion for one-man operation two years later, opens the door to modern, high capacity single decks on trunk routes

1967   General route renumbering converts two and four digit numbers to three

1969   Bristol Omnibus transfers from the British Transport Commission's successor to the National Bus Company, remaining in nationalised hands. Buses begin to be painted in corporate National leaf green livery from 1972

1969   Stroud Christmas Carol Bus launched in what was to be an annual event till 1993

1971   One of Stroud's diminutive 30 seat SUSs stars alongside John Mills and Carol White in the film "Dulcima"

1971   Gloucestershire County Council uses new powers to grant aid rural bus services – with an initial contribution of over £15,000 to Stroud's routes

1972   Following the construction of Merrywalks Shopping Centre, Stroud Bus Station rebuilding complete

1974   Black "SD" vehicle allocation plates introduced conforming to new Bristol Omnibus standards and replacing traditional yellow and red colour depot coding

1974   Last rear entrance double deck withdrawn in the shape of Bristol LD 8538

1975   First Bristol LH6Ls arrive. All have been withdrawn by the end of 1981

1978   First two Leyland Nationals arrive following improvements to the camber at the bus station exit which otherwise prevented such vehicles working at Stroud

1979   Withdrawal of all remaining Bristol FLF half-cab deckers and replacement with single deck Leyland Nationals. Some crew operations remain till 1981, however

1979   First two minibuses arrive at Stroud, purchased by Gloucestershire County Council, for Nailsworth locals and Stroud - Birdlip – Cheltenham. Initial Ford Transits replaced five years later by Mercedes Benz examples

1981   Market Analysis Project-inspired service changes see service reappraisal, reduction and vehicle withdrawals but the welcome re-introduction of double deck buses with new Bristol VRTs being added in August to Stroud's otherwise sole-surviving double deck, VR 5512

1983   Bristol Omnibus operations in the Northern Division of Stroud,

	Swindon, Gloucester and Cheltenham pass in September to the Cheltenham & Gloucester Omnibus Company Ltd
1983	"Stroud Valleys" brand name introduced. Coaches branded "Cotswold" and repainted in National "stripes style" red and green
1986	Commercial network introduced in May, ahead of deregulation in October. October sees some independent operator activity under contract to the county council
1986	Withdrawal of last RE single decks
1986	Cheltenham & Gloucester privatised in November following successful management-led buy-out. Holding company, Western Travel, formed
1986	Stroud's buses assume a bold, new local identity and new livery of mint green with mid-chrome yellow flash
1989	Stroud's buses become no-smoking
1991	Introduction of frequent minibuses on Metro route "C" to Cashes Green
1992	Stroud Bus Station branded "edge of town" and closes to passengers with a return to on-street running, save for the interchange of school children which continues on the site
1992	London Road bus garage and depot site sold to Waitrose for supermarket development. New largely open depot at Bowbridge in operation from summer 1993
1993	All private hire and excursions cease with the sale of Stroud's remaining Leyland Tiger coaches
1993	Stagecoach buys Western Travel and its subsidiary Cheltenham & Gloucester Omnibus. Stroud services to become "Stagecoach Stroud Valleys"
1995	All remaining evening services withdrawn
1996	Stroud's last green bus is repainted into Stagecoach white
1997	Following purchase of the site by Stroud District Council, all services again terminate at Stroud Bus Station
1997	Significant route changes improve a number of bus services, to be enhanced again a year later with the termination of the Bulk Scholars Agreement with the LEA
1999	First of four Volvo/Alexander ALX200s arrive for contract services and service 21, as Stroud's first ultra-low floor buses
2001	Adoption of "Stagecoach in the Cotswolds" new image and livery while Stroud operations form part of the new Stagecoach West & Wales
2001	Some services pass to Cotswold Experience. A year later, this operator withdraws from the Bus Station, to use Cornhill instead
2003	Double deck Volvo Olympians drafted in to improve quality of trunk services
2003	In preparation for the development of the bus station site, Stagecoach moves to vacant unit in Merrywalks Shopping Centre

APPENDIX 2

STROUD VEHICLE INFORMATION

This Appendix attempts to piece together the vehicles operating from the Stroud Depot of the Bristol Omnibus Company Ltd, its predecessor Bristol Tramways and its successors, at the time of the 1950 merger to date. It also considers some of the early buses operated by Red Bus and Western National.

The author gladly acknowledges the help given by Richard Waters in the production of these data. The author wishes to thank Richard Johnson for his permission to use his late father, David's material.

The Appendix is as accurate as possible but the reader is asked to remember that the task of assembling this information has been challenging because of both the frequent transfer of vehicles and conflicts between a number of information sources. If any reader is able to add or amend any of the information herein, they are asked to email daniels@stroudvalleys.co.uk.

(a) Red & White and Western National at 1950 Merger with BTCC

BTCC No.	Reg No.	Chassis	Body	Date New	Date to Stroud	Transfer Out	Notes
Red & White		**Double Decks**					
3782	AAX 129	Bristol GO6G	NCME H24/24R	1935	New	Oct-50	
3783	CWO 419	Albion CX19	Weymann H30/26R	1939	New	Dec-51	Repainted BTCC
L4139	EAX 632	Albion CX19	Duple L30/26R	1941	New	Aug-52	Repainted BTCC
L4140	EAX 633	Albion CX19	Duple L30/26R	1941	New	May-52	Repainted BTCC
L4141	EAX 634	Albion CX19	Duple L30/26R	1941	New	Sep-52	Repainted BTCC
L4142	EAX 636	Albion CX19	Duple L30/26R	1941	New	Jan-53	Repainted BTCC
L4143	EAX 637	Albion CX19	Duple L30/26R	1941	New	Jan-53	Repainted BTCC
L4144	EAX 638	Albion CX19	Duple L30/26R	1941	1948	Aug-52	Repainted BTCC
L4145	EAX 639	Albion CX19	Duple L30/26R	1941	New	Sep-52	Repainted BTCC
L4146	EAX 640	Albion CX19	Duple L30/26R	1941	New	Oct-53	Repainted BTCC
L4147	EAX 641	Albion CX19	Duple L30/26R	1942	New	Jan-51	
L4148	EAX 642	Albion CX19	Duple L30/26R	1942	1943	Mar-52	Repainted BTCC
L4149	EAX 643	Albion CX19	Duple L30/26R	1942	New	Jan-51	
Red & White		**Single Decks**					
230	GWO 876	Bedford OB	Duple C29F	1948	New	Sep-54	Repainted BTCC
2600	WO 6377	Albion PMB28	Duple C35F	1932		Jan-51	Rebodied 1938
2601	CAX 390	Albion PW141	Duple C32F	1938		Jan-51	
2602	CAX 391	Albion PW141	Duple C32F	1938		Jan-51	
2603	CAX 395	Albion CX13	Duple C32F	1938		Jan-51	
2604	CWO 401	Albion CX11	Duple B37C	1939		Jan-51	
2605	CWO 402	Albion CX11	Duple B37C	1939		Jan-51	
2606	CWO 428	Albion CX13	Duple B35C	1939	New	Jan-51	Repainted BTCC
2607	EXF 264	Albion CX13	Duple C35F	1938	1939	Jan-51	Rebodied 1934
2608	FLF 927	Albion CX13	Duple C32F	1939	1939	Jan-51	
2609	GWO 865	Albion CX13	Lydney B35F	1948	New	Jan-51	
2610	GWO 866	Albion CX13	Lydney B35F	1948	New	Jan-51	
2611	GWO 868	Albion CX13	Lydney B35F	1948	New	Jan-51	
2612	GWO 869	Albion CX13	Lydney B35F	1948	New	Jan-51	
2613	GWO 870	Albion CX13	Lydney B35F	1948	New	Jan-51	
2614	GWO 879	Albion CX13	Lydney B35F	1948	New	Jan-51	
2615	CAX 394	Albion PW141	Duple C32F	1938		Jan-51	
2616	BAX 330	Albion PV141	Duple C32F	1937		Jan-51	
Western National		**Double Decks**					
L3600	FJ 7835	Titan TD1	Beadle L26/26R	1931	1947	10/50	See below
L4127	DDV 18	Bristol K5G	Beadle L30/26R	1939	New	1954	
L4128	DOD 502	Bristol K5G	ECW L30/26R	1940	New	Apr-55	
L4129	DOD 504	Bristol K5G	ECW L30/26R	1940	New	Apr-55	
L4130	HTT 980	Bristol K5G	ECW L29/28R	1946	New	Dec-54	
L4131	KUO 932	Bristol K5G	ECW L29/28R	1949	New	Jan-66	
L4132	KUO 945	Bristol K6B	ECW L29/28R	1949	New	Aug-66	
L4133	KUO 959	Bristol K6B	ECW L29/28R	1950	New	Dec-66	

BTCC No.	Reg No.	Chassis	Body	Date New	Date to Stroud	Transfer Out	Notes
L4134	KUO 963	Bristol K6B	ECW L29/28R	1950	New	Dec-66	
L4135	KUO 964	Bristol K6B	ECW L29/28R	1950	New	1962	
L4136	LTA 723	Bristol K5G	ECW L29/28R	1949	New	Jan-66	
L4137	HTT 987	Bristol K5G	ECW L29/28R	1947	New	Dec-54	

Western National   Single Decks

BTCC No.	Reg No.	Chassis	Body	Date New	Date to Stroud	Transfer Out	Notes
165	GF 7297	Leyland TS2	Duple C31F	1930		Sep-50	Rebodied 1938
166	GF 7288	Leyland TS2	Duple C31F	1930		Sep-50	Rebodied 1938
167	GF 7289	Leyland TS2	Duple C31F	1930		Sep-50	Rebodied 1938
168	GF 7294	Leyland TS2	Duple C31F	1930		Sep-50	Rebodied 1941
169	DR 8562	Leyland TS2	Duple C31F	1931		Sep-50	Rebodied 1939
170	JY 88	Leyland TS1	Duple C31F	1932		Sep-50	Rebodied 1940
171	JY 89	Leyland TS1	Duple C31F	1932		Sep-50	Rebodied 1940
228	HOD 45	Bedford OB	Duple C29F	1949	New	Sep-54	
229	CTA 547	Bedford WTB	Duple C29F	1937	c. 1948	Sep-50	
290	JTA 201	Bedford OWB	Duple MOS B30F	1943	c.1949	Jan-51	
291	JTA 203	Bedford OWB	Duple MOS B30F	1943	c.1949	Jan-51	
292	JTA 205	Bedford OWB	Duple MOS B30F	1943	c.1949	Jan-51	
293	JTA 208	Bedford OWB	Duple MOS B30F	1943	c.1949	Dec-50	
294	JTA 210	Bedford OWB	Duple MOS B30F	1943	c.1949	Dec-50	
657	BTA 80	Dennis Mace	ECOC B26F	1935	New	Sep-50	
658	OD 7804	Dennis Ace	ECOC B20F	1934	New	Feb-51	
659	ATT 191	Dennis Ace	Brush B20F	1935		Dec-50	
660	ADV 337	Dennis Ace	Brush C20F	1936		Oct-50	
661	BDV 118	Dennis Ace	Mumford B14F	1936	New	Sep-50	
662	CTA 515	Dennis Ace	Mumford B20F	1937	New	Feb-51	
663	CTA 517	Dennis Ace	Mumford B20F	1937	New	Feb-51	
2485	FJ 8932	Bristol H	Bristol B35R	1933		Nov-50	Rebodied 1940
2486	FJ 8934	Bristol H	Bristol B35R	1933		Nov-50	Rebodied 1940
2487	FJ 8943	Bristol H	Bristol B35R	1934		Nov-51	Rebodied 1941
2488	FJ 8950	Bristol H	Bristol B35R	1934		Feb-51	Rebodied 1943
2489	FJ 8957	Bristol H	Bristol B35R	1934		Feb-51	Rebodied 1941
2490	FJ 8959	Bristol H	Bristol B35R	1934		Nov-51	Rebodied 1942
2491	FJ 8960	Bristol H	Bristol B35R	1934		Jun-51	Rebodied 1941
2492	ADV 110	Bristol J05G	Beadle B36R	1936	New	Nov-52	Rebodied 1948
2493	ADV 118	Bristol J05G	Beadle B36R	1936	c. 1949	Oct-58	Rebodied 1949
2494	ADV 119	Bristol J05G	Beadle B36R	1936	New	Sep-58	Rebodied 1949
2495	ADV 121	Bristol J05G	Beadle B36R	1936	New	Sep-58	Rebodied 1949
2496	ADV 123	Bristol J05G	Beadle B36R	1936	New	Sep-58	Rebodied 1949
2497	ADV 128	Bristol J05G	Beadle B36R	1936	New	Oct-58	Rebodied 1949

L3600: ex-Exeter Corporation 1945. Rebodied 1947. Gardner 5LW 1947

(b) Bristol Tramways & Bristol Omnibus and Successors

Bristol Gs

Fleet No.	Reg No.	Chassis	Body	Date New	Date to Stroud	Transfer Out	Notes
L4150	CHY 117	GO6A	ECW L27/26R	1936	Sep-52	1955	Formerly Gardner engined
L4151	CHY 115	GO6A	ECW L27/26R	1936	Aug-52	1955	Formerly Gardner engined
L4152	CHY 440	GO6A	ECW L27/26R	1936	Aug-52	1955	Formerly Gardner engined
L4153	CHY 441	GO6A	ECW L27/26R	1936	Aug-52	1955	Formerly Gardner engined
L4154	CHY 442	GO6A	ECW L27/26R	1936	Oct-52	1955	Formerly Gardner engined

L4150-4 replaced ex-Red & White Albions, some of which returned to their former owner or sister company United Welsh.
All had lowbridge Bristol relaxed MOS bodies fitted 5/46.

Bristol Ks

Fleet No.	Reg No.	Chassis	Body	Date New	Date to Stroud	Transfer Out	Notes
L3644	HHY 588	K6A	Strachan MOS L27/28R	1945	1952	1956	4/53 Received body from L4143
L3647	HHY 591	K6A	Strachan MOS L27/28R	1945	1952	1956	2/54 Received body from L4146. Reseated L27/26R
L3651	HHY 595	K6A	Strachan MOS L27/28R	1945	1952	1956	2/53 Received body from L4142
L3653	HHY 597	K6A	Strachan MOS L27/28R	1945	By 1951	??	
L3654	HHY 598	K6A	Strachan MOS L27/28R	1945	By 1951	??	
3622	HHT 143	K5G	BBW (MOS) H30/26R	1942	c. 1950	c. 1950	Temporary allocation
3687	KHT 522	K5G	ECW H30/26R	1947	By 1951	By 7/52	Temporary allocation
3688	KHU 613	K5G	ECW H30/26R	1947	c. 1950	c. 1950	Temporary allocation
3703	KHY 386	K5G	ECW H30/26R	1948	By 1951	??	Temporary allocation
3711	KHY 713	K6A	ECW H30/26R	1948	c. 1950	c. 1950	Temporary allocation
3778	LHY 942	K6B	ECW H31/28R	1950	c. 1950	c. 1950	Temporary allocation
3780	LHY 944	K6B	ECW H31/28R	1950	c. 1950	c. 1950	Temporary allocation
L4102	KHU 623	K6A	ECW L27/28R	1947	1951	8/59	Wooden framed bodywork
L4103	KHU 624	K6B	ECW L27/28R	1947	1952	2/59	Wooden framed bodywork
L4104	KHU 601	K6B	ECW L27/28R	1947	1951	8/59	Wooden framed bodywork
L4105	KHU 602	K6A	ECW L27/28R	1947	??	4/59	Wooden framed bodywork
L4106	KHU 603	K6B	ECW L27/28R	1947	2/59	11/59	Wooden framed bodywork
L4107	KHU 608	K6A	ECW L27/28R	1948	1952	5/61	Wooden framed bodywork
L4110	KHU 607	K6A	ECW L27/28R	1947	1951	12/59	Wooden framed bodywork
L4111	KHU 609	K6A	ECW L27/28R	1947	1953	1/60	Wooden framed bodywork
L4113	KHU 611	K6B	ECW L27/28R	1947	1953	3/59	Wooden framed bodywork
L4114	KHU 612	K6A	ECW L27/28R	1947	1951	8/59	Wooden framed bodywork
L4115	KHW 635	K6A	ECW L27/28R	1948	1953	4/59	Wooden framed bodywork. Also 12/60-2/61
L4116	KHW 636	K6A	ECW L27/28R	1948	4/50	11/50	First BTCC allocation while Albions repainted
L4118	LHU 511	K6B	ECW L27/28R	1948	11/59	12/65	Returned 5/62
L4121	LHU 517	K5G	ECW L27/28R	1948	1952	9/62	
L4122	LHU 518	K5G	ECW L27/28R	1948	1954	2/63	

Fleet No.	Reg No.	Chassis	Body	Date New	Date to Stroud	Transfer Out	Notes
L4125	LHU 515	K5G	ECW L27/28R	1948	1953	1964	
L4126	LHU 519	K6B	ECW L27/28R	1948	1952	10/66	
L4127	DDV 18	K5G	Beadle L30/26R	1939	New	1954	ex-Western National
L4128	DOD 502	K5G	ECW L30/26R	1940	New	4/55	ex-Western National
L4129	DOD 504	K5G	ECW L30/26R	1940	New	4/55	ex-Western National
L4130	HTT 980	K5G	ECW L27/28R	1946	New	12/54	ex-Western National
L4131	KUO 932	K5G	ECW L27/28R	1949	New	2/66	ex-Western National
L4132	KUO 945	K6B	ECW L27/28R	1949	New	3/66	ex-Western National
L4133	KUO 959	K6B	ECW L27/28R	1950	New	10/66	ex-Western National
L4134	KUO 963	K6B	ECW L27/28R	1950	New	11/66	ex-Western National
L4135	KUO 964	K6B	ECW L27/28R	1950	New	6/62	ex-Western National
L4136	LTA 723	K5G	ECW L27/28R	1949	New	2/66	ex-Western National
L4137	HTT 987	K5G	ECW L27/28R	1946	New	12/54	ex-Western National
L4138	GHU 489	K5G	1947 Beadle L27/26R	1941	1950	1955	Chassis ex C3352, Body ex L3600
L8092	OHY 935	KSW6B	ECW L27/28RD	1952	New	12/60	See below
L8093	OHY 932	KSW6G	ECW L27/28RD	1952	2/66	6/68	

3622 (K5G), 3688 (K5G), 3711 (K6A), 3778 (K6B) and 3780 (K6B) were temporarily allocated in 1950, leaving that year.
L3644/7/51 and 4102/4/10/14/21/15 replaced ex-Red & White Albions
L8092 First new BTCC vehicle and first at 8'0" wide. This and L8093 featured conductor operated rear platform doors

Bristol LDs

Fleet No.	Reg No.	Chassis	Body	Date New	Date to Stroud	Transfer Out	Notes
L8249	THW 739	LD6B	ECW H33/25RD	1955	New	6/62	
L8250	THW 740	LD6B	ECW H33/25RD	1955	2/68	10/70	Also deputised for 7275 12/70-11/71
L8251	THW 741	LD6B	ECW H33/25RD	1955	by 1958	12/60	
L8255	THW 745	LD6B	ECW H33/25RD	1955	New	5/63	
L8256	THW 746	LD6B	ECW H33/25RD	1955	by 1958	4/59	
L8259	THW 749	LD6B	ECW H33/25RD	1955	4/66	10/70	
L8260	THW 750	LD6B	ECW H33/25RD	1955	New	8/65	
L8262	THW 752	LD6B	ECW H33/25RD	1955	New	3/62	
L8280	UHY 409	LD6G	ECW H33/25RD	1955	New	10/65	See below
L8282	UHY 411	LD6G	ECW H33/25RD	1956	New	8/65	
L8287	UHY 416	LD6G	ECW H33/25RD	1956	8/67	9/67	
L8390	WHY 931	LD6G	ECW H33/25RD	1956	New	1961	
L8392	WHY 933	LD6G	ECW H33/25RD	1956	New	3/59	
L8395	WHY 948	LD6G	ECW H33/25RD	1956	New	3/58	
L8398	WHY 951	LD6G	ECW H33/25RD	1956	New	10/65	
L8463	YHT 959	LD6B	ECW H33/25RD	1958	11/70	9/71	
L8481	837 CHU	LD6G	ECW H33/25RD	1958	1969	7/70	
L8483	839 CHU	LD6G	ECW H33/25RD	1958	New	11/65	
L8499	859 CHU	LD6G	ECW H33/25RD	1959	New	2/72	
L8500	860 CHU	LD6G	ECW H33/25RD	1959	3/66	11/66	
L8510	964 EHW	LD6G	ECW H33/25RD	1959	8/59	11/66	

STROUD'S BUSES

Fleet No.	Reg No.	Chassis	Body	Date New	Date to Stroud	Transfer Out	Notes
L8511	965 EHW	LD6G	ECW H33/25RD	1959	8/59	11/65	
L8538	993 EHW	LD6G	ECW H33/25RD	1959	7/73	3/75	
L8542	432 FHW	LD6G	ECW H33/25RD	1959	New	10/69	
L8546	436 FHW	LD6G	ECW H33/25RD	1959	New	by 1964	

L8280 at Stroud 1955 to 9/61; 12/61 to 10/65; 4/66 to 7/67

Bristol FSFs/FLFs

Fleet No.	Reg No.	Chassis	Body	Date New	Date to Stroud	Transfer Out	Notes
6007	704 JHY	FSF6G	ECW H34/26F	1960	9/61	2/65	
6035	832 MHW	FSF6G	ECW H34/26F	1961	New	2/65	
7046	214 NAE	FLF6G	ECW H38/32F	1961	6/62	8/77	
7052	220 NAE	FLF6G	ECW H38/32F	1961	New	9/77	
7053	221 NAE	FLF6G	ECW H38/32F	1961	by 1964	6/72	
7062	507 OHU	FLF6B	ECW H38/32F	1962	1/78	5/78	
7063	508 OHU	FLF6B	ECW H38/32F	1962	New	9/76	
7083	526 OHU	FLF6G	ECW H38/32F	1962	2/65	4/66	
7107	552 OHU	FLF6G	ECW H38/32F	1962	5/63	2/72	Returned on short loan 1/78
7117	810 SHW	FLF6B	ECW H38/32F	1963	1964	6/78	
7123	816 SHW	FLF6G	ECW H38/32F	1963	10/77	11/77	Loan vehicle
7159	AAE 264B	FLF6G	ECW H38/32F	1964	11/66	4/78	
7160	AAE 265B	FLF6G	ECW H38/32F	1964	11/66	4/78	
7174	BHU 98C	FLF6G	ECW H38/32F	1965	2/65	6/72	
7203	DHT 783C	FLF6G	ECW H38/32F	1965	8/65	9/72	
7206	DHW 981C	FLF6B	ECW H38/32F	1965	8/65	3/79	See below
7212	DHW 982C	FLF6G	ECW H38/32F	1965	10/65	5/66	See below
7213	DHW 983C	FLF6G	ECW H38/32F	1965	10/65	5/66	
7215	DHW 985C	FLF6G	ECW H38/32F	1965	5/66	12/72	
7223	EHT 112C	FLF6G	ECW H38/32F	1965	5/66	5/77	
7225	EHT 114C	FLF6G	ECW H38/32F	1965	11/65	3/79	
7226	EHT 115C	FLF6B	ECW H38/32F	1965	11/65	9/76	
7239	EHW 191C	FLF6G	ECW H38/32F	1965	12/65	3/79	
7240	FHT 15D	FLF6G	ECW H38/32F	1965	5/77	3/79	See below
7274	HHW 457D	FLF6B	ECW H38/32F	1966	10/66	8/67	
7275	HHW 458D	FLF6B	ECW H38/32F	1966	10/66	3/79	Out of service 12/70 to 11/71. 8250 deputised
7282	HHY 185D	FLF6G	ECW H38/32F	1966	11/66	9/73	
7283	HHT 186D	FLF6G	ECW H38/32F	1966	9/77	9/77	

7206 at Stroud 8/65 to 11/74; 6/75 to 3/79. Vehicle used for a FLF Farewell Tour of Routes March 1979.
7212 at Stroud 10/65 to 5/66; 11/74 to 6/75 and was an all-over advertisement bus for Ebley Tyre Services, normally at Gloucester
7240 became a second Ebley Tyre Services all-over advertisement bus, allocated to Cheltenham and then Stroud from 5/77, reverting to standard livery 10/77 while remaining at Stroud

7062, 7101 and 7143 were each allocated to Stroud in 1978 for stand in duties. 7101 was involved in accident on Cowcombe Hill on its way to Cirencester dump 14/4/78

Bristol VRs

Fleet No.	Reg No.	Chassis	Body	Date New	Date to Stroud	Transfer Out	Notes
5065	MOU 739R	VRT/SL3/6LXB	H43/28F*	1976	2/90	3/93	* Rebuilt
5107	PHY 701S	VRT/SL3/6LXB	ECW H43/27D	1977	7/81	by 10/81	
5108	PHY 702S	VRT/SL3/6LXB	ECW H43/27D	1977	7/81	by 10/81	
5110	RHT 504S	VRT/SL3/6LXB	ECW H43/27D	1977	7/81	by 10/81	
5112	RHT 506S	VRT/SL3/6LXB	ECW H43/27D	1977	7/81	by 10/81	
5117	RHT 511S	VRT/SL3/6LXB	ECW H43/27D	1977	7/81	by 10/81	
5118	RHT 512S	VRT/SL3/6LXB	ECW H43/27D	1977	7/81	by 10/81	
5119	REU 309S	VRT/SL3/6LXB	H43/28F*	1977	1994	1995	* Rebuilt. Renumbered 211 7/94
5120	REU 310S	VRT/SL3/6LXB	H43/28F*	1977	9/91	1995	* Rebuilt. Renumbered 212 7/94
5132	TWS 913T	VRT/SL3/6LXB	H43/28F*	1979	2000	2000	* Rebuilt. Renumbered 223 7/94
5511	LHT 721P	VRT/SL3/501	ECW H39/31F	1976	9/77	10/77	Loan vehicle
5512	LHT 722P	VRT/SL3/501	ECW H39/31F	1976	3/78	10/83	Repainted from "Silver Jubilee" before Stroud service
5515	LHT 725P	VRT/SL3/501	ECW H39/31F	1976	Aug-82	10/82	All-over advertisement for Anchor Butter
5518	PEU 513R	VRT/SL3/6LXB	ECW H43/31F	1977	9/77	3/78	
5520	PEU 515R	VRT/SL3/6LXB	ECW H43/31F	1977	7/84	11/84	
5527	RFB 617S	VRT/SL3/6LXB	ECW H43/31F	1977	7/82	10/83	
5528	DHW 350W	VRT/SL3/0680	ECW H43/31F	1981	New	7/82	Returned 1986 to 1995. Renumbered 225 7/94
5530	DHW 352W	VRT/SL3/0680	ECW H43/31F	1981	New	1997	Renumbered 226 7/94
5532	EWS 740W	VRT/SL3/0680	ECW H43/31F	1981	New	1997	Renumbered 227 7/94
5535	EWS 743W	VRT/SL3/0680	ECW H43/31F	1981	New	2000	Renumbered 228 7/94
5538	EWS 746W	VRT/SL3/0680	ECW H43/31F	1981	New	1998	Renumbered 229 7/94
5540	EWS 748W	VRT/SL3/0680	ECW H43/31F	1981	New	See below	Metrocolour unibus advert. Renumbered 230 7/94
5543	EWS 750W	VRT/SL3/0680	ECW H43/31F	1981	8/82	1999	Also operated from 5/86. Renumbered 231 7/94
5603	JNU 129N	VRT/SL6G	ECW H39/31F	1975	2/84	4/84	Ex-East Midlands 1982
5605	HPT 83N	VRT/SL6G	ECW H43/31F	1975	??	5/86	Ex-United Automobile 1983
5606	HPT 84N	VRT/SL6G	ECW H43/31F	1975	2/83	See below	Ex-United Automobile 1983
5608	HPT 86N	VRT/SL6G	ECW H43/31F	1975	9/85	2/87	Ex-United Automobile 1983
5611	GUA 383N	VRT/SL6G	ECW H43/31F	1974	10/83	By 11/84	Ex-West Riding 1983
5612	GUA 384N	VRT/SL6G	ECW H43/31F	1974/5	10/83	By 12/84	Ex-West Riding 1983
5613	MUA 872P	VRT/SL3/6LX	ECW H43/31F	1974/5	10/83	9/91	
5616	MUA 875P	VRT/SL3/6LX	ECW H43/31F	1974/5	10/83	6/91	Ex-West Riding 1983
5618	ATA 551L	VRT/SL6G	ECW H43/32F	1973	9/88	11/91	Ex-Southern National 1985
5619	XDV 602S	VRT/SL3/6LXB	ECW H43/31F	1978	10/87	by 2/92	Ex-Devon General 1987
208	NWS 288R	VRT/SL3/6LXB	H43/28F	1977	1997	1998	
234	YEL 2T	VRT/SL3/6LXB	H43/31F	1978/79	1997	1998	Ex-Stagecoach South
235	HBD917T	VRT/SL3/6LXB	H43/31F	1978/79	1997	1998	Ex-United Counties

Dual door VRs from 5107 to 5118 were substituting for the late arrivals of single door vehicles from 5528. Most transferred out by 9/81

5540 operated between autumn 1981and 8/82 and again from 11/84-6/85; 9/85; 2/86-7/86 and from 2/87. Withdrawn 1999

5606 operated between 2/83 and 6/83 and again from 4/84-7/84; 5/85-2/86;7/86-11/86

5613 ex-West Riding 1983. First to Receive National Bus version of Stroud Valleys branding. Renumbered 202 7/94

Olympians

Fleet No.	Reg No.	Chassis	Body	Date New	Date to Stroud	Transfer Out	Notes
101	G101 AAD	Leyland	Alexander RL H51/36F	1990	2000	2001	
103	G103 AAD	Leyland	Alexander RL H51/36F	1990	1994	1995	Returned 2001 to 2002
104	G104 AAD	Leyland	Alexander RL H51/36F	1990	2001	Extant	R/n 14274 1/03
105	G105 AAD	Leyland	Alexander RL H51/36F	1990	2000	Extant	R/n 14275 1/03
112	JHU 899X	Leyland	Roe H47/29F	1982	2001	Extant	R/n 14282 1/03
115	LWS 33Y	Leyland	Roe H47/29F	1982	10/91	1999	R/n from 9517 7/94
116	LWS 34Y	Leyland	Roe H47/29F	1982	5/86	1994	Returned 2001 & extant. R/n from 9518 7/94 and 14286 1/03
118	LWS 36Y	Leyland	Roe H47/29F	1982	9/91	Extant	R/n from 9520 7/94
119	LWS 37Y	Leyland	Roe H47/29F	1982	11/96	2000	
120	LWS 38Y	Leyland	Roe H47/29F	1982	5/86	2001	R/n 9522 7/94
123	LWS 41Y	Leyland	Roe H47/29F	1982	1997	Extant	R/n 14293 1/03
130	C610 LFT	Leyland	Alexander RH H45/31F	1985	2003	Extant	R/n 14610 1/03
144	ANA 4Y	Leyland	NCME H43/30F	1982	2000	2000	Ex-Stagecoach Manchester
146	ANA 6Y	Leyland	NCME H43/30F	1982	2000	2000	Ex-Stagecoach Manchester
147	ANA 7Y	Leyland	NCME H43/30F	1982	2000	2000	Ex-Stagecoach Manchester
148	ANA 8Y	Leyland	NCME H43/30F	1982	2000	2000	Ex-Stagecoach Manchester
149	ANA 9Y	Leyland	NCME H43/30F	1982	2000	2000	Ex-Stagecoach Manchester
150	ANA 10Y	Leyland	NCME H43/30F	1982	2000	2000	Ex-Stagecoach Manchester
162	E502 LFL	Leyland	Optare DPH 43/27F	1988	2002	Extant	Ex-Stagecoach Cambus. R/n 14502 1/03
180	R128 EVX	Volvo	Alexander H51/32F	1988	2003	Extant	Ex-Stagecoach London. R/n 16128 2/03
181	R129 EVX	Volvo	Alexander H51/32F	1988	1988	Extant	Ex-Stagecoach London. R/n 16129 2/03
16127	R127 EVX	Volvo	Alexander H51/32F	1988	1988	Extant	Ex-Stagecoach London
16142	R142 EVX	Volvo	Alexander H51/32F	1988	1988	Extant	Ex-Stagecoach London
16180	R180 VPU	Volvo	Alexander H51/32F	1988	2003	Extant	Ex-Stagecoach London

Bristol J, H, Ls

Fleet No.	Reg No.	Chassis	Body	Date New	Date to Stroud	Transfer Out	Notes
2007	HY 8339	J(5LW)	BBW B35R	1933		1956	Rebodied 10/48
2010	HY 8253	J(5LW)	BBW B35R	1933	1/51		Rebodied 11/48
2011	HY 8254	J(5LW)	Longwell Green B35R	1933	1/51	1957	Rebodied 12/46
2014	HY 8257	J(5LW)	BBW B35R	1933	1/51		Rebodied 6/48
2019	AHU 26	J(5LW)	Longwell Green B35R	1934	1/51		Rebodied 1946
2020	AHT 969	J(5LW)	BBW B35R	1934	1/51	3/54	Rebodied 3/48
2043	CHU 568	JJW (5LW)	BBW B35R	1936	1/51	??	Rebodied 6/49
2046	CHU 571	JJW (5LW)	ECW B35R	1936	1/51	4/59	Rebodied 1/50
2060	EHT 98	J05G	BBW DP31R	1937	??	3/59	Rebodied 5/50. B35R from 10/54
2065	EHT 99	J05G	BBW B35R	1937	??	11/58??	Rebodied 10/50
2066	EHT 100	J05G	BBW B35R	1937	??	??	Rebodied 1/51
2070	EHT 550	J05G	BBW B35R	1937	??	By 9/51	Rebodied 4/51
2072	EHT 552	J05G	BBW B35R	1937	??	12/58	Rebodied 8/50

Fleet No.	Reg No.	Chassis	Body	Date New	Date to Stroud	Transfer Out	Notes
2076	EHT 538	J05G	BBW B35R	1937	1958??	10/59??	Rebodied 6/51. Reserve fleet
2078	EHT 540	J05G	BBW B35R	1937	??	1957	Rebodied 8/50
2079	EHT 541	J05G	BBW B35R	1937	??	??	Rebodied 11/49
2087	FAE 57	L5G	BBW B32D	1938	4/51	1951	
2147	FHT 784	L5G	Duple C32F	1939	1951	1952	
2152	FHT 789	L5G	Duple C32F	1939	1951	1952	
2153	FHT 790	L5G	Duple C32F	1939	1951	1952	
2154	FHT 791	L5G	Duple C32F	1939	1951	1952	
2160	CHT 336	JNW (5LW)	ECW B35R	1936	1951???	By 1955	Rebodied 11/49
2164	HAE 14	L5G	ECW B35R (Ex 2374)	1941	??	??	Formerly carried BBW B32F body to 1955
2172	DFH 451	L5G	ECW B35R (Ex 2197)	1941	3/56	8/60	Formerly carried BBW B32F body to 1956
2191	KHW 640	L5G	ECW DP31R	1948	12/52	7/60	Bus livery 12/52; B35R from 2/55
2194	BHU 978	JNW (5LW)	ECW B35R	1935	??	12/59	Rebodied 12/49
2195	BHU 981	JNW (5LW)	ECW B35R	1935	4/59	12/59	Rebodied 9/49
2201	DHY 653	J06A	BBW DP31R	1937	1950	??	Rebodied 5/50
2202	DHY 654	J06A	BBW DP31R	1937	1950	??	Rebodied 5/50
2204	DHY 656	J06A	BBW DP31R	1937	1950	??	Rebodied 5/50
2205	DHY 657	J06A	BBW DP31R	1937	1950	??	Rebodied 5/50
2206	DHY 658	J06A	BBW DP31R	1937??		1957	Rebodied 5/50
2207	DHY 659	J05G	BBW DP31R	1937??		??	Rebodied 5/50
2210	DHY 662	J05G	BBW B35R	1937??		??	Rebodied 5/50
2211	DHY 663	J05G	BBW B35R	1937	??	by 1/58	Rebodied 5/50
2367	CHW 567	J(5LW)	BBW C26F	1936	??	7/58	Rebodied 11/52 with 1948 Beadle body ex 2492
2370	HY 9379	J(5LW)	BBW B35R	1933??		2/59	Rebodied 1/51
2375	CHT 332	J(5LW)	ECW B35R	1936??		3/59	Rebodied 9/49
2381	KHY 382	L6B	BBW B35R	1948	1951-58	11/64	
2382	KHY 383	L6B	BBW B35R	1948	7/59	5/59	
2385	LHT 903	L6B (L5G)	BBW B35F	1948	2/62	11/62	L6B (L5G 9/57)
2386	LHT 904	L6B	BBW B35F	1948	3/62	10/62	
2388	LHT 911	L5G 3/52	BBW B35R	1948	7/59	4/61	ECW B35R (BBW B35R 10/58)
2389	LHT 912	L6B (L5G)	BBW B35R	1948	??	??	ECW B35R (BBW B35R 6/57). L5G 8/53
2391	LHT 914	L6B (L5G)	BBW B35R	1948	??	??	ECW B35R (BBW B35F 11/57). L5G 3/57
2394	LHU 502	L5G	ECW B35R	1948	1/60	2/60	
2396	LHU 504	L6B	ECW B35R	1949	1951-58	2/60	
2398	LHW 901	L5G	ECW B35R	1949	12/59	2/60	
2399	LHW 902	L5G	ECW B35R	1949	??	??	

Fleet No.	Reg No.	Chassis	Body	Date New	Date to Stroud	Transfer Out	Notes
2406	LHW 912	L5G	ECW B35R	1949	4/59	11/62	
2408	LHW 914	L6B	ECW B35R	1949	4/59	10/65	
2413	LHW 923	L5G	ECW B35R	1949	4/59	7/65	
2416	LHW 926	L5G	ECW B35R	1949	7/59	10/62	Returned 9/64 to 2/65 in
2431	LHY 951	L5G	ECW B35R	1949	11/50	1963	
2441	LHY 961	L5G	ECW B35R	1949	1/60	Oct-63	
2444	LHY 992	L6B	ECW B35R	1949	11/60	Oct-63	
2445	LHY 993	L6B	ECW B35R	1949	8/50	Jul-65	
2447	LHY 994	L5G	ECW B35R	1949	12/59	Sep-64	
2453	MHW 988	L5G	ECW B35R	1950	1/58	5/59	
2454	MHW 989	L5G	ECW B35R	1950	11/50	Jul-59	
2455	MHW 990	L5G	ECW B35R	1950	10/65	9/66	Reserve fleet
2456	MHW 991	L5G	ECW B35R	1950	2/51	by 1/58	
2457	MHW 992	L5G	ECW B35R	1950	2/51	by 1/58	
2458	MHW 993	L5G	ECW B35R	1950	1/58	Jan-59	
2459	MHW 994	L5G	ECW B35R	1950	1955	Jan-59	
2460	MHW 995	L5G	ECW B35R	1950	1955	Jul-59	
2461	MHW 996	L5G	ECW B35R	1950	1/58	Jul-59	
2462	MHW 997	L6B	ECW B35R	1950	1/58	Jul-59	
2463	MHW 998	L6B	ECW B35R	1950	6/51	Jul-59	
2470	CFH 608	L5G	BBW B33D	1939	12/51	12/53	
2474	MHW 985	L5G	ECW B35F	1950	10/62	12/62	
2482	LHY 984	L6B	ECW B35F	1950	1/62	7/63	
2485	FJ 8932	H(5LW)	Bristol B35R	1933	??	11/50	Ex-Western National
2486	FJ 8934	H(5LW)	Bristol B35R	1933	??	11/50	Ex-Western National
2487	FJ 8943	H(5LW)	Bristol B35R	1934	??	11/51	Ex-Western National
2488	FJ 8950	H(5LW)	Bristol B35R	1934	??	Feb-51	Ex-Western National
2489	FJ 8957	H(5LW)	Bristol B35R	1934	??	Feb-51	Ex-Western National
2490	FJ 8959	H(5LW)	Bristol B35R	1934	??	Nov-51	Ex-Western National
2491	FJ 8960	H(5LW)	Bristol B35R	1934	??	Jun-51	Ex-Western National
2492	ADV 110	J05G	Beadle B36R	1936	New	Nov-52	Ex-Western National
2493	ADV 118	J05G	Beadle B36R	1936	c. 1949	Oct-58	Ex-Western National
2494	ADV 119	J05G	Beadle B36R	1936	New	Sep-58	Ex-Western National
2495	ADV 121	J05G	Beadle B36R	1936	New	Sep-58	Ex-Western National
2496	ADV 123	J05G	Beadle B36R	1936	New	Sep-58	Ex-Western National
2497	ADV 128	J05G	Beadle B36R	1936	New	Oct-58	Ex-Western National
2487	LHY 988	L5G	ECW B35F	1950	4/64	9/65	Converted to OMO
2490	MHW 981	L5G	ECW B35F	1950	7/63	4/64	Returned 6/64 to 2/65. Converted to OMO
2491	LHY 972	L5G	ECW B33D	1949	2/60	7/63	
2492	LHY 973	L5G	ECW B33D	1949	2/60	8/65	B35R FROM 6/62
2498	LHW 931	L6B	ECW B35R	1949	2/60	5/65	

2381 DP31R (bus livery 10/53, B35R 3/54, BBW B35R 2/59)
2382 DP31R (bus livery 10/53, B35R 4/54, BBW B35R 11/58)
2385 DP31R (bus livery 10/53, B35R 3/54, BBW B35F 9/57)
2386 DP31R (bus livery 12/52, B35R 1/53, BBW B35F 3/59). In common with other OMO Ls, this vehicle was converted to OMO in the early 1960s by removing part of the saloon bulkhead, across the top of the engine and moving the entrance from the rear to the front

Bedford

Fleet No.	Reg No.	Chassis	Body	Date New	Date to Stroud	Transfer Out	Notes
207	MHU 49	OB	Duple B30F	1949	4/58	9/58	
208	MHU 50	OB	Duple B30F	1949	1/51	10/56	
209	MHU 51	OB	Duple B30F	1949	1/51	10/56	
210	MHU 52	OB	Duple B30F	1950	12/50	12/57	OMO fitted 12/57
211	MHU 53	OB	Duple B30F	1950	12/50	10/56	
212	MHU 54	OB	Duple B30F	1950	12/57	2/62	OMO 4/58. 12/57 Perkins P6 from ex-H&D vehicle
213	MHU 55	OB	Duple B30F	1950	11/51	11/62	OMO 3/58. 12/57 Perkins P6 from ex-H&D vehicle
214	MHU 56	OB	Duple B30F	1950	12/50	10/56	
215	MHU 57	OB	Duple B30F	1950	12/57	11/62	OMO 3/58. 12/57 Perkins P6 from ex-H&D vehicle
217	MHU 59	OB	Duple B30F	1950	12/57	11/61	OMO 6/58. 12/57 Perkins P6 from ex-H&D vehicle
230	GWO 876	OB	Duple C29F	1948	1948	9/54	Former RW 876
281	MJ 7681	WTL	Duple C26R	1935	10/50	1/51	Ex-Henry Russett 1950

OMO fitted OBs featured converted automatic sliding doors

Bristol LSs

Fleet No.	Reg No.	Chassis	Body	Date New	Date to Stroud	Transfer Out	Notes
2837	PHW 927	LS5G	ECW B45F	1954	1954?	9/71	OMO 9/58
2838	PHW 928	LS5G	ECW B45F	1954	1954?	by 1/58	OMO 9/58. Also at Stroud 1967
2841	PHW 931	LS5G	ECW B45F	1954	1954	by 1957	OMO 11/58
2849	PHW 939	LS5G	ECW B45F	1954	1954?	11/65	OMO 11/58
2852	PHW 942	LS5G	ECW B45F	1954	2/65	10/67	OMO 4/58
2890	XHW 406	LS5G	ECW B45F	1956	7/65	3/68	OMO 4/58
2893	XHW 409	LS5G	ECW B45F	1956	1957?	6/69	OMO 11/58
2895	XHW 411	LS5G	ECW B45F	1957	12/60	6/69	OMO 11/58
2896	XHW 412	LS5G	ECW B45F	1957	7/59	12/62	OMO 8/58
2897	XHW 413	LS5G	ECW B45F	1957	1958	7/63	OMO 12/58
2898	XHW 414	LS5G	ECW B45F	1957	1957	6/69	OMO 12/58
2900	XHW 416	LS5G	ECW B45F	1957	1957	5/68	OMO 12/58
2901	XHW 417	LS5G	ECW B45F	1957	1957?	1/59	OMO 11/58
2914	YHY 72	LS5G	ECW B45F	1957	8/71	2/72	OMO 10/58
2916	YHY 74	LS5G	ECW B45F	1957	9/65	7/66	OMO 5/58
2917	YHY 75	LS5G	ECW B45F	1957	1957	2/71	4/71 in; 3/72 out. OMO 12/58
2918	YHY 76	LS5G	ECW DP41F	1957	3/61	4/72	R/n 2000 3/61 to 4/63. OMO 3/59
2919	YHY 77	LS5G	ECW DP41F	1957	1964	6/72	R/n 2001. OMO 3/59
2921	YHY 79	LS5G	ECW DP41F	1957	5/70	4/72	R/n 2003. OMO 5/58
2924	YHY 82	LS5G	ECW DP41F	1957	9/67	10/67	R/n 2006. OMO 3/59
2926	YHY 84	LS5G	ECW DP41F	1957	4/59	7/72	R/n 2008 3/61 to 7/66. OMO 3/59
2927	YHY 85	LS5G	ECW DP41F	1957	9/67	10/67	R/n 2009. OMO 3/59

2918-2927 were fitted with DP seats from new and painted in bus livery. All were renumbered in the 2000 series in 3/61 and roofs painted cream in 11 and 12/59.
All demoted to bus duties in 3/63 (2919), 4/63 (2918), 7/66 (2926) and 8/66 (2921), reverting to bus livery and subsequently OMO livery.
DP seats from 2918 transferred to 2022, from 2919 to 2019. 2921 and 2926 retained DP seats till c.1971

Bristol MWs

Fleet No.	Reg No.	Chassis	Body	Date New	Date to Stroud	Transfer Out	Notes
2017	976 DAE	MW5G	ECW DP41F	1959	7/66	7/67	
2025	BHW 93C	MW5G	ECW DP41F	1965	7/67	4/68	
2027	BHW 95C	MW5G	ECW DP41F	1965	5/68	6/69	
2037	HAE 269D	MW6G	ECW DP41F	1966	4/68	7/70	Renumbered 2425 7/70
2040	HAE 272D	MW6G	ECW DP41F	1966	7/70	8/79	Renumbered 2435 10/73
2403	926 RAE	MW5G	ECW B45F	1963	New	7/76	See below
2420	HAE 264D	MW6G	ECW B43F	1966 ??	9/70	11/74	Ex-DP 2032. R/n when demoted to bus duties
2421	HAE 265D	MW6G	ECW B43F	1966 ??	9/70	3/79	Ex-DP 2033. R/n when demoted to bus duties
2422	HAE 266D	MW6G	ECW B43F	1966 ??	9/70	8/79	Ex-DP 2034. R/n when demoted to bus duties
2424	HAE 268D	MW6G	ECW B43F	1966	7/66	4/79	Ex- DP 2036 7/66 to 7/70. R/n when demoted
2432	BHU 96C	MW6G	ECW DP39F	1965	2/71	12/78	See below
2433	BHU 97C	MW6G	ECW DP39F	1965	8/74	12/78	See below
2435	HAE 272D	MW6G	ECW B45F	1966	7/70	8/79	Ex-DP 2040 7/70 to 10/73. R/m when demoted
2501	523 JHU	MW5G	ECW B45F	1960	10/74	1/76	
2502	524 JHU	MW5G	ECW B45F	1960	10/74	3/76	
2505	527 JHU	MW5G	ECW B45F	1961	10/63	8/67	
2512	534 JHU	MW5G	ECW B45F	1961	New	by 1964	
2523	362 MHU	MW5G	ECW B45F	1961	9/76	1/77	Retrieved Cirencester dump to replace 362 to 1/77
2537	372 MHU	MW5G	ECW B45F	1961	1/77	4/77	Used as 362 replacement
2540	375 MHU	MW5G	ECW B45F	1961	8/62	by 1964	
2543	378 MHU	MW5G	ECW B45F	1961	10/62	1963	
2544	379 MHU	MW5G	ECW B45F	1961	11/62	7/75	
2545	380 MHU	MW5G	ECW B45F	1961	12/62	3/76	
2548	383 MHU	MW5G	ECW B45F	1961	12/72	3/73	
2558	873 RAE	MW5G	ECW B45F	1963	1963	11/75	
2561	876 RAE	MW5G	ECW B45F	1963	10/63	10/75	
2570	929 RAE	MW5G	ECW B45F	1963	7/63	6/77	
2571	930 RAE	MW5G	ECW B45F	1963	7/63	8/77	
2574	933 RAE	MW5G	ECW B45F	1963	10/67	11/77	
2579	938 RAE	MW5G	ECW B45F	1963	10/67	11/77	
2585	945 RAE	MW5G	ECW B45F	1963	New?	11/77	
2589	982 UHW	MW5G	ECW B45F	1964	11/64	10/75	
2590	983 UHW	MW5G	ECW B45F	1964	3/78	2/79	

Fleet No.	Reg No.	Chassis	Body	Date New	Date to Stroud	Transfer Out	Notes
2602	BHU 970C	MW5G	ECW B43F	1965	2/65	3/76	
2611	BHY 718C	MW5G	ECW B43F	1965	5/65	6/76	
2617	CHY 410C	MW5G	ECW B43F	1965	6/78	1/79	
2622	CHY 415C	MW5G	ECW B43F	1965	7/65	6/76	
2626	DHW 992C	MW5G	ECW B43F	1965	1/79	1/79	
2627	DHW 993C	MW5G	ECW B43F	1965	1/79	1/79	
2628	DHW 994C	MW5G	ECW B43F	1965	New	9/67	
2630	EAE 469C	MW5G	ECW B43F	1965	10/67	2/79	
2631	EAE 740C	MW5G	ECW B43F	1965	11/65	9/67	
2636	HHW 452D	MW5G	ECW B45F	1966	10/66	9/67	Returned 4/75 to 2/79
2931	921 AHY	MW5G	ECW B45F	1958	9/67	10/67	
2933	923 AHY	MW5G	ECW B45F	1958	3/72	10/74	
2935	925 AHY	MW5G	ECW B45F	1958	2/65	10/66	
2936	926 AHY	MW5G	ECW B45F	1958	8/73	10/74	Last vehicle to wear BOC "OMO" livery
2942	932 AHY	MW5G	ECW B45F	1958	1/59	10/61	Experimental reversing aid window
2943	933 AHY	MW5G	ECW B45F	1958	3/59	4/59	
2949	939 AHY	MW5G	ECW B45F	4/59	New	9/70	
2954	974 DAE	MW5G	ECW B45F	1959	2/72	6/75	
2958	978 DAE	MW5G	ECW B45F	1959	6/72	6/75	Downgraded dual purpose
2959	979 DAE	MW5G	ECW B45F	1959	3/59	4/59	
2960	980 DAE	MW5G	ECW B45F	1959	4/59	9/70	
2961	981 DAE	MW5G	ECW B45F	1959	9/71	4/75	
2964	984 DAE	MW5G	ECW B45F	1960	1964	9/70	
2981	993 EHY	MW5G	ECW B45F	1960	7/71	7/71	2 weeks only
2991	513 JHU	MW5G	ECW B45F	10/60	New	10/75	
2997	519 JHU	MW5G	ECW B45F	11/60	10/67	Mar-68	
2998	520 JHU	MW5G	ECW B45F	11/60	New	10/70	

2403 ex-2022 4/63 to 4/68 DP41F using seats from LS 2000. 4/68, converted to B45F
2432 delivered as Greyhound coach on bus body as 2142. Retained single aperture destination
2433 delivered as Greyhound coach on bus body as 2143. Retained single aperture destination

Bristol SUSs

Fleet No.	Reg No.	Chassis	Body	Date New	Date to Stroud	Transfer Out	Notes
300	861 RAE	SUS4A	ECW B30F	11/62	New	4/72	
301	862 RAE	SUS4A	ECW B30F	11/62	New	4/71	
302	863 RAE	SUS4A	ECW B30F	11/62	New	4/71	
303	843 THY	SUS4A	ECW B30F	1963	4/71	3/78	
307	AHW 226B	SUS4A	ECW B30F	1964	4/72	11/77	Also 9/69 to 10/69

Bristol REs

Fleet No.	Reg No.	Chassis	Body	Date New	Date to Stroud	Transfer Out	Notes
500	THU 346G	RESL6G	ECW B43F	1969	6/69	12/69	
501	THU 347G	RESL6G	ECW B43F	1969	6/69	11/76	
502	THU 348G	RESL6G	ECW B43F	1969	6/69	7/77	
524	DAE 523K	RESL6G	ECW B43F	1971	6/75	1/78	
525	DAE 524K	RESL6G	ECW B43F	1971	6/75	8/77	
526	DAE 525K	RESL6G	ECW B43F	1971	1/78	1/78	Vehicle used 25-28 Jan while at Stroud for repair
1006	LAE 340E	RELL6L	ECW B53F	1967	10/79	4/83	
1007	LAE 342E	RELL6L	ECW B53F	1967	12/69	6/72	
1017	LAE 352E	RELL6L	ECW B53F	1967	7/67	4/83	Accident victim: away at CRW 2/11/77 to 13/7/78
1037	MHW 846F	RELL6L	ECW B53F	1968	8/77	7/81	
1038	MHW 847F	RELL6L	ECW B53F	1968	3/77	7/81	
1060	NHU 194F	RELL6L	ECW B53F	1968	11/76	7/81	
1067	OHU 766F	RELL6L	ECW B53F	1968	11/76	12/76	6/78 in; 7/81 out
1068	OHU 757F	RELL6L	ECW B53F	1968	7/77	7/81	1/82 in; 4/83 out
1070	OHU 769F	RELL6L	ECW B53F	1968	2/72	4/83	
1081	OHW 593F	RELL6L	ECW B53F	1968	6/68	6/72	4/78 to 1/79; 3/79 to 1/82
1093	RHT 142G	RELL6L	ECW B53F	1969	2/72	4/83	
1097	RHT 146G	RELL6L	ECW B53F	1969	7/70	10/70	
1100	RHT 149G	RELL6L	ECW B53F	1969	9/73	7/81	
1105	RHT 151G	RELL6L	ECW B50F	1969	10/70	7/81	Arrived with fully automatic gearbox
C1138	UHY 633H	RELL6L	ECW B44D	1969	1/75	1/76	
1216	YHY 596J	RELL6L	ECW B50F	1971	2/71	6/75	
1228	AHT 212J	RELL6L	ECW B44D	1971	2/82	9/82	
1273	EHU 374K	RELL6L	ECW B44D	1971	9/82	9/85	
1278	EHU 379K	RELL6L	ECW B44D	1971	12/76	3/77	Returned 1/78 to 4/78. Jason Hire Tools
1287	EHU 384K	RELL6L	ECW B50F	1972	1/78	2/86	
1293	EHU 387K	RELL6L	ECW B50F	1972	9/72	12/85	
1294	EHU 388K	RELL6L	ECW B50F	1972	6/72	12/85	
1295	EHU 389K	RELL6L	ECW B50F	1972	6/72	9/85	
1305	HHW 918L	RELL6L	ECW B50F	1972	6/84	5/86	
1306	HHW 919L	RELL6L	ECW B50F	1973	10/76	1976	Traffic pool vehicle
1314	LHT 168L	RELL6L	ECW B50F	1973	3/73	5/86	
1320	LHT 174L	RELL6L	ECW B50F	1973	9/76	5/86	
1333	OAE 955M	RELL6L	ECW B50F	1973	4/78	12/78	
1334	OAE 956M	RELL6L	ECW B50F	1973	4/78	9/78	
1337	OAE 959M	RELL6L	ECW B50F	1973	9/76	5/86	
1338	OAE 960M	RELL6L	ECW B50F	1974	2/74	5/86	
1340	OAE 962M	RELL6L	ECW B50F	1973	8/77	5/86	See below
2041	KHW 310E	RELH6L	ECW DP47F	1967	6/67	9/67	
2045	KHW 314E	RELH6L	ECW DP47F	1967	6/72	10/79	R/n 2440 4/79
2050	NHW 304F	RELH6L	ECW DP47F	1968	1969	5/79	
2051	NHW 305F	RELH6L	ECW DP47F	1968	6/72	11/81	
2057	TAE 418G	RELH6L	ECW DP49F	1969	3/78	1/79	
2062	WHW 374H	RELH6L	ECW DP49F	1970	4/83	12/83	

Fleet No.	Reg No.	Chassis	Body	Date New	Date to Stroud	Transfer Out	Notes
2064	WHW 376H	RELH6L	ECW DP49F	1970	11/81	1/82	
2072	GHY 134K	RELH6L	ECW DP49F	1972	1/77	1/77	On loan 3 days 13-15 Jan but with SD plates
2073	GHY 135K	RELH6L	ECW DP49F	1972	8/72	5/83	9/85 in; 5/86 out
2077	GHY 139K	RELH6L	ECW DP49F	1972	6/75	12/85	
2078	GHY 140K	RELH6L	ECW DP49F	1972	5/77	12/85	
2083	NHW 312F	RELH6L	ECW DP45F	1972	7/75	5/77	Demoted Greyhound coach
2089	EHW 313K	RELH6G	Panorama Elite DP47F	1972	5/79	6/82	Demoted coach
2436	KHW 310E	RELH6L	ECW DP47F	1967	5/79	10/79	Formerly 2041 and renumbered 5/79

Traffic pool vehicles 1102 and 1103 temporarily allocated to cover for 1017, 1070 and 1093's absence at Central Repair Works
Traffic pool vehicle 1306 temporarily allocated to cover for 1100 and 1105's absence at Central Repair Works
1340 stolen 16/11/77, damaged in suicide bid & returned 9/12/77

Bristol LHs

Fleet No.	Reg No.	Chassis	Body	Date New	Date to Stroud	Transfer Out	Notes
347	XRX 819H	LH6L	ECW B41F	1970	6/77	9/79	Ex-Alder Valley
362	JHW 122P	LH6L	ECW B43F	9/75	New	9/80	
363	JHW 123P	LH6L	ECW B43F	9/75	New	7/81	
364	JHW 124P	LH6L	ECW B43F	9/75	New	7/81	
365	KHU 315P	LH6L	ECW B43F	1975	1/76	7/81	
368	KHU 318P	LH6L	ECW B43F	1975	1/79	7/81	
384	JOU 163P	LH6L	ECW B43F	2/76	New	7/81	
388	KHY 431P	LH6L	ECW B43F	3/76	New	7/81	Delayed in service: rear damage on delivery
389	KHY 432P	LH6L	ECW B43F	2/76	New	7/81	
419	REU 3330S	LH6L	ECW B43F	1978	1/79	7/81	
421	REU 332S	LH6L	ECW B43F	1978	1/79	7/81	
440	WAE 192T	LH6L	ECW B43F	8/79	New	7/81	
441	WAE 193T	LH6L	ECW B43F	8/79	New	7/81	
448	YAE 515V	LH6L	ECW B43F	1979	9/79	7/81	

In addition, ex-Alder Valley 346 was used for a short period for evaluation and Wells 353, a semi-automatic version, was used while at Stroud for repair

Leyland Nationals

Fleet No.	Reg No.	Chassis	Body	Date New	Date to Stroud	Transfer Out	Notes
559	GEU 371N	Leyland National	B44F	1974	4/83	4/85	
576	HHU 639N	Leyland National	B44F	1975	12/85	1986	

Fleet No.	Reg No.	Chassis	Body	Date New	Date to Stroud	Transfer Out	Notes
700	VAE 499T	National B series	B44F	1978	10/87	by 9/88	R/n 500 7/94. Returned 1995 to 1997
701	VAE 500T	National B series	B44F	1979	5/86	by 9/88	
702	VAE 501T	National B series	B44F	1979	9/91	11/91	
705	VAE 504T	National B series	B44F	1979	7/81	5/86	
713	XEU 861T	National B series	B44F	1979	7/81	5/87	
714	YEU 446V	National B series	B44F	1979	4/85	5/87	
1456	NWS 903R	Leyland National	B44D	1976	12/78	2/79	Ex-Silver Jubilee livery used as all-over advert for tickets
3011	HEU 120N	Leyland National	B52F	1975	1991	2/92	Ex-Badgerline
3012	GOL 413N	Leyland National	B52F	1975	'9/91	1994	Ex-Midland Red South
3013	HEU 122N	Leyland National	B52F	1975	7/86	10/87	Returned 11/87 to 11/88; 12/88. 324 R/n 7/94
3016	JHW 104P	Leyland National	B52F	1975	5/83	5/86	Returned 9/85 to 5/86. R/n 325 7/94
3024	KHT 122P	Leyland National	B52F	1976	6/82	12/88	Returned 5/89 to 6/89in
3035	NFB 602R	Leyland National	B52F	1976	by 1986	1994	Renumbered 332 7/94
3037	NOE 551R	Leyland National	B52F	1977	11/91	11/93	Ex-Midland Red South
3044	PHW 986S	Leyland National	B52F	1977	12/85	1995	R/n 339 7/94
3045	PHW 987S	Leyland National	B52F	1977	10/87	1995	R/n 340 7/94
3046	PHW 988S	Leyland National	B52F	1977	5/86	12/91	Refurbished as "National 3" 3/91. R/n 306
3048	SAE 751S	Leyland National	B52F	1978	12/85	1995	R/n 341 7/94
3050	SAE 753S	Leyland National	B52F	1978	12/85	9/93	
3051	SAE 754S	Leyland National	B52F	1978	5/86	7/90	Refurbished 7/90, r/n 309 but not returning to Stroud
3052	SAE 755S	Leyland National	B52F	1978	11/78	11/82	Returned 1/83 to 8/93; 11/93. R/n 342 7/94
3053	SAE 756S	Leyland National	B52F	1978	11/78	9/82	Returned11/83 to 9/83. Refurb 11/91 and r/n 311
3055	SAE 758S	Leyland National	B52F	1978	11/82	1/83	
3056	TAE 638S	Leyland National	B52F	1978	9/82	9/82	Returned 9/83 to 11/83 . R/n 343 7/94
3057	TAE 639S	Leyland National	B52F	1978	12/85	10/89	Refurb 10/89, r/n 313 but not returning to Stroud
3062	TAE 644S	Leyland National	B52F	1978	May-86	8/86	
3073	VEU 228T	Leyland National	B52F	1979	3/79	1995	Returned 8/82 . R/n 347 7/94
3074	VEU 229T	Leyland National	B52F	1979	3/79	1995	R/n 348 7/94
3075	VEU 230T	Leyland National	B52F	1979	3/79	1995	R/n 349 7/94
3076	VEU 231T	Leyland National	B52F	1979	3/79	6/82	
3077	VEU 232T	Leyland National	B52F	1979	2/79	1995	R/n 350 7/94
3081	YFB 972V	Leyland National	B52F	1979	5/87	9/93	
3500	AAE 644V	National 2	B52F	1980	1984	5/86	
3502	AAE 646V	National 2	B52F	1980	4/90	1/92	R/n 362
3503	AAE 647V	National 2	B52F	1980	7/90	2/92	In 1994; out 1999. R/n 363 and reregistered 511 OHU
3514	AAE 658V	National 2	B52F	1980	8/86	2000	R/n 368 7/94. Reregistered YJV 806

Fleet No.	Reg No.	Chassis	Body	Date New	Date to Stroud	Transfer Out	Notes
376	ARN 892Y	National 2	DP52F	1983	1994	1997	Ex-Ribble/Cumberland
377	RHG 880X	National 2	B52F	1982	1994	1997	Ex-Ribble/Cumberland
378	NHH 382W	National 2	B52F	1981	1994	1997	Ex-Ribble/Cumberland
379	CHH 389X	National 2	B52F	1982	1994	1997	Ex-Ribble/Cumberland
381	SNS 825W	National 2	B52F	1981	1995	1998	Ex-Ribble/Cumberland
382	KHH 376W	National 2	B52F	1980	1995	1998	Ex-Ribble/Cumberland
393	LFR 873X	National 2 10.6	B44F	1981	1997	1999	Ex-Ribble/Cumberland

Minibuses

Fleet No.	Reg No.	Chassis	Body	Date New	Date to Stroud	Transfer Out	Notes
301	PHU 647M	Leyland Redline 440EA	Ascough Clubman B16F	1973	9/80	6/82	
302	VFB 188T	Ford Transit	Reebur DP17F	1979	2/79	10/84	Owned by GCC
303	VFB 189T	Ford Transit	Reebur DP17F	1979	2/79	10/84	Owned by GCC
600	A871 KDF	Mercedes L608D	PMT DP18F	1984	10/84	1994	Dlvrd new to GCC
601	B601 OBF	Mercedes L608D	PMT DP18F	1984	10/84	9/91	Dlvrd new to GCC
602	B602 OBF	Mercedes L608D	PMT DP18F	1984	10/84	9/91	Dlvrd new to GCC
607	C705 FKE	Ford Transit 190	Dormobile B16F	1986	12/91	1994	Ex-East Kent
608	C718 FKE	Ford Transit 190	Dormobile B16F	1986	12/91	1994	Ex-East Kent
609	C716 FKE	Ford Transit 190	Dormobile B16F	1986	12/91	1994	Ex-East Kent
610	C724 FKE	Ford Transit 190	Dormobile B16F	1986	7/92	9/92	Ex-East Kent
611	B205 GNL	Ford Transit 190	Alexander B16F	1985	12/91	1994	Ex-Northern General
612	B206 GNL	Ford Transit 190	Alexander DP16F	1985	6/91	1994	Ex-Northern General
614	C614 SFH	Ford Transit 190	Alexander B16F	1985	1/89	1994	
615	C615 SFH	Ford Transit 190	Alexander B16F	1985	1/89	1994	
616	C616 SFH	Ford Transit 190	Alexander B16F	1985	12/91 ??	1994	
606	R606 KDD	Iveco Daily 49.10	Mellor B17F	1997	1997	1998	
607	R607 KDD	Iveco Daily 49.10	Mellor B17F	1997	1997	1999	
608	R608 KDD	Iveco Daily 49.10	Mellor B17F	1997	1997	1999	
609	R609 KDD	Iveco Daily 49.10	Mellor B17F	1997	1997	1998	
610	R610 KDD	Iveco Daily 49.10	Mellor B17F	1997	1997	1998	
618	C618 SFH	Ford Transit 190	Alexander B16F	1985	1993	1994	
621	C619 SFH	Ford Transit 190	Alexander B16F	1985	1994	1996	
631	C631 SFH	Ford Transit 190	Alexander B16F	1985	1994	1995	
632	C632 SFH	Ford Transit 190	Alexander B16F	1985	1995	1997	
644	C644 SFH	Ford Transit 190	Alexander B16F	1985	1994	1997	
645	C645 SFH	Ford Transit 190	Alexander B20F	1985	1994	1997	
651	C651 XDF	Mercedes-Benz L608D	Alexander B16F	1986	1994	1997	
655	C655 XDF	Mercedes-Benz L608D	Alexander B16F	1986	1993	1996	

Fleet No.	Reg No.	Chassis	Body	Date New	Date to Stroud	Transfer Out	Notes
659	C659 XDF	Mercedes-Benz L608D	Alexander B16F	1986	1996	1997	
660	C660 XDF	Mercedes-Benz L608D	Alexander B16F	1986	1995	1995	
677	F677 PDF	Mercedes-Benz 709D	PMT B25F	1988	1992	1999	
678	F311 DET	Mercedes-Benz 709D	Reeve Burgess B25F	1989	1994	1996	Ex-Demonstrator
679	G679 AAD	Mercedes-Benz 709D	PMT B25F	1989	1994	1996	1997 in
683	G683 AAD	Mercedes-Benz 709D	PMT B25F	1989	1993	1995	
685	L685 CDD	Mercedes-Benz 709D	Alexander Sprint B25F	1994	1994	1994	
686	L686 CDD	Mercedes-Benz 709D	Alexander Sprint B25F	1994	1994	2000	in 1998
687	L687 CDD	Mercedes-Benz 709D	Alexander Sprint B25F	1994	1999	2000	
688	L688 CDD	Mercedes-Benz 709D	Alexander Sprint B25F	1994	1999	2000	
689	L689 CDD	Mercedes-Benz 709D	Alexander Sprint B25F	1994	1998	2000	
691	L691 CDD	Mercedes-Benz 709D	Alexander Sprint B25F	1994	1998	1999	
704	M702 JDG	Mercedes-Benz 709D	Alexander Sprint B25F	1995	1995	2001	
718	N718 RDD	Mercedes-Benz 709D	Alexander Sprint B25F	1996	1996	1996	2000 in
719	N719 RDD	Mercedes-Benz 709D	Alexander Sprint B25F	1996	1996	2001	
720	N720 RDD	Mercedes-Benz 709D	Alexander Sprint B25F	1996	1996	Extant	R/n 40720 1/03
721	N721 RDD	Mercedes-Benz 709D	Alexander Sprint B25F	1996	1996	Extant	R/n 40721 1/03
722	N722 RDD	Mercedes-Benz 709D	Alexander Sprint B25F	1996	1996	Extant	R/n 40722 1/03
725	N725 RDD	Mercedes-Benz 709D	Alexander Sprint B25F	1996	1997	Extant	R/n 40725 1/03
726	N726 RDD	Mercedes-Benz 709D	Alexander Sprint B25F	1996	2002	Extant	R/n 40726 1/03
727	N727 RDD	Mercedes-Benz 709D	Alexander Sprint B25F	1996	2002	Extant	R/n 40727 1/03
735	N735 RDD	Mercedes-Benz 709D	Alexander Sprint DP25F	1996	1996	Extant	R/n 40735 1/03
736	N644 VSS	Mercedes-Benz 709D	Alexander Sprint B23F	1996	2001	2002	Ex-Stagecoach Cambus 1999
737	N618 VSS	Mercedes-Benz 709D	Alexander Sprint B23F	1996	1999	2002	Ex-Stagecoach Cambus 1999
738	N643 VSS	Mercedes-Benz 709D	Alexander Sprint B23F	1996	2001	2001	Ex-Stagecoach Cambus 1999
803	L803XDG	Mercedes-Benz 811D	Marshall C16 B33F	1993	9/93	Extant	R/n 41803 1/03
804	L804XDG	Mercedes-Benz 811D	Marshall C16 B33F	1993	9/93	Extant	R/n 41804 1/03
805	L805XDG	Mercedes-Benz 811D	Marshall C16 B33F	1993	9/93	Extant	R/n 41805 1/03
806	L806XDG	Mercedes-Benz 811D	Marshall C16 B33F	1993	9/93	Extant	R/n 41806 1/03
807	L330CHB	Mercedes-Benz 811D	Marshall C16 B33F	1993	1995	Extant	Ex-Red & White 1994. R/n 41330 1/03
808	K308YKG	Mercedes-Benz 811D	Wright NimBus B33F	1992	1995	Extant	Ex-Red & White 1995. R/n 41308 in 1/03
809	J413PRW	Mercedes-Benz 811D	Wright NimBus B33F	1991	1998	2001	Ex-Stagecoach Midland Red 1997
811	J417PRW	Mercedes-Benz 811D	Wright NimBus B33F	1991	1998	1999	Ex-Stagecoach Midland Red 1998
1403	H403 MRW	Mercedes-Benz 811D	Wright NimBus B33F	1991	2001	2002	Ex-Stagecoach Midland Red 1998 via Red & White

Coaches

Fleet No.	Reg No.	Chassis	Body	Date New	Date to Stroud	Transfer Out	Notes
281	MJ 7681	WTL	Duple C26R	1935	10/50	1/51	Ex-Henry Russett
2200	LAE 906	Foden PVS5	Plaxton C33F	1948	5/51	1951	Ex-Henry Russett
2806	NAE 9	LL6B	ECW FC35F	1951	??	??	R/n 2058
2809	NHY 941	LWL6B	ECW FC35F	1951	4/59	10/62	R/n 2061
2813	NHY 945	LWL6B	ECW FC35F	1951	4/59	10/62	R/n 2065
2815	LHY 972	LWL6B	ECW C35F	1951	??	??	
2069	NHY 949	LWL6B	ECW C35F	1951	4/63	10/64	Ex-2817
2820	OHY 992	LWL6B	ECW FC35F	1951	??	??	R/n 2072
2082	PHW 950	LS6B	ECW C39F	1953	By 10/64	6/65	Ex-2860
2866	PHW 956	LS6B	ECW C39F	1953	??	??	R/n 2088
2873	SHT 346	LS6G	ECW C39F	1954	4/59	1965	R/n 2095
2876	SHT 349	LS6G	ECW C39F	1954	10/59	4/63	R/n 2098
2877	SHT 350	LS6G	ECW C39F	1954	11/60	10/65	R/n 2099
2102	THY 954	LS6G	ECW C39F	1955	5/66	6/66	Ex 2880
2103	THY 955	LS6G	ECW C39F	1955	5/66	6/67	Ex 2881
2882	THY 956	LS6G	ECW C39F	1955	??	??	R/n 2104
2984	289 HHU	MW6G	ECW C39F	1960	??	??	R/n 2105
2106	290 HHU	MW6G	ECW C39F	1960	6/65	5/66	Ex-2985
2108	292 HHU	MW6G	ECW C39F	1960	4/66	10/66	Ex-2987. Returned 11/66; out 10/67
2112	405 LHT	MW6G	ECW C39F	1961	5/66	10/67	Returned 12/67 to 1/68
2117	863 UAE	RELH6G	ECW C47F	1964	5/69	10/69	
2136	280 ECY	MW6G	ECW C39F	1962	5/67	11/67	
2141	BHU 95C	MW6G	ECW DP39F	1965	3/66	5/66	
2144	FHW 150D	MW6G	ECW C39F	1966	6/67	5/68	
2087	BHW 84J	Leopard PSU3A/4R	Paramount Elite II C47F	1971	10/79	7/80	OMO. Returned 5/83 to 1/85
2088	BHW 85J	Leopard PSU3A/4R	Paramount Elite II C47F	1971	4/79	7/80	OMO
2088	YDF 325K	Leopard PSU3A/4R	Paramount Elite II C47F	1971	1/85	3/86	OMO. Ex-Black & White
2173	RHY 761M	Leopard PSU3B/4R	Panorama Elite III C47F	1974	7/76	10/76	
2174	RHY 762M	Leopard PSU3B/4R	Panorama Elite III C47F	1974	8/76	9/76	
2111	AFH 198T	Leopard PSU5C/4R	Dominant II C50F	1979	3/86	7/87	Ex-Black & White
2112	SND 299X	Leopard PSU5D/4R	Supreme V C53F	1981	5/87	5/89	Ex-Black & White
2113	SND 300X	Leopard PSU5D/4R	Supreme V C53F	1981	5/87	5/89	Ex-Black & White
2211	A211 SAE	Tiger TRCTL 11/3R	Paramount 3200 C53F	1983	12/83	2/93	
2214	A214 SAE	Tiger TRCTL 11/3R	Paramount 3200 C53F	1983	5/89	3/93	
2224	CDG 207Y	Tiger TRCTL11/3R	Paramount 3200 C50F	1983	5/89	2/93	Ex-Black & White

Modern Single Decks

Fleet No.	Reg No.	Chassis	Body	Date New	Date to Stroud	Transfer Out	Notes
423	P823FVU	Volvo B10M-55	Alexander PS B49F	1996	1999	2001	Ex-Stagecoach Manchester 1999
424	P824FVU	Volvo B10M-55	Alexander PS B49F	1996	1999	Extant	Ex-Stagecoach Manchester 1999. R/n 40824 1/03
425	P825FVU	Volvo B10M-55	Alexander PS B49F	1996	1999	Extant	Ex-Stagecoach Manchester 1999. R/n 40825 1/03
426	P826FVU	Volvo B10M-55	Alexander PS B49F	1996	1999	Extant	Ex-Stagecoach Manchester 1999. R/n 40826 1/03
427	P827FVU	Volvo B10M-55	Alexander PS B49F	1996	1999	Extant	Ex-Stagecoach Manchester 1999. R/n 40827 1/03
428	P828FVU	Volvo B10M-55	Alexander PS B49F	1996	1999	1/03	Ex-Stagecoach Manchester 1999. R/n 40828 1/03
846	L248CCK	Volvo B6-50	Alexander Dash DP40F	1993/94	2000	2001	Ex-Ribble in 1995
847	M847HDF	Volvo B6-50	Alexander Dash B40F	1994/95	2000	2001	
850	L711FWO	Volvo B6-50	Alexander Dash B40F	1993/94	2000	2001	Ex-Red & White in 1995
901	P901SMR	Dennis Dart	Alexander Dash B40F	1997	2000	Extant	R/n 32901 1/03
902	P902SMR	Dennis Dart	Alexander Dash B40F	1997	2000	Extant	R/n 32902 1/03
903	P903SMR	Dennis Dart	Alexander Dash B40F	1997	2000	Extant	R/n 32903 1/03
932	R809YUD	Dart SLF	Alexander ALX200 B37F	1998	2000	Extant	Ex-Stagecoach Oxford 1998. R/n 33809 1/03
933	R810YUD	Dart SLF	Alexander ALX200 B37F	1998	1999	Extant	Ex-Stagecoach Oxford 1998. R/n 33810 1/03
934	R811YUD	Dart SLF	Alexander ALX200 B37F	1998	1998	Extant	Ex-Stagecoach Oxford 1998. R/n 33811 1/03
935	R812YUD	Dart SLF	Alexander ALX200 B37F	1998	1998	Extant	Ex-Stagecoach Oxford 1998. R/n 33812 1/03
936	M85DEW	Dennis Dart	Marshall C37 B40F	1994	1999	Extant	Ex-Stagecoach Manchester 1999, ex-Glossopdale. R/n 32936 1/03
937	M86DEW	Dennis Dart	Marshall C37 B40F	1994	1999	Extant	Ex-Stagecoach Manchester 1999, ex-Glossopdale. R/n 32937 1/03

(c) Known and Likely Red Bus and Early Western National Vehicles

Known and Likely Red Bus Vehicles

Reg No.	Chassis	Body	Date New	Red & White No. upon transfer	Notes
DF 296	Albion PK26		1926	60	
DF 260	Albion PK26		1926	61	
DF 576	Albion PK26		1926	62	
DF 577	Albion PK26		1926	63	
DF 747	Albion PK26		1926	64	
DF 1833	Albion PK26		1926	65	
DF 2529	Albion PM28		1927	66	
DF 3260	Albion PM28		1927	67	
DF 6916	Leyland Lion		1929	102	
DF 5218	Albion PM28	30 seat	1928	113	
??	Albion PM28		??	123	
DF 6961	Albion Viking	32 seat	1929	126	
DF 6960	Albion LB40	14 seat	1929	127	
DF 6809	Leyland Lion			12	
AD 8571	Albion PH24			14	
DF 4605	Thornycroft A6			44	
DF 3958	Albion PM28			69	
DF 4561	Albion SPLB24			78	
DF 7946	Albion LB40			92	
DF 9186	Leyland Tiger TS3			100	
DF 7945	Albion			135	
DG 6945	Albion Viking Six		1932	204	

Early vehicles of the National and Western National Omnibus Companies understood to have been based at Stroud

Date built	Fleet No.	Reg. No.	Chassis	Body		Notes
1919	2023	BM 7768	AEC YC		B31	
1919	2026	BM 7813	AEC YC		OT28/26RO	
1920	2049	HK 7287	AEC YC	NOTC	OT22/2RO	
1920	2052	AD 6654	AEC YC	NOTC	OT22/22RO	
1920	2053	AD 6863	AEC YC	NOTC	OT22/22RO	
1920	2063	AD 7261	AEC YC	Ch28		
1920	2064	AD 7262	AEC YC	Ch28		
1920	2065	AD 7310	AEC YC	NOTC	OT22/22RO	
1920	2070	AD 7480	AEC YC	NOTC	OT22/22RO	
1920	2084	HK 8636	AEC YC		Ch28	
1920	2091	AD 8060	AEC YC	Dodson	B36	
1920	2095	AD 8136	AEC YC	NOTC	OT22/22RO	
1920	2096	AD 8262	AEC YC		B36	
1920	2103	AD 8453	AEC YC	NOTC	OT22/22RO	
1920	2104	AD 8461	AEC YC	Dodson	B36R	

Date built	Fleet No.	Reg. No.	Chassis	Body	Notes	
1921	2113	YA 920	AEC YC	Hurst Nelson	OT18/16RO	
1921	2112	AD 5710	Caledon			EX-Arnold
1922	2159	DD 787	Burford 30cwt	Hickman	B14F	
1924	2210	DD 5891	Chevrolet	London Lorries	B14F	
1922	2161	NM 1908	Burford 30cwt Hickman		B14F	
1925	2217	DD 7070	Guy BA	Dodson	B20F	
1925	2218	DD 7069	Guy BA	Dodson	B20F	
1925	2219	DD 7068	Guy BA	Dodson	B20F	
1926	2280??	LX 9170	AEC YC		OT30/26RO	
1926	2298	YB 6479	Guy B	Hickman	B26F	
1927	2333	TW 8931	Leyland PLC1	Strachan & Brown	B26R	
1927	2334	YB 9809	Leyland PLC1	Strachan & Brown	B26R	
1927	2347	TW 8579	Guy BA	Short	B20R	
1927	2348	TW 8580	Guy BA	Short	B20R	
1927	2363	TW 9336	Guy BA	Beadle	C20F	
1927	2367	TW 9856	Leyland PLC1	Beadle	C26D	
1927	2371	VW 109	ADC 416A	Strachan & Brown	C28D	
1927	2410	TW 9345	Guy BB	London Lorries	C26D	
1927	2411	TW 9344	Guy BB	London Lorries	C26D	
1927	2413	TW 9346	Guy BB	London Lorries	C26D	
1927	2394	DD 6205	Morris T2		B14	
1927	2395	DD 6204	Morris T2		B14	
1927	2396	DD 5149	Vulcan		B20	
1927	2397	DD 4292	Vulcan		B20	
1928	2529	DF 4743	Leyland PLSC3	Strachan	B32R	
1928	2534	DF 4744	Leyland PLSC3	Strachan	B28R	
1928	2549	DF 4977	Leyland PLC1	Beadle	C26D	
1929	2855	DF 7647	Guy BA	Hoyal	C20	
1929	2879	DF 7475	AEC Reliance	Strachan	B32F	
1929	2881	DF 7523	AEC Reliance	Strachan	B32F	
1929	2887	DF 7916	AEC Reliance	Strachan	B32F	
1929	2891	DF 7917	AEC Reliance	Strachan	B32F	
1931	3127	DG 2630	Leyland TD1	Strachan	H24/24R	Rebodied L26/26R 5/43
1931	3128	DG 2671	Leyland TD1	Strachan	H24/24R	Rebodied L24/24R 2/42